ACTION IN THE SOUTH ATLANTIC

THE SINKING OF THE GERMAN RAIDER *STIER*
BY
THE LIBERTY SHIP
STEPHEN HOPKINS

by
Gerald Reminick

ACTION IN THE SOUTH ATLANTIC

THE SINKING OF THE GERMAN RAIDER *STIER*
BY
THE LIBERTY SHIP STEPHEN HOPKINS

by
Gerald Reminick

THE GLENCANNON PRESS
MARITIME BOOKS

Palo Alto
2006

This book is copyright © 2006.

Published by The Glencannon Press
P.O. Box 341, Palo Alto, CA 94302
Tel. 800-711-8985, Fax. 510-528-3194
www.glencannon.com

First Edition, first printing.

ISBN 978-1-889901-38-1   1-889901-38-5

Library of Congress Control Number: 2006932603

Publisher's note: Every effort is made to obtain and reproduce the best quality photographs. Due to wartime conditions, and the age of the photos available, a number are of lesser quality. They have nevertheless been used.

There is nothing more precious than life itself.

Dedication

To the U.S. Navy men and merchant mariners who died during the battle of the SS *Stephen Hopkins* against the German raider and its aftermath, who gave the ultimate sacrifice.

By the same author:

Patriots and Heroes, True Stories of the U.S. Merchant Marine in World War II, Vol. 1

Patriots and Heroes, True Stories of the U.S. Merchant Marine in World War II, Vol. 2

Nightmare In Bari, The World War II Liberty Ship Poison Gas Disaster and Coverup

Death's Railway: A Merchant Mariner POW on the River Kwai

No Surrender: True Stories of the U.S. Navy Armed Guard in World War II

Our Pond: A Year in the Life of St. John's Pond

ACKNOWLEDGEMENTS

Many people helped me write this book. A very special thank you to my colleague and editor, Professor Joyce Gabriele who has assisted with all my writings. Thanks also to Professor Kevin Peterman for his technical knowledge involving the photographs supporting the text. This book wouldn't have been possible without the support of the libraries of Suffolk County Community College and the emotional backing of my wife, Gail, and family.

Special thank-yous also for Rodger H. Piercy, ordinary seaman aboard the S.S. *Stephen Hopkins,* for the use of his manuscript concerning the voyage; Moses N. Barker and Paul B. Porter, Navy Armed Guard survivors from the S.S. *Stephen Hopkins*; Dan and Toni Horodysky, editors of the fabulous *American Merchant Marine at War* website; Captains Arthur R. Moore and Walter W. Jaffee for their reference works; and Capt. Charles Renick for his support, and for James Patrick Conroy's manuscript concerning the battle.

I would also like to express my appreciation to the relatives of the merchant seamen who were aboard *Hopkins,* for their assistance: Dorothy O. Norris, Robert T. Chamberlin, Jean Dierkes-Carlisle, Susan Cordova, Cecelia Layman, Linda Pizzuto, Maxine Spence, and Imogene Trembowicz.

The following people and organizations helped me in my research: Merchant Marine poet and writer, Ian A. Millar; William Bentley of the S.S. *Stephen Hopkins* A.M.M.V. Chapter; William Kooiman, San Francisco Maritime Library Technician; Linda Phillippe, director of the Robinson Public Library District, Robinson, Ill.; William Chubb, Chief Main Personnel Branch, Marine Personnel Division, U.S.C.G.; Robin Cookson and Sandy Smith of the National Archives and Records Administration; Dr. George Billy and Donald Gill of the Schuyler Otis Bland Library at the U.S. Merchant Marine Academy; The Reverend Clint Padgitt of the German Seamen's Mission of New York City for his terrific job of translating German records, and Herb Lowenthal who also helped in this regard; German war correspondent Friedrich Weber who, I believe, was the photographer responsible for the incredible photographs taken aboard *Stier*.

Finally, a special thanks to my editor, Bill Harris, for his patience and skill in bringing this book to fruition. Thank you, Bill!

Contents

PREFACE

Stephen Hopkins was born on March 7, 1707 in Scituate, Rhode Island. Although he had little formal education, he was an avid reader of Greek, Roman and English history.

In 1742 he sold the farm he had inherited from his father and bought a store in Providence, Rhode Island that led to a successful career as a merchant and ship builder. He married Sarah Scott and they had seven children.

He was elected town clerk, then chosen as a representative from Scituate to the General Assembly and was re-elected to that post fourteen times. In 1751, he was appointed Chief Justice of the superior court and in 1756 was elected governor of the colony.

Stephen Hopkins was one of the most vigorous champions of the colonies' rights. In 1765 he wrote a pamphlet, "The Grievances of the American Colonies Candidly Examined," which was printed by the General Assembly and reissued in London later that year. He was elected chair of the committee in Providence to draft instructions to the General Assembly on the Stamp Act. The resolutions that were adopted were almost identical to those Patrick Henry produced in Virginia.

Stephen Hopkins freed his slaves in 1773 and the following year he sponsored a bill that prohibited the importation of slaves into the colony.

Hopkins was elected to represent Rhode Island in the Continental Congress in 1774, 1775 and 1776 and had the courage and honor of signing his name to the Declaration of Independence. He then served in the Congress, distinguishing himself as a powerful orator. As a member of the naval committee, his knowledge of the shipping business served him well in planning for the armament of vessels and in framing regulations for the nation's new navy.

Stephen Hopkins died at his home in Providence, Rhode Island on July 13, 1785, at the age of seventy-eight.

In 1942 a ship that bore his name served the nation he helped to found with a distinction that was never equalled.

Portrait of Rhode Island's Stephen Hopkins, and his signature on the Declaration of Independence. National Archives.

PART I

1

THE LIBERTY SHIP

In 1936 Congress passed the Merchant Marine Act. This became the cornerstone of a new American merchant marine — one capable of carrying its own trade, competing globally and providing transport for troops and war materials. The Act called for five hundred ships to be built over a ten year period. The U. S. Maritime Commission was created to oversee this enormous program which included the training of new officers and seamen to crew the ships.

Ship construction commenced but wasn't adequate when World War II broke out. Even as late as 1941, "some 92 per cent of the 1,422 U.S.-Flag ocean-going ships of over 2,000 tons were more than twenty years old."[1] However, in only four years, American industry would complete a building task that will never be duplicated.

Within a year and a half after the United States entered the war in 1941 eighteen shipyards were building ships faster

3

Liberty ships were the workhorses of World War II and would become the foundation of many of the world's merchant fleets after the war. Richmond Museum of History.

than the enemy was able to sink them. From 1942 through 1945 United States shipyards built 5,592 merchant ships, of which 2,710 were Liberty ships, 534 were the faster Victory type, 651 were tankers, 417 were standard cargo ships, and the remaining 1,409 were military or minor types.[2]

The Liberty ship, known as the "Ugly Duckling" because of her straight lines and old-fashioned appearance, became the "bridge of ships" that supplied the Allies around the world and was a major factor in winning the war. Liberty ships were propelled by "old-fashioned triple-expansion steam engines

The operating side of a Liberty ship steam reciprocating engine. Produced to the same design specifications by several manufacturers, the engine weighed 271,000 pounds and produced 2,500 horsepower. Baldwin, Lima, Hamilton Corp.

(easier to produce in wartime than the high-tech turbines used in warships)…"[3] These "old-fashioned" machines were capable of 2,500 horsepower.

Whereas it took almost a year to build a cargo ship during World War I, in 1943 Liberty ships were being built "in as little as sixteen days in regular production in one of the most efficient yards."[4] This yard belonged to the Richmond Ship Building Corporation in California, a subsidiary of Kaiser Permanente Metal Corporation. Yard Number 2 would become famous as her work force set an incredible record for building a Liberty ship. "Richmond No. 2 responded with an effort which established a Liberty building record, assembling a ship in just over four days and outfitting her in another three. This was yard hull No. 440, the *Robert E. Peary*, on slip between 8 and 12 November 1942."[5]

The secret to Kaiser's construction prowess was fully-welded hulls welded to large pre-fabricated sections, a process never used before. It was a risky business because Kaiser's background was in constructing dams, not ships. The new technique and construction speed was accomplished by replacing much of the older riveting

Part of the preassembled after end of the Robert E. Peary *is lowered into place at Richmond No. 2. This ship set a record for the shortest construction time — four days, fifteen hours and twenty-six minutes from keel-laying to launching.* San Francisco Maritime National Historical Park.

construction with modern welding. The Liberty ship was copied from British designs. Although slow (11 knots top speed), they had tremendous cargo-carrying capacities amounting to over 9,000 tons. "A Liberty ship could carry an amount of cargo equal to four trains of seventy-five cars each."[6] The war objective for the Liberty ship was solely to transport cargo to its destination. If this was accomplished, the return voyage was considered a bonus.

The 351 Liberty ships built by Richmond Ship Building Corporation were prefabricated and cost an average of $1,667,500 each.[7]

Taken in 1944, this photo shows the four Kaiser shipyards at Richmond, California. There are twenty-seven building ways. Richmond No. 2 is the basin at the right. Richmond Museum of History.

2

THE GERMAN
RAIDER

The German raider was a war ship disguised to look like a merchant ship. This enabled them to approach unsuspecting enemy merchant ships and attack and sink them. During World War I, German raiders were responsible for 108 ships of some 379,178 tons[1] being sunk or damaged. The precedent was set and the German commerce raider would take an even greater toll in World War II. The raiders "accounted for nearly three times the surface tonnage of merchant shipping sunk by the German surface ships…"[2]

Building new vessels or converting existing ships into raiders gave Germany an admirable return on investment. Despite only nine raiders making it to sea, the damage they accounted for was equal to seven percent of the impressive U-boat total[3] attributed to 1,100 submarines. The raiders:

...sank or captured 142 ships (more than 870,000 tons of standard gross weight) in a total of 3,769 days at sea (an average of more than 230 tons of enemy ships sunk or captured per day). If this is impressive, then the economic figures are even more so. This performance was achieved by a little more than 3,000 sailors, nine second-hand ships built as freighters, armed with third-hand old weapons and whose total cost of ownership and fitting out didn't reach one percent of *Bismarck*.[4]

Whereas German U-boats often struck in wolf packs, the German raiders were, for the most part, "lone wolves," as they sneaked away from German ports and put out to sea on their own. The mission of the raider was simple: to disrupt merchant shipping and destroy merchant ships. This process created havoc with the already spread-out British naval forces which were committed to protecting their own merchant ships. In accomplishing their mission, the raiders created an immense amount of psychological stress because a merchant captain not only had to contend with mines, submarines and plane attacks, but the possibility of a disguised raider on the horizon as well.

HSK Orion *was in the first wave of raiders to put to sea in 1940 and responsible for sinking sixteen Allied ships.* Henry Keatts.

The raiders were expected to be at sea for at least a year. Periodically they would rendezvous with their supply ships for armament, fuel and supplies. On several occasions two raiders hunted together. Two raiders against a lone merchant ship created a desperate situation for the merchantman. On the other hand, it was not considered a good tactic to put two raiders in jeopardy so close together.

A total of eleven raiders were converted by the Kriegsmarine. Two, the *Coronel* and the *Hansa,* never made it to open sea. The seven raiders who did break out early in the war in 1940 (in what was the first wave) were *Atlantis, Orion, Widder, Thor, Pinguin, Komet* and *Kormoran.*

The remaining two raiders, *Michel* and *Stier,* put to sea along with *Thor,* on her second cruise, in the second wave in 1942. But the day of the raider was rapidly drawing to a close, although as long as the raiders could seek refuge, re-arm, re-fuel, re-supply and drop their prisoners-of-war off in the far eastern ports controlled by the Japanese, they could still cause significant losses for the Allies. The three ships were credited with sinking thirty-one Allied ships.

Because of the strength of the British Navy, getting to open sea from Germany was not an easy task, and it became more difficult as Germany changed her military objectives. In 1941-42 Hitler attacked Russia. It then became imperative for the Allies to supply Russia via the Murmansk convoys. To combat this Allied maneuver, Hitler moved his small surface naval fleet northward. Simultaneously, Germany dispatched "38 VIIC U-boats to attack

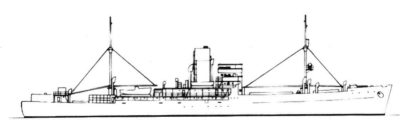

Line drawing of the Thor *as she appeared in 1940.* Conway Maritime Press.

the convoys in the Arctic area during the period of July 1941 to July 1942."[5]

As the German naval surface fleet became more concentrated in a smaller area, the Allies (especially with the entry of America into the war) were better able to defend against and contain it. The Allies, for the most part, closed the escape routes used by the raiders to leave and return to Germany via the English Channel and North Sea routes.

A raider might have a crew of between 350 and 400 men. In addition to regular sea duties, a specialized crew was needed to attend to prisoners-of-war and any captured ships and bring them safely back to port.

The raiders were elaborately disguised. Their derricks and masts were movable and quickly changed to look like Allied configurations. Raider funnels were moved and made to smoke as if they were coal-fired, not diesel operated. The smaller short-range anti-aircraft guns were hidden on deck by various means. RADM William H. Langenberg (Ret.):

> Falsework or screens topside hid the lighter guns and other combat equipment such as searchlights, range finders and smoke generators. Holds were fitted as crews' quarters, mine rooms, aircraft storage, ammunition magazines, reefers, auxiliary power supply storage, fuel bunkers, prisoners quarters, or dry stores compartments... The crews of necessity became versatile and innovative. Most were skilled at changing their vessel's identity and appearance while at sea with false masts, stacks or superstructures. Ships were frequently painted different colors, and sophisticated disguises, such as the impersonation of female figures on deck, became commonplace. Because most voyages involved independent steaming with little logistical support, crews occasionally careened their ships in mid-ocean to clean and paint their hulls. Trained divers worked on underwater repairs while unavailable spare parts were fabricated in the on-board machine shop.[6]

Below deck were surplus water and fuel tanks to accommodate the long voyages and the quarters for several hundred men. "Below innocent-looking hatches were stowed scouting planes.

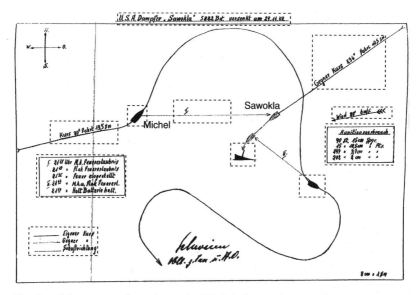

This hand drawn map from the raider Michel *depicts her attack on the* Sawolka. Stanley Willner.

Sideports opened to put guns in action. In the holds were stowed mines to sow off harbors and capes."[7]

The tactics used by the merchant raiders were varied. Usually a victim was signaled to stop. If this failed, a warning shot was fired across its bow to reinforce the signaled command. If the victim tried to make a run for it, the raider would fire upon it using the smaller 20mm and 37mm guns to pepper the deck. The bridge, radio room and waterline of the merchant vessel would be fired upon by the larger 5.9 guns in fire-controlled sequences usually every four to six seconds. Torpedo tubes in the ship could also be used and several of the raiders had fast motor launches which also had torpedo capability. No torpedo launch was more successful than the raider *Michel*'s *Esau*, which was responsible for sinking at least two Allied ships.

Some of the raiders attacked by night, notably *Michel.* This was a favorite tactic used by Kapitan Hellmuth von Ruckteschell, who tracked by day and maneuvered behind a merchant ship to initiate a frontal or beam attack. "Usually *Esau* would be lowered at dusk with Officer von Schack instructed to either shadow the enemy until the raider went into action or to act independently. Once an engagement was over, the boat would be handy in picking up survivors."[8]

The German raiders also used the Arado (AR) 231 sea planes to scout for enemy targets. The plane was not well-suited for the task. It was originally designed to be housed inside, and catapulted off, a submarine. Therefore it was small and could be made even smaller by folding its wings. "The plane was very difficult to handle in the air, even more so on water since it was so delicate and fragile. The AR 231 could not take off save in the lightest winds and calmest seas."[9] These planes were also equipped with machine guns and bombs. A favorite tactic was to disguise the plane, fly over an enemy ship and grab the communications equipment with a grappling hook thereby destroying the ship's ability to communicate.

The commerce raiders were a well-equiped, highly-effective yet little-known part of the German Navy.

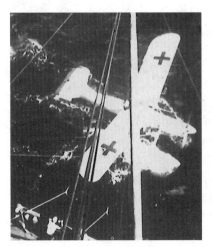

The Arado (AR) 231 seaplane was difficult to manage but was small enough (with wings folded for storage) to be carried aboard the raiders. National Archives.

3

THE

SS *STEPHEN HOPKINS*

Se", eptember 1942. World War II, now in its third year, continued to go badly for the Allies as the Axis powers tightened their stranglehold on conquered lands and German bombers pummeled Britain nightly. At sea, Germany was sinking Allied ships by the score. More ships were sunk in 1942 than in any other year of the war. During the first six months a total of "364 U.S. merchant ships were sunk or damaged. The last six months of that year resulted in 207 more U.S. ships sunk or damaged. The worst month was eighty-two ships in June."[1]

The toll, mostly due to German submarines, was so great that the devastating facts were kept from the American public to avoid demoralizing a nation so newly involved in the war. The typical newspaper headline for any given week might read, "Two ships sunk… In reality the average for 1942 was thirty-three Allied ships sunk each week."[2]

EXTRA!

Journal NEW YORK American

7TH SPORT RACING

SPORTS COMPLETE

WEDNESDAY JANUARY 21, 1942

SUBS SINK 2 MORE EAST COAST SHIPS

WASHINGTON, Jan. 21 (UP).—The Navy announced today that the American steamer City of Atlanta was sunk and the Latvian freighter Ciltvaira was attacked and believed sunk by an enemy submarine off the U. S. Atlantic Coast.

These were the fifth and sixth announced U-boat victims since the undersea raiders became active off the Eastern Coast a week ago.

The City of Atlanta was sunk by a submarine off Cape Hatteras on the morning of Jan. 19 with an apparent loss of 44 of its estimated crew of 46.

Newspapers frequently minimized the number of sinkings in order to keep morale up. Courtesy of Lou Cafiero.

Great Britain by contrast, rallying the will of the British people by providing the grim facts, reported that a total of 1,859 British, Allied, and neutral ships were sunk by enemy vessels (mostly U-boats) in 1942 in what became known as The Battle of the Atlantic.[3]

~~~

On January 2, 1942, less than a month after Japan's attack on Pearl Harbor, construction commenced on Hull No. 247, in Yard Number 2 of the Richmond Ship Building Corporation. Named SS *Stephen Hopkins* she was one of the first twenty Liberty ships built in World War II in what became known as the EC-2 (Emergency Cargo) class vessel. Measuring 7,176 gross tons, she was launched on April 14, 1942, outfitted and completed for service on May 11 and was operated by the Luckenbach Steamship Company of New York for the War Shipping Administration.

Armament was scarce and what was available was going to the Navy ships. In fact, some of the earliest Liberty ships carried wooden replicas of guns and cannons. Although the *Hopkins* was armed, she was considered to be lightly armed compared

Launching day and the Stephen Hopkins *slides into the water at Richmond Yard No. 2 in California.* William F. Hultgren.

Alongside the outfitting dock, the Stephen Hopkins *is prepared for her first voyage.* U.S. Navy.

Below, a 4-inch gun being lowered into place. Left, Armed Guard crew firing the 4-inch. Note the size of the shell at bottom of photo. Below, U.S. Navy, left Al Lowe.

to the later built Liberty ships. Her armament consisted of one World War I vintage 4-inch cannon surrounded by a three-foot steel protective plate on the stern located in the aft house gun platform. Directly below this cannon was the magazine whereby the ammunition was hoisted to the surface. There were two 37mm guns on the bow on the forepeak gun platform. In between these forward weapons were four .50 caliber Browning machine guns (two aft, two on the bridge), and two .30 caliber Colt machine

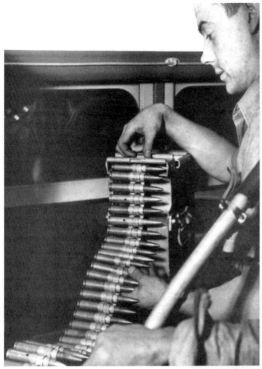

Fifty caliber machine-gun being loaded by Armed Guard. U.S. Navy

Merchant crew is given instruction in the operation of the .30 caliber machine-gun. U.S. Navy.

guns located on the flying bridge. Degaussing* installation was completed May 1, 1942 and all guns were canvas covered and in place by May 10, 1942.

Other armament installation details included:

Item	Detail
1. Splinter Protection	Wheel house, radio room, chart room, and all guns.
2. Gun Foundations & Magazines	All guns had steel foundations. 1 magazine aft, 1 magazine fwd.
3. Painting	Blue Grey.
4. Darkening Ship facilities	Light locks, blue lights, automatic switches, portholes darkened.
5. Reinforce Sea Chests	Has steel sea valves.
6. Fire Control Com. System	3 sets of phones; 1 aft, 1 forward, 1 flying bridge
7. Sky Look Out Stations	Use aft and forward.
8. Results D.M.O.	Not available
9. Messing Facilities	Good.[4]

---

* Degaussing consisted of thick copper wiring strung along the inside of the vessel's shell plating and connected to an electronic device which caused the wiring to neutralize the magnetism of the ship's hull. This prevented the ship from setting off magnetic mines.

Officially delivered on May 11, 1942, the *Stephen Hopkins* sailed to San Francisco to begin what would become one of the most historic voyages in the annals of maritime history.

4

THE GERMAN
RAIDER *STIER*

Stier's coat of arms.
National Archives

In official documents *Stier* was listed as "Hilfskreuzer (Auxiliary Cruiser) *Stier* — HSK 6, Schiff 23, Raider J.*" Each raider had five possible identifications: her name before conversion, her raider name, the shipyard conversion number beginning with HSK (Handels-Stor-Kreuzer or "commerce-disruption cruiser"), ship (*Schiff*) number used in communication, and a letter given to the ship by the British based on when the ship was converted.

Stier ("Bull"), originally named the *Cairo* when she was a merchant ship, was built in 1936 by Krupp Germania Werft and launched on July 10, 1936 at Kiel. She weighed 4,778 tons. As a

21

Kapitan Horst Gerlach was the only wartime captain to command Stier. National Archives.

merchant ship, she was owned by the Atlas-Levant Line. When the war began in September 1939 she was laid up for several months pending requisition by the German Navy. This occurred in November 1939. *Stier* began her Kriegsmarine service as an icebreaker during the summer of 1940. The only wartime captain to command *Stier* was Kapitan Zur See Horst Gerlach, beginning in May 1940.

Stier's next duties were as a minelayer in the Bay of Biscay* during the summer of 1941. Her time in this area was brief because she was slated for bigger and better things — she was to become a commerce raider.

From November 1941 into 1942, *Stier* was converted into a raider at Gdynia, Poland, the largest port in the Baltic Sea which was taken by the Germans earlier in the war.[+]

---

* Later in the war, the Bay of Biscay became "known as the Valley of Death" among U-boat men. By 1943 the RAF had gained total air supremacy all over the bay and was sinking U-boats only a few hours from their bunkers."[1]

[+] It was occupied until 1945 when it was destroyed by the Allies.

Convincingly disguised, Stier *looked like a typical ill-kept wartime freighter.* National Archives.

Stier was 439 ½ feet long with a 56 ½ foot beam. She had a clipper bow and a cruiser stern (designed more for aesthetics than function). Displacing nearly 11,000 tons, *Stier* was propelled by an oil powered diesel that generated 3,750 horsepower allowing for a top speed of 14 ½ knots. Her cruising capability at 12 knots was between 50,000 and 60,000 miles. She was built to remain at sea for 175 days. Her crew was officially listed at 324, but she could carry up to 350.

Two of Stier*'s camouflaged gunmounts, nearly unrecognizable as such.* National Archives.

Stier's outward appearance was convincingly that of a dirty-gray freighter with splotches of red-lead paint scattered over the ship.

Inwardly, *Stier* was a deadly warship. All armament could be centrally controlled by a fire director. Armament consisted of:

(6) 5.9 inch guns with a range of 10 miles.
(2) 37 mm twin flak antiaircraft guns.
(2) 37 mm antiaircraft guns
(4) 20 mm antiaircraft guns.
(2) 21-inch underwater torpedo tubes.
(2) AR-231 seaplanes stowed inside the ship.

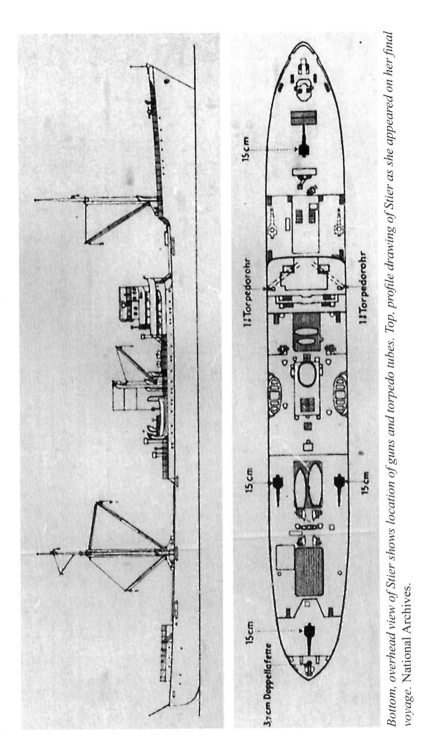

Bottom, overhead view of Stier shows location of guns and torpedo tubes. Top, profile drawing of Stier as she appeared on her final voyage. National Archives.

5

THE BLOCKADE RUNNER *TANNENFELS*

*T*annenfels translates literally from German as Fir Rock, presumably meaning a cliff topped by fir trees. Built for the Hansa Lines of Bremen in 1938, she measured 7,840 tons. Propulsion came from two six-cylinder diesels, configured to power a single propeller. Armament was light, consisting of 20mm antiaircraft guns.

In 1940, the German Navy requisitioned her for duty. *Tannenfels* was used to make the long voyage from French ports to the Far East for vitally needed rubber. She was also to supply the German commerce raiders at sea (*Michel, Stier* and *Thor*) and receive prisoners-of-war from these raiders for transport back to Germany.

Early in 1942 *Tannenfels* began duty as a blockade runner and supply ship for the auxiliary cruisers. As she steamed toward Yokohama for a load of rubber and other war supplies for the home front, bad luck seemed to "dog" the voyage. Two large fires

Tannenfels as she appeared at the time of her meeting with Stier in the South Atlantic in September 1942. National Archives.

broke out in hatch No. 2 causing violent explosions. Dozens of barrels of chemical potash were blown into the air. The first and second officers donned gas masks and went into the poisonous atmosphere of the inferno. They succeeded in separating the fire from its sources. Then the deck personnel heaved the still dangerous and charged portion of the chemical barrels overboard. During this heroic operation, not only was a howling storm taking place, but stowed in the secondary room of hatch No. 2 were hundreds of barrels of potentially poisonous ether-chloroform. *Tannenfels* escaped disaster and finally arrived in Yokohama on May 15, 1942, despite enduring a second violent storm enroute.[1]

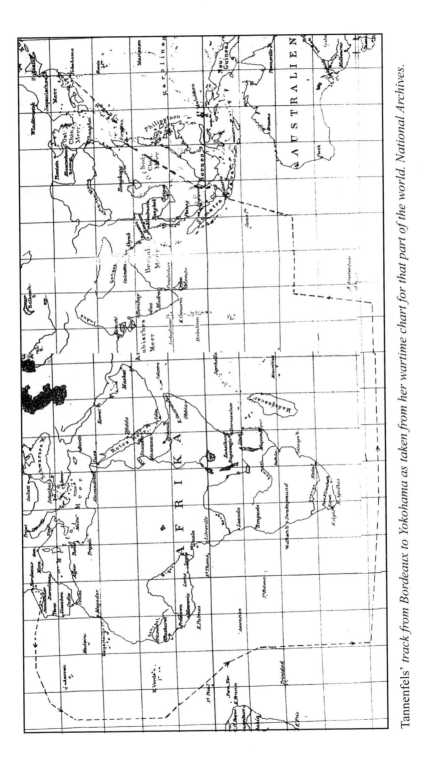

Tannenfels' track from Bordeaux to Yokohama as taken from her wartime chart for that part of the world. National Archives.

PART II

6

STEPHEN HOPKINS:
THE MERCHANT CREW

May 1942. The crew for the new ship began reporting to their assignment. They were typical of the crews that manned the early Liberty ships: eight officers and thirty-three unlicensed men, including veteran seamen and new graduates from the upgrading schools and academies established to fill the ever-expanding need for mariners.[*]

Newly-licensed officers came from the U.S. Merchant Marine Academy at Kings Point, New York. Dedicated in 1941, the Merchant Marine Academy joined the other Federal academies, at West Point, New York (Army); New London, Connecticut (Coast Guard); and Annapolis, Maryland (Navy), in training highly-qualified officers for the nation's wartime needs. Cadet-Midshipmen received their final training and sea experience at

---

[*] When the war began, only 55,000 mariners manned American ships. By war's end approximately 243,000 mariners would be trained and serve.

Capt. Paul Buck, master, SS Stephen Hopkins. U.S. Navy.

Kings Point. Basic training feeder schools for the U.S. Merchant Marine Academy were established at Pass Christian, Mississippi and San Mateo, California. In addition, there were four State Maritime Academies (California, Maine, Massachusetts and New York) which also trained future officers.

United States Maritime Service Training Stations for unlicensed personnel were established in Avalon on Catalina Island, California; St. Petersburg, Florida; and Sheepshead Bay, New York. These schools provided deck, engine and steward's department personnel including galley crews (bakers, messmen and cooks). Other facilities were established to train purser/medical seamen and radiomen (Gallops Island, Boston, Massachusetts; Hoffman Island, New York; and Huntington, New York) along with other licensed men who wanted to upgrade their ratings.

Paul Buck was the *Stephen Hopkins'* captain. From Merrimac, Massachusetts, he was thirty-nine years old. Buck had been a captain in the U.S. Merchant Marine for a year, most recently for United Fruit Lines. He had "followed the sea since he was sixteen."[1]

In the crew were:

Deck Department:
Chief Mate:	Richard Moczkowski
Second Mate:	Joseph E. Layman
Third Mate:	Walter H. Nyberg
Boatswain:	Allyn D. Phelps
Carpenter:	Hugh Kuhl

Able-bodied Seamen (AB):
Walter Manning

William J. Adrian
Karl G. Largergren
August Reese
George Papas
Ordinary Seamen (OS):
Archie Carlson
Antonio Moran
Rodger H. Piercy
James H. Burke

Deck Cadet: Arthur R. Chamberlin, Jr.

Engine Department:

Ch. Engineer: Rudolph A. Rutz
1st Asst. Eng.: Charles L. "Leo" Fitzgerald
2nd Asst. Eng.: George Cronk
3rd Asst. Eng.: Kenneth Vaughan

Oilers: Gus Tsiforos
Nicholas Kokalis
Andrew Tsigonis
Firemen Watertenders (FWT):
George Gelogotes
Michael J. Fitzpatrick
Athanosio A. Demetrades
Wipers: Henry O. Engel
Pedro Valdez
Deck Eng.:   Neek Makres

Eng. Cadet: Edwin J. O'Hara

Steward's Department:

Ch. Steward: Ford Stilson
Ch. Cook: Jack Troches
2nd Cook: Jean Ziesel
2nd Cook: Eugene Darrel "Mac" McDaniel

Asst. Cook:	Albert Eltiste
Messman:	Peter Enos
	Carlos G. Sanchez
	Herbert Lowe
Utility Men:	Gerald E. McQuality
	Leonardo Romero

Radio Operator – Hudson A. Hewey

The forty-one man crew* was a mixed group of seasoned mariners and neophytes on their first voyage. The oldest crew member was sixty-year-old George Papas. Born in Greece, he was a naturalized U.S. citizen sailing as an AB (Able Bodied Seaman).

There were other Greek mariners in the crew: Anthanasio Demetrades, Gus Tsiforos and Andrew Tsigonis. Having lost their homes when the Germans invaded Greece, they had been living in an immigrant camp located on the San Mateo coast after signing off their Greek-flag ship in San Francisco.[2] Transferred to the Immigration Station on Angel Island, they were selected to serve aboard the *Hopkins*. Only one, George Gelogotes, spoke English. He acted as interpreter for his countrymen.[3] Thirteen other foreign-born seamen had also signed the ship's articles. They represented Denmark, Germany, Spain, Switzerland and Sweden. Of this group, five had become U.S. citizens.

Captain Buck's two most senior officers were the chief mate and the chief engineer. Chief Mate (First Officer) Richard Moczkowski, thirty-eight years old, was born in Providence, Rhode

---

* Crews on commercial ships became larger as the war progressed, but seldom were more than seventy including the Navy Armed Guard. Navy vessels carried much larger crews. The U.S. Merchant Marine suffered a higher casualty percentage than any of the armed services. Based on the War Shipping Administration's statistic of 243,000 mariners serving, "9,521 merchant mariners were killed (3.9%) or a (1 in 26) ratio which was greater than any of the other services."[4]

Island. He had spent ten years in the Navy prior to his merchant marine service which was then almost six years. He was one promotion away from earning his own ship. Moczkowski had four other brothers in the service: Victor and Henry in the merchant marine, Walter in the Army Air Corps, and a twin brother, Theodore, in the Navy.

The second mate was thirty-year-old Joseph E. Layman, known as Earl, from Kentucky. Layman had also served in the Navy before joining the Merchant Marine. At one point in his early naval career he was commended by his former commanding officer:

U.S. Naval Training Station
San Diego, California
11 October 1929

Mrs. C. D. Layman
Louisville, Kentucky

My Dear Madam:

It gives me great pleasure to inform you that your son, Joseph E. Layman has been selected weekly honor man of his company at this station.

This means that he stood out in a group of approximately one hundred men in his company. Honor men are selected because of their neat appearance, initiative, and their ability to profit from instructions received during their recruit training.

Permit me, therefore, to congratulate you on having a son who demonstrated so early in his naval career that he possesses qualities that the Navy seeks to develop.

Sincerely yours,
C.W. Cole
Captain, U.S. Navy
Commanding.[5]

The Third Mate, Walter H. Nyberg, was thirty-four and lived in the state of Washington. Nyberg had previously worked on tankers and passenger liners.

Radio Officer Hudson A. Hewey, in merchant marine uniform. Courtesy Ian A. Millar.

The Radioman was forty-three-year-old Hudson A. Hewey, a twenty-year maritime service veteran. He often stayed with his brother, a prominent physician in the Washington D.C. area, when he was on leave. A third brother was in the Navy.

Swiss-born Rudolph Rutz, was the Stephen Hopkins' *chief engineer.* Courtesy Ian A. Millar.

Charles L. Fitzgerald, the Stephen Hopkins *' first assistant engineer, had sailed as chief engineer on the* President Johnson *(American President Lines) in 1930. This 1936 photo shows him holding his daughter Jean (dark hair) and a family friend on his right. After a long trip at sea, "Leo" Fitzgerald bought the best tricycle he could find in San Francisco for his daughter. She is not happy because her legs couldn't reach the pedals.* Courtesy Jean Dierkes-Carlisle.

Chief Engineer Rudolph A. Rutz was thirty-three-years-old, born in Switzerland. After his family moved to New Jersey his father started a successful business in which Rudolph had been expected to follow. Instead, "In time he decided that it was to be the seafarer's life for him and starting out as a wiper he worked his way up the ladder to chief engineer. He was one of those men who were very good at their calling and while success came to others through apple polishing, his came through hard work."[6] He was well-known and had been a longtime member of the Firemen's Union.

A report filed with Admiral Emory Scott Land, head of the Maritime Commission, stated: "A full [unlicensed] crew for the engine-room was hired through the Marine Firemen's Union hall; and it so happened that most of the licensed men were active members of the Marine Firemen's Union or former members."[7]

The First Assistant Engineer was forty-three-year-old Charles L. (Leo) Fitzgerald. Leo and his two brothers left home at an early

George Cronk's photo from his Seaman's Certificate of American Citizenship, and a Certificate of Discharge from the President Jackson *in 1929 (when he was eighteen).* Courtesy George Cronk, Jr.

age to join the merchant marine. Along the way Leo became a skilled boxer and fought matches as a welterweight between voyages. He also was an engineer and advanced quickly, receiving his chief engineer's license by 1930. Leo was an active union member, first in the Marine-Firemen's union and later in the MEBA (Marine Engineers Beneficial Association). He was a veteran of the 1934 San Francisco Longshoremen's strike.[8]

Thirty-two-year-old second engineer George Cronk lived in Bessemer, Alabama where he attended grammar school and high school. He had served in the merchant marine for fifteen years.

The third assistant engineer was Kenneth Vaughan, also an ardent union member, known far and wide as "Blacky" Vaughan.[9]

Eugene Darrel McDaniel (Mac) was twenty-three years old and was the second cook and baker. His earlier seagoing experience included two voyages on a troop ship to Australia. He hailed from Palestine, Illinois, and had recently returned from a furlough in early May. He would become fast friends with Gerald Eugene McQuality, a twenty-year-old utility man from Elkhorn, Wisconsin.

Twenty-four year old ordinary seaman (OS) James H. Burke, one of four OS's aboard, "was proud to be serving on an American freighter and of following in his father's footsteps. James Burke Sr. was at this time Chief Engineer on the transport ship *President Johnson.*"[10]

Ordinary Seaman Antonio Moran's brother Chris had also signed on the ship. However, Antonio felt that he and his brother should not be on the same ship together, thus Chris didn't make the trip.[11]

Rodger H. Piercy, ordinary seaman, grew up in Ores, near Fresno, California. In 1940 he joined the Merchant Marine, making trips to Hawaii on the Matson Lines. "Before the war ended I graduated from the Merchant Marine officers' school in Alameda, California. I became an Ensign and a licensed deck officer and spent three years in the Pacific. I was aboard a merchant ship in Tokyo Bay when the Japanese surrendered to General Douglas MacArthur."[12]

It was, and still is, the practice to have Cadet-Midshipmen aboard merchant ships. Working aboard ship under realistic conditions is important in their training. Known less formally as "Kings Point," the U.S. Merchant Marine Academy is the only federal academy to send their students to war.[*]

The *Stephen Hopkins'* Cadet-Midshipmen were eighteen-year-old engine cadet, Edwin J. O'Hara, and twenty-year-old deck-cadet, Arthur R. Chamberlin, Jr. O'Hara was the youngest member of the crew.

Edwin O'Hara's family lived in an orange grove in the small town of Lindsey, California, midway between Fresno and Bakersfield in the San Joaquin Valley. O'Hara had one brother, Donald, and one sister, Dorothy. Church was an important part of the O'Hara family's life. Both Edwin and Donald were altar boys, and Donald entered the seminary in 1939 in preparation for the priesthood. Edwin was more adventurous and mechanical-minded.

---

[*] "During times of war, members of the Army, Navy, Air Force and Coast Guard engage in combat, but the students at their respective service academies do not. However, the students of the U.S.M.M.A. received an integral part of their training at sea, and in the Second World War often found their lives in peril as they sailed through enemy-controlled waters or unloaded cargo in overseas combat areas. In all, 142 Cadet-midshipmen never returned to home port."[13]

One evening he took the family car, and with his friends, decided to ride down the railroad track having removed the tires beforehand. Later in the week, the town newspaper ran an article about a most unusual incident reported by members of the school board returning late from a meeting and subsequent visit to the local bar for a nightcap. As they approached the railroad crossing, they were surprised to see what they assumed to be an unscheduled train coming down the track. But they were puzzled to see that this train had two headlights. And then they 'rose to a man' as the train turned in front of them and drove down the street. Mr. O'Hara enjoyed showing this article to his friends at the coffee shop while having morning coffee.[14]

Edwin was active in several sports in high school. After being injured while playing football he switched to tennis. He was a member of the Future Farmers of America and when not plowing the family wheat field, or filling smudge pots (lit to warm the orchard air when orange trees were threatened by frost), he worked on an old jalopy in the backyard. He also built a shortwave radio in his bedroom.

In 1939, when Donald O'Hara left for the seminary, Edwin had two years to go before high school graduation. He began sending for information on Navy and Merchant Marine training programs. After his graduation from Lindsey High School in the summer of 1941, his parents persuaded him to enter the local community college (Visalia Junior College). Edwin's interest in the Merchant Marine prompted him to take math and physics courses in order to prepare him to become an engineer in the Merchant Marine Cadet Corps at Kings Point. He sent an application and was selected.

O'Hara promptly withdrew from Visalia Junior College and in January 1942, one month after the attack on Pearl Harbor, reported to Hunter Liggett Barracks, the new Merchant Marine Training School on Treasure Island in San Francisco Bay. Treasure Island had been developed as the site of the 1939-40 World's Fair. Edwin was familiar with the Fair as he and his family had visited it both summers.

Edwin was sworn in January 8, 1942 as a deck cadet. On February 14, he changed his major from deck (navigation and

Edwin J. O'Hara's first ship assignment was the SS Mariposa, *which, with Matson Lines'* Lurline, *provided liner service to the Territory of Hawaii.* Offshore Radio Fleet.

cargo stowage) to engine (propulsion and mechanics). His grades ranged from superior to good. While at Treasure Island, Edwin wrote home about the fog-shrouded Bay and of the sound of the foghorns which made him homesick for his valley town. However, he was able to get leave and visit home twice before being assigned to his first ship, the SS *Mariposa,* on March 12.[15]

The SS *Mariposa* was a passenger liner built by the Bethlehem Steel Corporation in 1931 and owned by Matson Navigation Company of Los Angeles. She could accommodate 800 passengers and sailed the San Francisco-Honolulu-Sydney, Australia run. In 1941 the *Mariposa* became a Troop Transport.

As a Cadet-Midshipman, E-2, this sea-training was a major part of O'Hara's education in the U.S. Merchant Marine Cadet Corps and essential to his graduation from the Academy. However, O'Hara was soon detached from the *Mariposa* to the U.S. Marine Hospital in San Francisco with an infected knee. Upon release, he was assigned to the new Liberty ship, SS *Stephen Hopkins.*

Arthur R. Chamberlin, Jr., the other Cadet-Midshipman, was born in Detroit, Michigan. Soon thereafter the family moved to Piedmont, [part of Oakland] California. Arthur had two brothers, John and Robert. Arthur Jr., or "Artie" as he was called, excelled in school as he prepared himself for college. He loved the water and had a small boat on Lake Merritt in Oakland. Later he owned a Snipe (15 ½ ft. racing dinghy) which he kept at the Berkeley Yacht Harbor on San Francisco Bay. After graduating from Piedmont High School, he enrolled at Polytechnic College and then transferred to San Francisco Junior College, but the war soon changed his career plans. He enrolled in the Merchant Marine Cadet Training School, first at Vallejo and then at Treasure Island, California reporting in March 1942. Two months later he was assigned to sea duty.

Arthur's parents and his brother John drove Artie from Piedmont to San Francisco to pick up his first ship, the brand-new SS *Stephen Hopkins*. Artie used to play a game with his younger brothers called "Last Look." As kids, this involved one brother poking his head around a corner, the icebox, stove, or a door, and a holler "Last Look!" would be shouted whenever one brother saw another. When the family returned home, they said that Artie had told them to tell Robert, his youngest brother, "Last Look!"[16]

Arthur R. Chamberlin, Jr., deck cadet on the Stephen Hopkins. Courtesy of Robert T. Chamberlin.

7

STEPHEN HOPKINS:
THE ARMED GUARD

T he U.S. Navy Armed Guard was established in World War I.

During 1917-18, the navy furnished a total of 30,000 men to the AG. They compiled a record of 1,832 transatlantic crossings in AG status, 347 sightings of submarines, and 227 attacks by submarines, of which 197 were repulsed. Of 2,738,000 tons of American marine shipping on which they served, only 168,458 were lost. Attacks repulsed by the AG saved 1,140,000 tons. Not a single troop ship was lost, although over 300,000 men were transported to Europe per month. The AG gun crews, of fifteen to thirty-two men usually under command of a chief petty officer, served on practically every American vessel that plied the war zones ...[1]

With the end of World War I, the Navy Armed Guard was disbanded, but not forgotten.

On November 17, 1941, following attacks by Germany against American ships, the U.S. Congress repealed Sections 2, 3, and 6 of the 1939 Neutrality Act:*

> ... the President is authorized, through such agency as he may designate, to arm, or to permit or cause to be armed, any American vessel as defined in such Act ...

Secretary of the Navy Frank Knox announced:

> ... many guns and trained crews were already on hand for the arming of American merchant vessels.
> Most merchant ships will have two large guns each. One mounted on the foredeck and one on the stern. Anti-aircraft machine guns will also be used.
> The actual arming of the ships will be a slow business at first. And there are not enough guns ready for all of them. Because of this the Navy has set up a system of priorities. Vessels which will carry munitions to Britain and Russia through the North Atlantic will be the first to receive guns and gun crews.[2]

Once again the U.S. Navy Armed Guard was charged with protecting the ships that delivered American troops, food, machinery, munitions and supplies in the Allied war effort.

Following the training of 100 reserve officers in the summer of 1941 at the U.S. Naval Academy, a camp for Armed Guard gunnery training was established at Little Creek, Virginia on September 17, 1941.

After repeal of the Neutrality Act, Chief of Naval Operations Admiral Harold Stark appointed USNR Cdr. Edward Cleave to head up the Armed Guard program. "By the end of November, 1941 Cleave had supervised, under the Vice Chief of Naval Operations, the arming of fifty-five American owned ships. By the end of January 1942 the number totaled 112. By June 1942 it was in

---

* The Neutrality Acts were legislation designed to maintain the United States' isolationist policy toward the war in Europe.

Interior of the newly finished barracks at Little Creek, Virginia, taken in October 1941. Geo. J. Paquette

high gear with 1,064 merchant ships boasting some kind of defensive armament."[3] At first, the newest and heaviest armament was placed on the Navy's surface warships. Many merchant ships had fake guns made out of concrete or wood in hopes of convincing German ships that they were better armed than they were.

Three Basic Training Armed Guard Schools were established: Little Creek, Virginia (later moved to Camp Shelton, Virginia in 1943), Gulfport, Mississippi (initially in Chicago and moved because of winter weather), and San Diego, California. In addition to these Basic Training sites, anti-aircraft gun ranges were located in nearby locations to these centers: Dam Neck, Virginia; Shell Beach and New Orleans, Louisiana; Pacific Beach, Point Montara and San Francisco (Treasure Island), California; and in Washington, and Lido Beach, New York. Refresher courses were also taught at these locations.

The Armed Guard's mandate was explicit:

> <u>There shall be no surrender and no abandoning ship so long as the guns can be fought</u>. In case of casualty to members of the gun crew the remaining men shall continue to serve the gun. The Navy Department considers that so long as there remains a chance to save the ship, the Armed Guard should remain thereon and take every opportunity that may present itself to destroy the submarine.[4]

All ship captains received equally explicit instructions from Secretary of the Navy, Frank Knox:

C O P Y

N A V Y   D E P A R T M E N T   Op-23L-JH
                                        (SC)S76-3
W A S H I N G T O N   Serial 097923

March 30, 1942   **DECLASSIFIED**

From: The Secretary of the Navy

To: Master S.S. **STEPHEN HOPKINS**   7,184 Gross Tons

SUBJECT: Instructions for Scuttling Merchant Ships.

      1.   It is the policy of the United States Government
that no U.S. Flag merchant ship be permitted to fall into the hands
of the enemy.

      2.   The ship shall be defended by her armament, by
maneuver, and by every available means as long as possible.
When, in the judgment of the Master, capture is inevitable, he
shall scuttle the ship. Provision should be made to open sea
valves, and to flood holds and compartments adjacent to
machinery spaces, start numerous fires and employ any additional
measures available to insure certain scuttling of the vessel.

      3.   In case the Master is relieved of command of his
ship, he shall transfer this letter to his successor, and
obtain a receipt for it.

D. W. **Fuller,**   FRANK KNOX
**Comdr. (Ret.) U.S.N.
for**   *Paul Buck*

Port Director, Naval Transportation Service.

Port of San Francisco.
May 24, 1942

———————————————
Date
Copy: COMINCH (Routing & Convoy)

*"Instruction For Scuttling Merchant Ships" from the Secretary of the Navy to
Capt. Paul Buck. U.S. Navy.[5]*

    It is the policy of the U.S. Government that **no U.S. flag
merchant ship be permitted to fall into enemy hands.**
The ship shall be defended by her armament, by maneuver,
and by every available means as long as possible. When, in
the judgment of the Master, capture is inevitable, provision
should be made to open sea valves and to flood holds and
compartments adjacent to machinery spaces, start numerous

fires and employ any additional measures available to insure certain scuttling of the vessel....

After Basic Training, the novice armed guard was sent to one of three Navy Armed Guard Centers in the country: Brooklyn, New York for the East Coast; New Orleans, Louisiana for the Gulf Coast; and Treasure Island, California for the West Coast. These Centers handled records, mail, and payroll along with administering discipline, furnishing recreation, health, legal problems, additional training.[6]

The Brooklyn Armed Guard Center which opened in May 1941 was originally a U.S. Navy receiving station for British ship crews in for repairs. On November 10, 1941, this center received the first Navy Armed Guard Officers. Following rapid expansion it "became one of the largest military commands in the Navy ... By March 1944, 47,000 men and 2,800 officers with a payroll of over $2,000,000 a month. Over 5,000 men were fed each day ... By November 1944, 59,062 men were attached to the Center."[7]

The U.S. Navy Armed Guard Center at 1st Avenue and 52nd Street, Brooklyn, New York, as it appeared in the winter of 1945. U.S. Navy Armed Guard World War II Veterans.

The Treasure Island Armed Guard Center was established in December 1941 and rapidly expanded

> ... from zero to reach peak capacity of personnel of 46,817 on June 2, 1945. The Center had personnel on board 2,106 vessels. The men had to be cared for like those of the other Centers and Waves [women Navy personnel] took over the duties of men as gunnery instructors in many cases ... By the middle of 1945, the process of shifting battle tired veterans from the Atlantic to the Pacific center in the buildup for the Japanese invasion was well underway. Many of the crew were trained in Seattle, Washington, San Diego, California, Farragut, Idaho, and many more places, too numerous to mention...[8]

The New Orleans Armed Guard Center, also known as NOLA, was established in March 1942.

> The purpose of the Center was to provide at one central location, facilities for receiving, berthing, messing, equipping and training men in the Naval Service assigned to duty as Armed Guard gun crews on Merchant ships. A program of training was begun in June 1942, in an enlisted barrack which was equipped with one 20 MM, one .50 caliber and two .30 caliber guns. Transient officers with combat experience

Treasure Island, California in San Francisco Bay, as it appeared in 1945. U.S. Navy Armed Guard World War II Veterans.

were assigned to instructional work for brief periods between voyages.[9]

From these training facilities, especially the Treasure Island Armed Guard Center in California, came the sixteen-man Navy Armed Guard Crew for the SS *Stephen Hopkins*:

Willett, Kenneth M.	Ensign	USNR
Barker, Moses Nathanial, Jr.	Seaman 2/c	USNR
Barnes, Ted Eugene	"	"
Berry, Lyle Mennen	"	"
Beyer, William Max	"	"
Breck, Wallace Ellsworth	"	"
*Brown, Robert Vernon	"	"
Bullock, Virgil Orville	"	"
Cleveland, Charles Thomas	"	"
DeMars, Peter Oral	"	"
Jackson, Vernice Edward	"	"
Little, Otto Marshal, Jr.	"	USN
Porter, Paul Boyer	"	USNR
Smith, Phillip Edward	"	"
Tingle, Jack Bascom	"	"
Yanez, Andrew Paz	"	"

* Taken off ship 8/2/42 (Follow-up to "Commanding Officer's Report- Arming of Merchant Vessels Serial No. 311-R)" 5/25/42.

This Armed Guard crew total was small compared to crews manning merchant ships later in the war which could easily number over thirty-five men.

The officer in charge of the Armed Guard crew was Ensign Kenneth Willett, from Sacramento, California. Willett was born in Overland, Missouri in 1919. On July 9, 1940, he enlisted in the Naval Reserve as an apprentice seaman. "... Appointed to the Naval Reserve Midshipmen's School 9 August, he was commissioned Ensign 14 November and assigned to battleship USS *California* (*BB-14*), where he served until 24 November 1941. He then reported to the 12th Naval District for duty at the Armed Guard Center, San Francisco, 22 January 1942."[10] Willett was promoted to Lieutenant (j.g.) on June 15, 1942 while at sea.

Seaman 2/c Moses Barker was born in Ft. Worth, Texas. There were six children in the household and school for Moses was considered a waste of time. However, he received a first-rate education in the military. Immediately after Pearl Harbor he joined the Navy and became a Navy Armed Guard on January 19, 1942. After the war, he worked for his father in the painting business and then went into business for himself, eventually owning three Dairy Queens before he retired.[11]

Seaman 2/c Paul Porter was born in Glendale, Arizona. Prior to graduating from Glendale High School, he worked on a dairy farm. After Paul was drafted, he trained at the Armed Guard base which was also the destroyer base in San Diego. After the war, Porter went into the sheet metal business.[12]

Virgil Orville Bullock was twenty-four-years old, born in Bixby, Oklahoma. He was one of eight children. He loved tinkering with cars, so much so that he became a car salesman after the war. He trained and became an Armed Guard in San Diego. The ordeal that would ensue weighed so heavily on him that he rarely talked about it throughout the remainder of his life.[13]

Wallace Ellsworth Breck had never seen a 37mm gun. However, "he would become killingly proficient in using the weapon. In late May 1942, he was billeted on Treasure Island with other members of the Navy Armed Guard so that he could become familiar with the intricacies of this Army cannon at the Presidio, across the Bay Bridge, in San Francisco. Learning how to fire the piece in a few days, Breck awaited assignment to a ship. At midnight the night she sailed, he boarded the S.S. *Stephen Hopkins*, a brand new Liberty ship with two 37mm guns...."[14]

During training, Armed Guards had to put up with being referred to as "fish food"[15], because their duty was considered by fellow sailors as hazardous and undesirable. The Armed Guard Navy man also had to swallow his pride as duty aboard a battleship, aircraft carrier, or destroyer held much more prestige than serving on a merchant ship; a ship that often looked like a "rust-bucket."

After training, one of the first orders of business was to integrate the gun crew with the merchant crew. Team work was crucial to the success of their mission. Initially the merchant crews looked down at the young, inexperienced Armed Guards. Most of these new navy men had never been to sea while many of the veteran merchant seamen had suffered through the Depression with low wages and poor shipboard conditions.

Conversely, the navy men resented the loose command and lack of military discipline (including not wearing uniforms) under which the seamen lived.

There was also friction from a command perspective. An often young and inexperienced Navy Armed Guard Ensign was responsible for the security and safety of the whole ship both at sea in combat situations and in port. The Navy Ensign had to walk a delicate line and establish camaraderie with the captain of the ship who, in most instances, was many years older and far more experienced. The following excerpt details the instructions in which Naval Armed Guard officer Willett was to operate his command:

> <u>General Instructions for Commanding Officer of Naval Armed Guard on Merchant Ships</u>
> As Commander of the Armed Guard you have been placed in command of a detachment of men of the United States Navy assigned to important detached and dangerous duty. You will be closely associated with officers and men who are not under your command; who may know little of naval customs and tradition. The hearty cooperation of the officers and men of the ship on which you are to serve will be essential to your success. Such cooperation can be best by showing toward all officers and men of the Merchant Service a uniform courtesy and respect. The

Merchant Service has its customs and traditions which should receive your respect and observance; inform yourself of these customs and instruct your men in their observance.[16]

Willett was also to uphold Article 1 of the Articles for Governing the U.S. Navy:

> The commanders of all fleets, squadrons, naval stations, and vessels belonging to the Navy are required to show themselves a good example of virtue, honor, patriotism, and subordination; to be vigilant inspecting the conduct of all persons who are placed under their command; to guard against and suppress all dissolute and immoral practices; and to correct, according to the laws and regulations of the Navy, all persons who are guilty of them; and any such commander who offends against this article shall be punished as a court-martial may direct.[17]

On most ships, however, it didn't take long for the two crews to realize that their safety and very existence depended upon each other.

~~~

A plaque dedicated in 1986 at Little Creek, (Norfolk) Virginia defines the enormous contribution of the U.S. Navy Armed Guard to the war effort in World War II. It is reproduced on the next page:

DEDICATED
TO
U.S.N. ARMED GUARD OF WORLD WAR II

THE ARMED GUARD OF WW II CAME INTO EXISTENCE ON APRIL 15, 1941. AS USN NAVAL RESERVES BEGAN SPECIAL GUNNERY TRAINING ON SEPTEMBER 25, 1941, ORDERS WERE GIVEN TO TRAIN 200 OFFICERS AND 1000 MEN BY JANUARY 16, 1942. THE BASE WAS OFFICIALLY ESTABLISHED ON OCTOBER 15, 1941. THE FIRST CLASS OF 23 OFFICERS AND 184 MEN BEGAN TRAINING 300 YARDS EAST OF THIS POINT, KNOWN AS NAVAL SECTION BASE, WITH A STAFF OF FOUR GUNNER'S MATES. U.S.S. PADUCAH, U.S.S. DUBUQUE, AND THE U.S.S. EAGLE 19 WERE THE GUNSHIPS USED FOR TRAINING.

ARMED GUARD CREWS CONSISTED OF OFFICERS, GUNNERS, SIGNALMEN, RADIOMEN, MEDICS, WAVES AND SHIP'S COMPANY, WITH A TOTAL OF 144,970 PERSONNEL SERVING ON 6236 SHIPS. OF THESE SHIPS, 710 WERE SUNK AND DAMAGED, WITH 1810* KILLED IN ACTION AND UNKNOWN INJURIES. ARMED GUARD P.O.W. TOTAL WAS 27 WITH 14 SURVIVORS. 86,198 ARMED GUARDS WERE TRANSFERRED TO THE FLEET AS NEEDED ON LST, LCI, PT BOATS, SUBS AND LARGER SHIPS.

TO THE 1810 ARMED GUARDS WHO GAVE THEIR LIVES, TO THEIR FAMILIES AND FRIENDS, THE ARMY AND MERCHANT CREW THAT ASSISTED US SO WELL, THIS MEMORIAL IS DEDICATED BY THEIR SURVIVING SHIPMATES.

OUR MOTTO "WE AIM – TO DELIVER" AND WE DID!

---

* Recent statistics show about 2,085 died, and at least 1,127 were wounded.[18]

8

STIER BREAKS OUT

What became known as the "Second Wave" of German merchant raiders to rally against the Allies began in January 1942 as *Thor* embarked on her second cruise from Gironde to Yokohama. *Michel* left March 13, 1942 and, despite a protective flotilla of some fourteen ships, encountered enemy action. The British had been laying mines in the German channel which were blown up by the attendant German minesweepers. Early the next morning there was a four-minute action with British Motor Torpedo Boats (MTB) off Le Touquet, France. Star shells lit up British MTBs and four destroyers at just under two miles. Although both sets of forces closed, no effective action took place. British MTBs and Motor Gun Boats, plus four destroyers ranged across *Michel*'s path. The destroyers went into action, and HMS *Windsor* and HMS *Fernie* suffered slight damage, but eight crew aboard *Michel* died. *Michel* was able to reach Le Havre, and then Gironde. She made it out of European waters on the 20th of March, and set out for the Azores.[1]

Although it was not known at the time, *Stier* would hold the distinction of being the last raider to make it to open sea. Her one and only voyage disguised as a raider began on May 1st. *Stier*'s captain, Horst Gerlach was eager to sail. He was confident of a successful voyage, but there were other officers aboard who had their doubts. Author and editor Jon Guttman wrote:

> One of his officers, *Fregattenleutnant* Ludolf Petersen, did not share his optimism. A veteran who had served as prize officer aboard the *Panzerschiffe Lutzow* and *Admiral Scheer*, as well as the raider *Pinguin*, Petersen felt that *Stier*'s maximum speed of 14.5 knots was too slow, her crew too inexperienced, and the mounting of all her armament above decks severely limited their ability to disguise her – all of which were factors to take into consideration if the ship was to play a useful role in the 'second wave' of disguised raiders that the *Kriegsmarine* was about to unleash in 1942.[2]

Moreover, the German naval command (SKL – Seekriegsleitung) knew that the British had become more vigilant in defense of the Channel especially in the Calais Strait. *Michel's* fight to get to open sea was clear indication of action to follow.

On May 1st, *Stier* was docked in the Polish port of Gdynia, renamed Gotenhafen by the Germans. This was a large port in the Southern Baltic Sea, where, according to her *War Diary, Stier* had adjustments made to her propeller. The results were evident as she sailed at 0800 to Stettin, Poland, making improved time. Since the prop was more efficient, the RPM rate could be reduced.[3]

Stier entered Stettin and immediately docked at Dock H of the Stettiner-Oderwerke Ship Building Company for more repairs on May 2-3. The shipyard personnel made the repairs quickly. In addition, 655 tons of coal were loaded in Hedwigshutte-Stettin. On the following day *Stier* left Stettin at 0138 and sailed past Cape Arkona at 0600. Here, *Stier* picked up Sperrbrecher *165* as

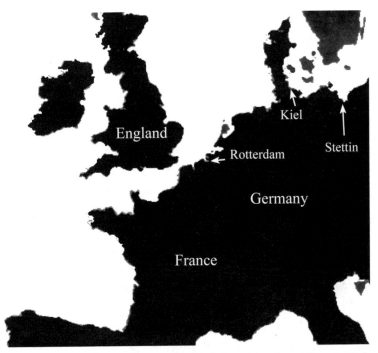

Stier's breakout included transiting the Kiel Canal and avoiding British warships in the English Channel.

· an escort at 0915.[4]

By 1940 magnetic mines were the biggest threat for ships entering or leaving German bases. Laid by Allied aircraft during the night they could cause severe damage. Sperrbrechers were heavy, specially constructed minesweepers that sailed in front

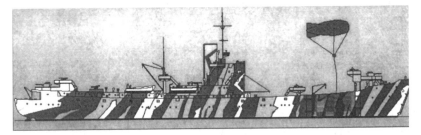

Pathmakers or Sperrbrechers were heavily armed with antiaircraft guns and served as minesweepers, escorts and provided harbor protection.

of German convoys and detonated mines. They were equipped with a VES System, basically a huge magnetic field generator that exploded magnetic mines at a safe distance.[5]

On the morning of May 5, 1942 *Stier* arrived at Scheerhafen (the approach to Kiel, Germany) and tied up at 0910. Later that day she took on more oil and from 1830 to early the next morning, loaded ammunition including ten E (electronic) torpedoes and twelve G7a torpedoes.[6] These were also known as 'Ato' and considered to be very reliable. "They were capable of doing 44 knots @ 6,560 yards, 40 knots @ 8,750 yards, and 30 knots @ 15,300 yards."[7] These torpedoes were part of the lethal weaponry system aboard *Stier*.

At 0850 on May 8, *Stier* tied up in the *air-loch* canal in Scheerhafen for testing of her MES System (Magnetischer Eigenschutz). MES was a magnetic self-protection system in which cables were attached to the ship's hull in order to demagnetize the ship against mines or torpedoes.

A problem developed with the amperage needed to operate the MES system. It was found that 46 amps were too weak for the system to operate. The system needed at least 52 amps, with

A G7a or Ato torpedo being loaded aboard Stier *at Scheerhafen.* National Archives.

60 being optimal. This increase required a new equipment switch and more cable turns around the ship and at least five to six days of precious time to complete. In the opinion of the commanders the delay would be detrimental because preparations for the breakout to open sea had already begun. It was suggested that the ship be taken to Rotterdam in the escort of two Sperrbrechers and have the MES system installed there in the larger loop. This would create only a one day delay. Two Sperrbrechers, *11* and *161*, were detached to escort *Stier*.[8]

On May 9 *Stier* arrived in the Kiel Canal and Scheerhafen for refueling and the process of re-disguising her as Sperrbrecher *171* was begun in preparation for her breakout to sea. Late that evening Sperrbrecher *161* lay at anchor in Brunsbuttel with the disguised *Stier*. Both ships cleared anchor on May 10 at 0558 and met Sperrbrecher *11* near Cuxhaven.[9]

It was decided at this point not to use escort merchant steamers as additional camouflage (although that was part of the original breakout plan) for the following reasons:

View of the forward deck as Stier *passed through the Kiel Canal en route from Kiel to Brunsbuttel.* National Archives.

Stier's officers discussing aspects of disguising their vessel as a merchant ship. National Archives.

1. Their average speed of 7 knots was too slow for the trip's length.
2. The use of a leading merchant ship flying a trade or realm flag was bound to be considered suspicious by the enemy. It was recommended that future escorts consist of fast armed forces and Sperrbrechers with completely intact MES systems.
3. The difficulty sending reference signals to a HSK disguised as steamer XY.
4. The camouflage of the ship's name as Sperrbrecher was bound to draw attention.[10]

On May 11 at 0400, HSK 23, *Stier* set sail for Rotterdam where she requested de-magnetization as soon as possible. This was accomplished between 1645 and 1845. *Stier* then tied up in Petroleumhaven, Netherlands for refueling on May 12. There was more discussion concerning exposing the ship's name and the dangers inherent with this exposure. Camouflage would be difficult in the homeland because HSK 23 had the same name formerly on another ship designed for a different purpose. It was ordered that, despite tradition, Ship 23 had to take on another name.[11]

At 2131, Sperrbrecher *171* (*Stier*), left Hoek van Holland with an escort of four fast and powerful motor torpedo boats from the 5th Torpedo Flotilla (*Falke, Iltis, Kondor and Seeadler*). Fourteen miles out she met up with six minesweepers, to which six more were added from the 2nd Minesweeper Flotilla. Finally, three more ships were added from the 8th Minesweeper Flotilla. The protective shield in a winged-diamond formation was a formidable one. And, at the center, was the disguised raider *Stier*.[12]

On the morning of May 13 the wind was out of the north and the visibility was poor due to rain. Soon thereafter, *Stier* received a warning that attacks from British MTBs (Motor Torpedo Boats) were imminent as the convoy approached the Strait of Dover.

At 0327 the convoy was abeam of Cape Griz Nez. Several salvos from the British 14-inch artillery batteries in Dover were fired but fell short of their mark. At 0347 the lead ship came into battle contact with a previously unknown armed enemy. The artillery alarm was issued on board *Stier*. Although the 15 centimeter (5.9-inch) battery remained camouflaged, the artillery personnel stood near their battle stations ready for action. When the forward minesweepers moved to the portside and fired the first flares, Capt.

One of the minesweepers which made up the flotilla that accompanied Stier *on her breakout to the Atlantic.* National Archives.

Gerlach ordered a series of flares for the forward 15-centimeter artillery from port to beam. Immediately after the flares went off, the English torpedo boats were seen to port but were a fairly long distance away. The distance was too great for the 3.7 (37mm) and 2 (20mm) centimeter artillery.[13]

The first guns now shot flares in a series of salvos and it soon became clear that because of the cloud cover the barrel height and the explosion point were too high. The height was reduced to 40 and 14 degrees. Thereafter, the flares lit up the immediate foreground. At 0353 the first enemy boats came into shooting distance so that the 2 cm. four-barrel and the other portside artillery could be used, except for the 3.7 double gun, whose forward shooting angle was too short.[14]

From the start of active combat, *Stier* followed closely in *Seeadler*'s wake. The course varied from 210-230 degrees. At 0353 hours, an English boat (*MTB-221*) that had been shot at and

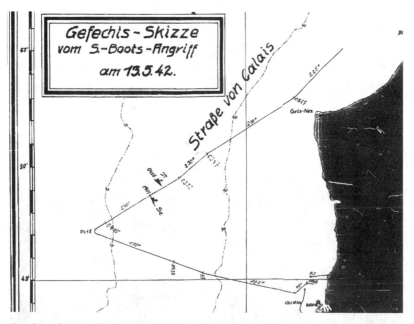

Combat sketch of the S-boat attack on the morning of May 13, 1942 in the Road of Calais. The Germans lost two ships: Seeadler *at 0401 and* Iltis *at 0406.* National Archives.

set on fire by other vessels was so close to *Seeadler* that the German ship was able to come alongside and illuminate the English boat with spotlights and shoot at it with long bursts of fire from her artillery. The English ship altered course several times, trying to avoid *Seeadler*'s artillery barrage.[15]

Suddenly, *Seeadler* was rocked with a large explosion. She was torn in two at midship, and tilted up with bow and stern pointing skyward. The British ship came past at a slow speed and a distance of about 100 meters, and it was seen that this boat, which was earlier on fire, also had its stern deep in the water and its bow upright. *Stier*'s artillery shot at the British boat, since it was certain that this vessel, which had previously been badly damaged by *Seeadler*, was in no position to damage *Stier*. Capt. Gerlach surmised that there must have been another fast boat (*MTB-219*) behind the first enemy boat (*MTB-221*) that torpedoed *Seeadler*. With this realization, *Stier* went forward at triple speed and a course of 240 degrees in order to re-join the convoy. The gunners kept firing as additional British S-boats were spotted. It was not possible to determine whether any hits were scored. By 0415 hours no more S-boats could be seen. The ships in the convoy ahead also stopped shooting at aircraft so that their antiaircraft fire would not reveal their position.

At 0418 hours, the convoy had not been reached. At the same time aircraft were again in the air and heavy gunfire was heard. *Stier*'s captain decided to head for Boulogne at full speed in accordance with orders not to engage his ship with the enemy any further. One of the German motor torpedo boats served as an escort.[16]

The officers aboard *Stier* were unaware that one of their torpedo boat escorts (*Iltis*) had been destroyed and sunk; no one had observed the sinking. At 0418 a telegraphic message was received stating that a T-Boat had been sunk in quadrant BF 3329.[17]

The final toll included the German *Iltis* and *Seeadler* and the British torpedo boat *MTB-220*. After the battle, "the torpedo boats and minesweepers returned to the scene of the battle where they rescued from the sea eighty-eight Germans, and three British who

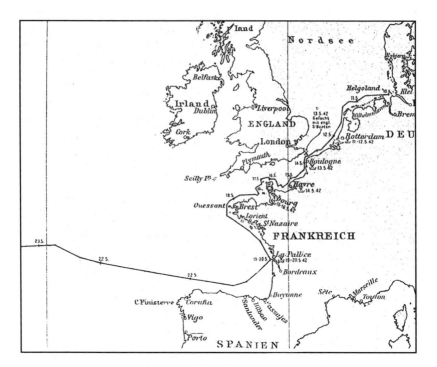

Stier's breakout into the Atlantic from France as shown on her chart. Noon each day is shown on her track, followed by the month. National Archives.

had been on the only British loss, the *MTB 220*. The total German losses in this battle had numbered over 200 lives."[18]

Stier arrived at Boulogne at 0507 but it took a long time to open the submarine nets to the port. This created some tension until 0533 when she anchored. In the course of the afternoon the entire escort group entered Boulogne, where a conference followed to decide how to handle the westward march. At 2000 hours, they sailed out of Boulogne in formation, the only incident that occurred was one of the minesweepers hitting a mine at 2115 hours.[19]

On May 15 at 0340 artillery fire was heard and seen at a distance. Since the captain was unable to determine the number of enemy units, he turned *Stier* to port and headed to Cherbourg for refuge. It was soon discovered that Vp-Boote *204* and *205* (fast auxiliary armed-trawler escorts) had been fired upon. At 0510 *Stier* fastened to Quai homet (pier) in Cherbourg.[20]

Departing Cherbourg, *Stier* worked her way down the French coast with her escorts, finally reaching the port of Royan in the mouth of the Gironde estuary on May 19. After adding fuel and supplies *Stier* finally sailed out westward into the Atlantic to fulfill her mission to destroy Allied shipping in the South Atlantic.

9

STEPHEN HOPKINS

TO THE

SOUTH PACIFIC

In early May 1942, the *Stephen Hopkins* was outfitted and made ready to sail "as soon as possible." After delivery, she began loading cargo in Oakland, California. Supplies were badly needed in the South Pacific.

From Oakland, the *Hopkins* shifted to San Francisco, loaded on May 25th and departed for San Pedro, California for final loading. Rodger H. Piercy, Ordinary Seaman, recalled the pervasive sense of urgency in the war effort, "In fact, we left port with a two degree list which we didn't have time to correct."[1]

On the way down the coast, the *Hopkins* experienced the first of two storms on her maiden voyage. Rodger Piercy: "She wallowed and rolled something fiercely being in the Pacific trough. The journey took three nights and two days to complete."[2]

In San Pedro, over 100 troops and passengers were taken aboard along with more cargo and supplies. The additional weight corrected the list.

Rodger Piercy:

We were only there a few days and were tightly restricted to the ship for security reasons. Naturally the ship was all buzzing with scuttlebutt rumors about our destination and our chances of seeing real action. Remember, this was all very shortly after Pearl Harbor, and we all felt like we were going out for vengeance. Our specific destination was unknown, but even if it had been in Tokyo Bay, we would have gone. We were all proud and cocksure.[3]

Shortly after midnight on May 28, 1942, the *Hopkins* left San Pedro and turned her bow toward the South Pacific to begin her maiden voyage in earnest. Her destination was Bora Bora, Society Islands in the South Pacific.

Capt. Buck called all his officers together, including Navy Armed Guard Ensign Willett. His discussion was brief and to the point: the success and safety of their mission depended upon all crewmembers and officers working and sacrificing together. Soon thereafter, the emergency fire, lifeboat and General Quarters drills began. The Navy Armed Guard held gunnery drills. A special relationship was developing between Capt. Buck and Ensign Willett and all communications were made available to the young ensign to use in guiding his command.

James Patrick Conroy explained how it worked:

"A plan of action for any type of emergency had to be drawn up between Lt. Willett and Capt. Buck, and the merchant officer who was on watch on the bridge had to be advised accordingly. In formulating these plans the following points had to be borne in mind:

(1) Weather conditions likely to be encountered;

(2) The areas and times in which the enemy attacks might be expected; and

(3) The types of enemy forces likely to be employed. Particular caution had to be exercised during the morning and evening twilight.

For his part, Captain Buck would keep Lt. Willett informed at all times concerning the following:

(1) The ship's position.
(2) The course.
(3) Location of mine fields of which the Captain had knowledge.
(4) All war warnings received.
(5) Confidential instructions received from naval authorities as to measures tending to the safety of the ship."[4]

The merchant marine crew, being sworn-in naval auxiliaries, were given gunnery assignments to back up the Armed Guard crew and subsequently participated in their drills.

Rodger Piercy:

Shortly after leaving the States we had to begin our new duties. The merchant crew, of course, was used to fire drills and lifeboat drills, but now we were divided into crews under navy personnel and assigned to gun positions and duties. We were instructed in ammunition handling, how to take the guns apart and reassemble them, how to load them, oil them, and keep them covered from the weather. We were taught our stations and duties in a very serious manner, learning such things as how to get someplace in the dark with no lights of any type ever being shown, how to uncover, load, and fire by sense of feel. It was intensely interesting and practically everyone aboard was serious about doing their jobs well. I think most of us felt like we were going out to avenge Pearl Harbor personally.

Captain Buck was a quiet, likeable type, but a strict disciplinarian and his officers were much the same. They were friendly, helpful and yet aloof, as officers should be. They had the respect of the entire crew. They knew their business and didn't have to run around blowing horns.

Ensign Willett had charge of the gun crew and the merchant gun crew when we were at battle stations. The Second Mate, Earl Layman, had charge of the bow gun which we called the one pounder. I think he had five men with him up there. Chief

Officer Richard Moczkowski was in control of the midship guns, which were two fifty caliber machine guns and two thirty caliber machine guns. The fifty caliber guns were protected by tubs, but the thirty caliber machine guns were on a stand at shoulder height and were fired by placing shoulder against butt as with a rifle. They had no protection.

The stern gun was called a 4-inch 50 (450). We were told that it was a seven mile range gun. It had seats on each side of it, like you would find on a tractor. By each seat was a wheel. One wheel would cause the gun to rise and lower, while the other would swing the barrel left and right. It took one man on each side. One man would open the breech while another slammed home the shell. The same man closed the breech, and the fire control officer would determine range and fire. Two men were down in the ammo locker below deck by the steering engine sending up shells. Others were receiving them and placing them nearby for use. Various jobs were rotated from time to time so all could familiarize themselves with the routine. It was all new to us and even the naval gun crew was quite green, but we got to be rather adept at our stations and felt that certain pride of accomplishment.[5]

It was during these training sessions that Armed Guard Ensign Willett and Cadet-Midshipman O'Hara formed a close friendship. O'Hara, always mechanically inclined, was fascinated

by the firearms, ordnance and duties of the Navy Armed Guard. This interest was sparked while O'Hara was training in gunnery at the Merchant Marine base and he relayed these thoughts home.[6] O'Hara's interest peaked even more on board *Hopkins* while practicing with the Navy gun crew. He especially took keen interest and enjoyed practice-firing the 4-inch 50 stern gun and he did so at every opportunity, even while off-duty.

Cadet-Midshipman Edwin O'Hara at the Presidio Army Base in San Francisco in 1942. American Merchant Marine at War Website.

Navy Armed Guard gunner Wallace Breck also developed a strong friendship with Cadet-Midshipman Arthur

Chamberlin. "Wally" was interested in attending O.T.S. (Officer Training School) in the Navy and asked "Artie" to teach him navigation principles, which he did. In his V-mail letters home, Artie spoke often of Wallace Breck.[7]

While not on duty or drilling, both the merchant and Navy Armed Guard crews could relax, play games, read or sleep. Before departing, the Navy Armed Guard crew was equipped with "Welfare and Recreation Equipment":

> 1 set of boxing gloves
> 1 set of horseshoes
> 1 Chinese checker board
> 1 sack of marbles
> 2 checker boards
> 2 sets of checkers
> 2 cribbage boards
> 1 Acey-Ducey game
> 2 sets of dominoes.[8]

The merchant crew provided their own recreation equipment — books, magazines, cards, dice, cribbage, chess and checkers were the most common diversions.

On June 20, 1942 after an uneventful Pacific crossing, S.S. *Stephen Hopkins* sailed through the submarine nets of Bora Bora into a protective bay. Bora Bora was an incredibly beautiful, reef-surrounded island, a picture-postcard vista of palm trees, flowers, blue skies and blue water. This paradise was a supplying and staging point for the westward advance to the strategically valuable Solomon Islands (Guadalcanal becoming the most famous). Early in the war, huge 7-inch guns were installed on Bora Bora to thwart any Japanese invasion.

Here, the *Hopkins* had her first alert. Rodger Piercy:

> We stayed about a week, discharged some material and a few men, and then got ready to leave. Just before we were ready, the alarms went off out at the sub net. Something was

trying to enter! Mines were immediately dropped and up came a huge ray fish that weighed about a ton. Everyone felt a little sheepish and a lot of good-natured kidding went on, but it was generally conceded that the correct action had been taken. That was the first action of the war for us.[9]

The *Hopkins* next port of call was Wellington, New Zealand, scheduled to arrive on July 5th. On the way, the *Hopkins* experienced another alert, the possible sighting of a submarine.

It was about 4:30 P.M. when the lookout reported a possible submarine off our port quarter. Battle stations sounded, and all positions were manned for the next few hours, but nothing positive was ever sighted. There were so many whales and large sharks in the area that we were constantly spotting something. We were instructed that if we spotted anything and were in the slightest doubt, to notify the bridge and our officers would determine what course to pursue.[10]

The *Hopkins* stayed in Wellington for only a few days unloading more troops and passengers. Then it was on to Melbourne, Australia arriving there on July 14th for some shore leave. Piercy writes:

We entered the bay which is some 50 miles from Melbourne and proceeded up to a berth. We picked up a pilot for the last 20 miles or so as we had to go up in a narrow channel to our dock. Here we received the greatest surprise of our trip thus far. Many people who were near the bank waved and cheered to us. Australia had been at war since 1939 and had sent so many men overseas that they were in bad shape to defend themselves and were more than glad to see any help arriving. There was great excitement aboard the ship.[11]

There were more surprises in store for the crew of the *Hopkins*; they received orders for a well-deserved liberty!
Rodger Piercy:

After we berthed, we were allowed our first Liberty in nearly two months. I will never forget that liberty. When we walked out to the street after passing through customs, we found several hundred people waiting to welcome us. I think the Australian people are the nicest and friendliest people anywhere. There were invitations to their homes, social clubs, and a warm welcome for all of us.

One gentleman and his wife approached me and introduced themselves. They told me their son was in North Africa. They also told me that they had a spare bedroom at their home which was the son's, and that they would deem it a real pleasure if I would use it and make myself welcome with them.

They took Eugene (Mac) McDaniel and me to their home, served us dinner and treated us like royalty. They called in their neighbors, and it seemed like we met everyone in that part of Melbourne. We spent the night with them and had a wonderful time.

Then they made arrangements for a group of us to go to their social club. Here we met more people, had music and dancing, food and entertainment, and a wonderful time. These were the greatest people I had ever met anywhere. Someone always wanted us to visit them and spend a night or two. Time passed so quickly that before we knew it, it was time to move on. We had gone on shopping tours, and had bought koala bear souvenirs, etc. We were taken to the Melbourne museum which is terrific. The great Australian race horse *Phar Lap** is mounted there.[12]

Time passed quickly and after discharging the remaining cargo and troops, the *Hopkins* sailed for Port Lincoln, Australia, arriving there on July 27th. There, she received orders to take a shipment of grain to South Africa. The SS *Robert G. Harper* was supposed to have taken the shipment but had been damaged at sea by another vessel.

Rodger Piercy:

The trip to Port Lincoln only took about four days. Here we were to pick up a cargo of grain, which was badly needed in

---

* Phar Lap was an exceptional champion racehorse. He was brought to the U.S. and won his first and only race in Mexico. Like the American racehorse, Sea Biscuit, he brought cheer and solace to his devoted fans during the Depression.

Liberty ship SS Robert G. Harper. U.S. Navy Armed Guard Veterans.

South Africa, as they had become a supply center for operations in North Africa.

Port Lincoln became almost a repetition of Melbourne. We were the first American ship to enter the small harbor in quite a few years. It was a small country town, but also the shipping center for thousands of acres of grain in the surrounding area. This was kangaroo and wallaby country. They are like the jack rabbits in California and are somewhat destructive to crops.

For a few days we had a pet young wallaby aboard ship, but as you must have a permit to take one from the country, we had to release him before leaving. I was surprised to learn that they are considerably meaner and harder to handle than I thought.[13]

The wallaby was a popular pet. In a letter to his family, Cadet-Midshipman Edwin O'Hara wrote:

This is where the shipmates acquired a young kangaroo. However, the little guy would slip on the deck and get a nosebleed, so they had to return him. Also on board were a parrot and other exotic birds. They hoped to find two koalas as well.

Edwin also wrote home about the friendliness of the people. Some new friends drove him out to the bush country, and he was struck by how much undeveloped land he saw and of the red clay soil. He wrote that the Australians were rationed for nearly everything including clothing, which he thought was strange because of their abundance of wool and leather goods. He added that he was homesick and anxious to come home. He had a camera and had been taking pictures to put in a scrapbook of his journeys.[14]

Navy gunner Wallace Breck, who was engaged to be married, had the strangest experience of all one day when he walked into a cafe. "I met a girl who asked me how old I was. I told her, twenty-two. And she said: 'Let's get married.'"[15]

Rodger Piercy:

The Lord Mayor of Port Lincoln arranged a social affair with dinner and dancing for the entire community and invited the ship's crew. Captain Buck sat at his right side and was introduced by him to the people. They greeted him with quite an ovation, and he spoke for a few minutes. All were pleased with him.

The dance that followed was quite an affair. Many Australian men and our crew got a little tight. The women did not drink but stayed, danced, and enjoyed themselves. The dancing of the men became more hilarious as the night moved on. I felt sorry for the women. I'll bet half of them could not walk the next day because of barked shins and stepped on feet, but they were good sports and just laughed it off. Everyone had a good time. Three or four of the crew even had to be carried back to the ship ... we never again had the greeting that was given the *Stephen Hopkins*. Of course, this was early after our entry into the war, and later on many ships came to Australia and their entry just became routine.[16]

Only a week was spent in Port Lincoln. The next port of call for the SS *Stephen Hopkins* was Durban, South Africa. She sailed on August 3, 1942 at 8 AM, with a full load of wheat, totaling 64,020 bags, heading for the South Atlantic.

10

ATLANTIC HUNTING GROUNDS

The South Atlantic was an important theater for the German Kriegsmarine. Allied cargo ships and tankers traversed these waters carrying armament, foodstuffs, gasoline, supplies, and other war matériel to war zones throughout the globe. Sinking these vessels was of prime importance in the Axis' need to control what moved eastward, north along the African coasts to the Mediterranean and across the Indian Ocean, and back again. "The Axis sank seventy U.S. ships in this theater, thirty-four in 1942 alone from torpedoing and shelling."[1]

As May turned into June, *Stier* was opposite the Kap-Verdische (Cape Verde) Islands* and continued on a course of 180 degrees at an average speed of 14 knots as she passed these islands.

---

* The Cape Verde Islands were colonized by Portugal in the fifteenth century. Set in the mid-Atlantic, these nine islands played an important role during the slave-trade era and they also served as a port for refueling and resupply. The islands received their independence from Portugal in 1975.

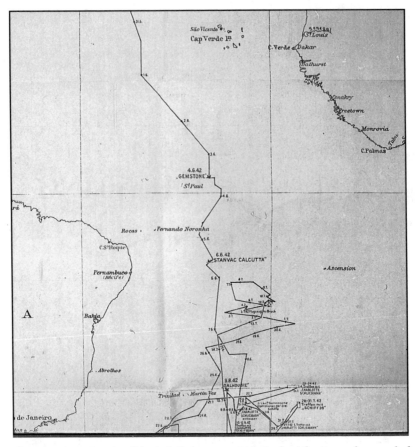

German chart showing Stier's *daily noon position in the Atlantic as she prowled for enemy ships. Note the postions of ships encountered:* Gemstone, Stanvac Calcutta, Dalhousie, Charlotte Schliemann, Schiff 28. National Archives.

Late in the evening of June 3, transmissions were received indicating that the U-boats hadn't seen any shipping off the west coast of Africa in the last ten days and that Allied ship traffic was shifting more to the center of the South Atlantic and away from the coast. This was good news for *Stier* as she was traveling southward toward the Atlantic narrows. At this point, *Stier was* about 500 miles north of St. Peter and St. Paul's Rocks.

At 0730 on June 4, an enemy ship suddenly came into view bearing on a 30 degree reciprocal heading. The alert command was given immediately to the artillery. *Stier* held her course and measured the steamer's speed at 10 knots. The enemy still hadn't seen *Stier* as Capt. Gerlach was shrewdly using the rising sun as a screen. Finally, at 0809 the command was given to fire a salvo across the steamer's bow. At the same time *Stier*'s war flag was raised and a flag signal given to the other ship to stop immediately. The steamer turned hard to port to show her stern and present a smaller target. *Stier*'s port artillery opened fire and Capt. Gerlach then matched the steamer's subsequent turn to starboard with the starboard artillery opening fire.[2] The steamer returned fire with her stern gun.

After the first salvo was fired the steamer tried to send a Q (under attack) message which was thwarted by *Stier*. The steamer

Top, the British freighter Gemstone *was pursued and fired upon, center. Bottom, the* Stier's *crew watches the bombardment from the main deck.* National Archives.

The crew of the Gemstone *come alongside and are taken aboard after their ship was torpedoed and sunk.* National Archives.

made two more course changes and once more showed her stern to *Stier*. *Stier* fired her cannon. The opponent stopped returning fire. The steamer was dead in the water. Her crew lowered the lifeboats, boarded them and came alongside *Stier*. The steamer's captain, E.J. Griffiths, handed over the ship's papers indicating that she was the 4,986 BRT British freight steamer *Gemstone*, loaded with ore and sailing from Durban to Baltimore. Captain Gerlach believed the area was too dangerous to remain in and decided to sink the *Gemstone* quickly. At 0906, a G7a torpedo was fired. The ship sank stern first.[3]

Since there was no further attempt to send a Q message, Capt. Gerlach believed the steamer sank unnoticed at 1349. However, *Gemstone* had sent off a second message.

An accounting of the prisoners taken aboard was: one captain, three radio officers, three watch officers, four engineers, fourteen white men and nineteen colored men. The prisoners were examined and the injured, including the captain and one radio officer, were treated. Separate accommodation areas were set up — colored, white, and officers — in a tarpaulin area and partitioned from each other.*

At 2315 the captain put *Stier* on a longer zig zag course as she passed St. Peter and St. Paul's Rocks on June 5.[4]

At 2330 three planes flew high overhead and the captain stopped the ship to avoid creating a wake that might be seen. *Stier* was undetected and thirty minutes later she entered the trade-wind zone.[5]

At 0915 on June 6, *Stier* was approximately 600 miles off the coast of Natal, Brazil. [just north of Pernambuco on the map on p. 80] A lookout suddenly spotted a ship moving out of a rain squall about two miles away. The lookout reported that the ship was a tanker. Using the rain squalls as cover, *Stier* was able to track the vessel for another thirty-four minutes covering about 14 ½ miles. At 0949, as the sun broke out, the other ship came back into view and continued on the same course. Capt. Gerlach positioned his ship, again using the sun as a screen. At 0954 the *Stier* fired the first salvo and the stop signal was flashed to the tanker. The tanker refused to stop and immediately set the Panamanian flag. *Stier* set her flag to inform the tanker that she was a German warship. The tanker immediately began turning to starboard. Capt. Gerlach ordered a hard turn to port and *Stier*'s starboard battery opened fire.[6]

After *Stier*'s first salvo, the tanker answered with two cannons from aft, one 12cm. and an 8cm. At 1001, *Stier* fired a G7a torpedo from the starboard pipe, hitting the tanker in the stern. No more resistance was encountered. A total of 148 rounds of 15cm were fired and the tanker received numerous hits throughout the ship. *Stier* received two 8cm hits, one by the forward mast not detonating, and a second shot detonating on the starboard side

---

* *Gemstone*'s captain, E.J. Griffiths, spent seven weeks aboard *Stier*, was transferred to an oil tanker, then returned to *Stier* in late September 1942. He ended up on *Tannenfels* and was taken to France as a prisoner-of-war.

This unique series of photos show the Stanvac Calcutta *being chased and fired upon, two upper photos; taking on a heavy list, center; rolling over, second from bottom, and sinking, bottom.* National Archives.

near the No. 5 hatch. Two crewmen in this area were wounded; one lightly in the face and the other in the foot and calf.[7]

At 1028 the tanker began to settle at the stern. The tanker's crew left the burning ship and boarded a lifeboat and two rafts. *Stier* now exposed her port side to allow the men in the boats and those swimming in the oily water to board.

According to the prisoners their ship was the 10,170 BRT American ship *Stanvac Calcutta* with a capacity of 16,000 tons of oil, traveling in ballast enroute from Montevideo to Aruba. Of the fifty-two man crew, the first and third officers [mates] and thirty-five men were saved. The captain and the radio operator were killed in the midship house. Interrogation of the prisoners revealed that the tanker received approximately forty hits with the 15cm and some hits from the 3.7.[8] No Q messages had been transmitted. Eight of the prisoners and two officers were seriously injured and most likely would not live. The two physicians aboard *Stier* took over immediately.

The crew of the Stanvac Calcutta *approach in boats and rafts and are taken aboard.* National Archives

According to Capt. Arthur Moore in A Careless Word…, A Needless Sinking …: *"The raider was first seen about 1012 ship's time after she had fired the first salvo. She was about 4 miles away off the port bow. The Captain gave orders for full speed ahead and ordered the gun crews to open fire. The gun crew fought back firing 20-25 rounds from the forward and after guns. The broadsides from the raider made a shambles of the midship house, killing the Captain* (Gustaf O. Karlsson)*, Radio Operator* (Philip A. Heath) *and the AB at the wheel* (Nelden W. Okander)*. The raider also put a torpedo into the ship. The engines were stopped and the ship lay dead in the water with a rapidly increasing list.*

The thirty-seven survivors of the battle were picked up by Stier.* *An ordinary seaman* (Martin W. Hyde) *died after being rescued.*[9]

At 1200 on June 6 *Stier* left the area. The next day, Capt. Gerlach gave out three E.K. II awards (*Iron Cross – Second Class*) to the lookout, physician and second cannon operator for their bravery during combat.

It was an auspicious beginning for *Stier* with her early sinking of two enemy vessels over a two-day period.

On June 8, a suspicious looking ship with a black smoke trail was spotted. Capt. Gerlach thought it was possibly a warship because of the unusual configuration of its masts. He observed the ship for forty minutes until it disappeared in the rain gusts.

At 2219, *Stanvac Calcutta* crewmember Martin W. Hyde succumbed to his injuries. At 0650 the next morning the ship was stopped for his burial at sea, an American flag covering his body. Those prisoners well enough to attend were on hand. The oldest American crewmember gave a short speech.

---

* Most of the survivors ended up in Japanese prison camps and one in a German camp. One prisoner remained on *Stier*. Since no Q message had been sent, no one knew what happened to the vessel or crew until almost a year later when this one prisoner was hospitalized. *Stanvac Calcutta* would receive the Gallant Ship award. See chapter 19 for details about the Gallant Ship award.

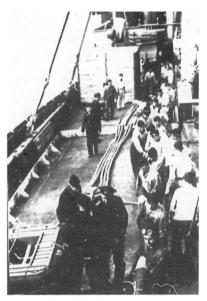

Much-needed fuel oil was pumped from the Charlotte Schliemann. *The process involved running fuel lines from the tanker, above, to the deck of the* Stier, *right.* National Archives.

A new course was set in preparation of meeting supply tanker *Charlotte Schliemann* on June 10.[10]

Early on the morning of June 11 the two ships met in the open ocean and began transferring oil. However, pumping oil from *Schliemann* to *Stier* was delayed because of a problem with the flange collar. It took almost three hours to correct before pumping could be resumed at 0920. Then, it was discovered that instead of oil, ninety-eight percent of what was being pumped was sea-water. Capt. Gerlach was furious and considered the act close to sabotage, blaming the tanker for the problem. The effect of this failure was that sixty tons of oil in tank No. 3 had to be evacuated until the water disappeared, a waste of time and precious fuel. Once the oil was transferred, provisions and sixty-eight prisoners from *Gemstone* and *Stanvac Calcutta* were transferred to the tanker the next day, June 12.[11]

Now, *Stier* would criss-cross the South Atlantic shipping lanes looking for quarry (*See map*).

On July 3 Capt. Gerlach decided to use one of his Arado 231 seaplanes to scout for enemy shipping. The ship stopped at 0750 hours in order to prepare the plane for launch in a moderate swell. The preparations lasted an hour-and-a-half. After launching the plane, the ship did a "duck pond" maneuver* to starboard and the plane attempted to take off. Although the sea conditions had diminished almost to zero and the plane's engine was revved up to maximum, the plane kept coming down in the swell before it reached maximum speed. It lost its momentum and was unable to rise above the water. The attempt to take off was repeated three times, all without success. Although the plane could handle the shock of hitting waves and was stable enough, the motor was too weak to lift the fully loaded aircraft with a full tank of fuel out of the water.[12]

It was decided to fill the fuel tank half way and lighten the plane by removing all equipment that was not absolutely necessary. In the middle of the day, both wind and sea became calmer. The plane was again launched at 1420 hours with a three-quarters full fuel tank, unnecessary parts removed and without emergency rations. The weight had been reduced approximately 50 kilograms (110 lbs.) After a rather long take-off in which the plane hit the swell in the duck pond with hard bumps, it was able to gain altitude and fly the one-hour prescribed reconnaissance route to the south, east and north. Following the assignment, the plane landed in the duck pond by putting down very carefully on a high swell.

The plane taxied to the ship and everything seemed to be in order. But when the motor stopped shortly before the plane was lifted by the hoisting hook, a rear strut of the starboard pontoon suddenly broke, the plane tilted down onto the starboard wing, and the tail went into the sea and slowly filled up with water. A rubber boat failed to pull the plane under the hook, and the plane was about to sink. The portside motorboat was launched. The plane had been driven about fifty meters back to portside by the wind and had to be towed carefully by the boat. Slight damage to the plane's starboard wing was unavoidable. The plane was

* With the engines going ahead, the ship makes a sharp turn which causes the sea surface on the inboard side of the turn to become calm, like a "duck pond."

The Stier*'s float plane, intended for reconnaisance, was more trouble than it was worth.* National Archives.

Launch and retrieval were supposed to be by boom, left, but in at least one instance, the plane had to be towed back alongside and almost sank in the process, below. National Archives.

lifted and placed on board but the tail and starboard wing were completely filled with water.[13]

The break may have been caused by the rear strut of the plane's starboard pontoon being partially damaged due to the three takeoff attempts in the morning, but any break was not visible in spite of a careful investigation of the plane and after the first flight attempts. There was also a possibility that, when the plane landed after the flight, the starboard rear pontoon strut was broken and held in position by the pressure exerted on the break by the plane's fairly rapid taxiing on the water. When this pressure ceased (the plane's motor was turned off shortly before it was to be hoisted), the strut collapsed and the plane tipped over toward starboard.

An investigation of all the struts and wing areas was immediately begun. A final verdict on whether the Arado 231 was still usable could not be delivered.[14] For Capt. Gerlach, aerial reconnaissance was no longer an option. *Stier* would go back to the hunt for enemy shipping without the use of the two airplanes.

No sooner had this decision been made when, on July 6, the lookout spotted a ship's mast bearing 310 degrees. Since the airplanes could not be used, the ship, which was fourteen sea miles away, was unapproachable. July 7 found *Stier* zigzagging slowly southward in what was thought to be promising hunting grounds according to U-boat reports. During this 2-3 day period the other airplane was repaired (parts from an Arado 196 were on board and used for repairs), but the sea swell was poor and the attempt was not made. With no action, the ship received a coat of light-gray paint.[15]

On July 9, a message was intercepted at 1600 from the British steamer *Tordene*. A zigzag course was set the next day to intercept *Tordene* on a southerly course but at 1800, the plan to run overnight for nine miles on *Tordene*'s course was abandoned because *Stier* would have traveled too far out of her patrolling area.

Adjustments to the other airplane's floats and lines were strengthened and completed that day but again the second plane couldn't be launched because of the weather.[16]

The plane's fuel capacity was reduced by deleting forty liters from its supply. However, this also meant cutting down on aerial reconnaissance by forty minutes.

Without the use of its second airplane, *Stier* was dependent on her lookouts. Capt. Gerlach had already determined that the AR 231 was unsuitable for the Atlantic, even under the best of weather conditions. Nonetheless, on July 14 another attempt was made to launch the airplane but was suspended because of a two foot swell with a moderate heave. The pilot was unable to break loose from the water and further damage occurred to the lines and struts holding the plane together. Three more attempts were made before the project was totally abandoned.

Charlotte Schliemann came into view on July 17 bearing 310 degrees at 0625. Because of the continuing high seas, oil transfer was impossible and both captains agreed to meet on the 23rd.[17]

On July 21, a special report was prepared for SKL concerning statements made by prisoners during their interrogations. The captain of the English steamer *Gemstone* and the remainder of the prisoners of the American tanker *Stanvac Calcutta* had now been aboard 1½ months.

Statements by *Gemstone* Captain (translated from German):
Gemstone was enroute from Durban to Baltimore. The captain admitted the ship had been in Cape Town after his papers had been examined. In Cape City the ship's route had been assigned by a naval authority. The Captain was trusted in his interrogation but appeared very reserved with his statements. The remaining crew members appointed themselves again and again to their captain and he said you'll not gain anything from them. Later the captain told in a conversation that there had been problems with the mine deflector and he had lost a day's travel causing him to take the route he had just taken...

In October 1941, *Gemstone* sailed from Glasgow to Archangel with eleven ships under the escort of HMS *King George V*, HMS *Ark Royal*, HMS *Suffolk*, HMS *Norfolk* and nine destroyers. They carried tanks and airplanes. There were nineteen English ships in Archangel at the time. The Communists had given a large celebration for the English captain. The captain also said that the best escort courses were from Canada to England and from England to Russia.

The English captain did not know of an HSK ship in the South Atlantic and had not counted on one being at the equator.

The Captain's General Sentiment:

England must win the war because Germany wants to control the whole world.

His earnings would be £70 sterling but 50% of this was deducted for the war tax. His family received £32. This relationship is very depressing.

Statements of the *Stanvac Calcutta* Prisoners:

Crew had been on the *Stanvac Calcutta* for two years and was glad to be traveling between Venezuela and Montevideo because of no U-boat activity. They hadn't counted on any auxiliary cruisers traveling from Venezuela to La Plata. Only the captain knew the ship's route. In America, sailors are heavily recruited; fifty percent of *Stanvac Calcutta*'s crew were on their first voyage. They were asked why they go to sea when they live in such a rich country. Their answer: "only a few are rich. The people are poor and if you want to provide for your family, you have to go to sea. You had some good years in Germany, but with us it was even worse."

Nothing was learned from interrogating the officers and further attempts were abandoned. These statements were skillfully taken by Lt.z.S. Petersen. In general, all the prisoners behaved politely and decently and gave no, nor caused any, complaints.

The wounded Americans (only one of them died) showed the most gratitude daily for their medical support. The prisoners did not receive the same meat as their captain or the German crew. This was a common practice and, from the point of view of the captain, for the prisoners who do not carry out manual labor, their provisions were sufficient. It was felt that they would adapt themselves to the quantities assigned in Germany.[18]

On July 23, the tanker *Charlotte Schliemann* returned. The captains discussed oil transfer, prisoner exchange and the possible voyage of *Charlotte Schliemann* to Japan. Another meeting was scheduled for the 28th but the tanker arrived on the 27th. The captain and the officer of the prisoners came on board. The remaining thirteen prisoners, including *Gemstone*'s captain, were transferred to the *Charlotte Schliemann* with the exception of the one prisoner who was still injured.

11

STIER

TO THE

ATLANTIC NARROWS

On July 27, 1942 *Stier* received instructions from SKL to rendezvous the next day, the 28th, with Ship No. 28 (the raider *Michel*) at specified coordinates.[1]

During the evening of July 28, a ship ten miles away was sighted in the evening darkness. A few minutes later another light was seen blinking about thirteen miles away. Morse contact was attempted with this ship but to no avail. The second ship seemed much smaller and traveled very fast. A call was made to this boat by lamp and the boat responded with "Heil Hitler." This greeting was not considered to be 100 percent accurate. The vessel could still be an opponent and the signal needed to be answered accurately. Finally, Ship No. 28, the raider *Michel* communicated directly with Capt. Gerlach stating that they carried an LS boat.

Then Ship 28 approached. Their captain, Hellmuth von Ruckteschell, informed Capt. Gerlach that the alarm had been set after they sighted *Stier* and the S-boat *Esau* was launched to

The captain of the Michel *boards the* Stier *to discuss raider strategy. National Archives.*

investigate. This confirmed to Capt. Gerlach that future meetings must be avoided at night if at all possible. At 1930 spontaneous greetings were exchanged by the crews. Both ships lay in close proximity to each other.

At 0930 the next morning, *Michel*'s captain and an aide came aboard *Stier* for discussion. Capt. von Ruchteschell said that the size of the operation area was too large and it had almost been two months since there were any results. Both captains agreed that a coordinated operation of both ships would be more effective. Plans were worked up the next day and detailed discussions and exchanges took place between the officers on logistics and strategies.[2]

Esau

The LS (Leicht-Schnellboot) *Esau*, named after the Biblical wandering hunter, was particularly effective in her career. She carried torpedoes that could travel thirty knots and in 1942 she was responsible for sinking the American ships *Connecticut* and *George Clymer* and the Norwegian ship, *Aramis*. Captain von Ruckteschell's favorite mode of attack was to track the opponent during the day and then move ahead at night so that the enemy sailed into *Michel*. Attack could be made outright or in many cases, *Esau,* after being lowered into the water, would then be let loose to initiate the attack or to monitor the opposing vessel. After an attack, *Esau* would be used to pick up survivors.

On July 30, *Michel's* captain returned and discussions continued. Both captains agreed to operate together for a more successful hunt. A message was sent to SKL. Another meeting was scheduled with *Charlotte Schliemann* for August 1. *Michel* prepared for prisoner delivery and oil transfer, and further discussions. Both raiders then proceeded on a 210 degree course separated by a distance of ten miles. [3]

On August 2, the commanders of the two raiders discussed tactical details with common employment of execution during day or night attack. These discussions lasted seven hours, curtailed only because of deteriorating weather conditions, which continued the next day, making it impossible for boat traffic, so measuring exercises were conducted on course headings and range finders. Practice drills were later carried out.[4]

During the early morning hours the seas and wind began to calm and discussions resumed the following day at 0800, continuing into the afternoon. Capt. Gerlach sent the following message to SKL:

1. There is no more steamer traffic in the (7) Quadrants that the two ships had been assigned to — GS, FS, FL, FM, FN, FU and GG (see page 98). The HSK's are heavy and slow to catch the faster ships.

2. Ship 23 (*Stier*) wants to operate in Quadrants FR, FK, FD and FE (*This is the Atlantic Narrows area between Natal, Brazil and Freetown, Sierra Leone – See map on page 80*). Captain Gerlach was awaiting a reply by noon for permission to carry out this plan or go either to the east coast of South America or hunt in the restricted area off Freetown. If permission was not granted, then the two ships would continue to operate together.

3. If the two ships continue to operate together they will do so in the fast traffic areas of FL, FM, FU and GG. Exclusive operation is hopeless.

4. If SKL rejects joint operations, then Ship 23 requests to be sent to the west coast of South America.

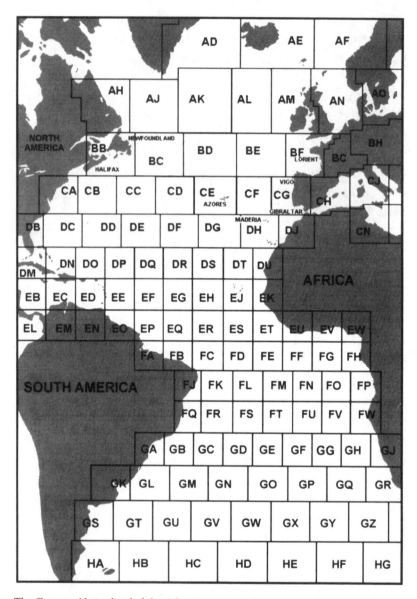

The German Navy divided the Atlantic into quadrants to provide easy reference and to prevent locations from being discovered by the enemy. The Quadrants known as Marinequadratkarte (Naval Square Map) divided the ocean into grids. The double letter grid consisted of 486 nautical miles per side. This square was then divided into 9 squares of 162 miles per side and, finally, this square was divided into 9 squares of 54 nautical miles per side. Copyright Rodney J. Martin 2005.

SKL's message: Ship 28 will refuel with *Charlotte Schliemann* and exchange its prisoners. If hunting improves on the east coast, Ship 28 will operate in FU and GG and will again join *Stier.*[5]

12

Stephen Hopkins

TO THE

South Atlantic

Departing Australia August 3, 1942, the *Stephen Hopkins* steamed westward. The voyage to Durban, South Africa was approximately eighteen days. The first week was clear of problems or submarine menace.

Rodger Piercy:

> For the next week, we sailed without incident. Weather was fine and seas fairly calm. Of course, we were under tight blackout restrictions, constant gun watches, and had our fire and lifeboat drills regularly. These precautions eventually paid off.
>
> Then the weather began to change. The seas began to roughen, wind blew, and the skies grew gray and darker. We were instructed to batten down for a typhoon and possible hurricane. By the following afternoon we were into it.[1]

Capt. Buck, seeing the barometer drop, ordered his officers and crew to prepare for the storm. Everything movable was

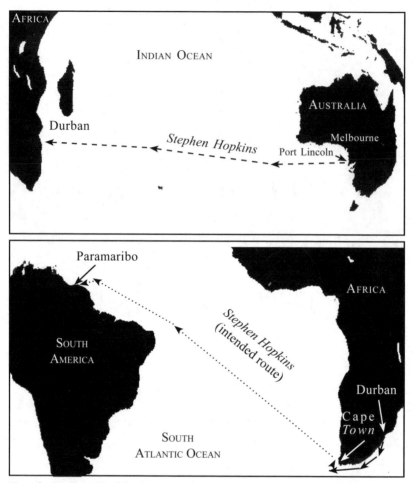

Top, the Stephen Hopkins *'approximate route from Australia to Africa; above, her intended route across the South Atlantic.*

secured and all the hatches were re-battened. The ship's speed was reduced to half as *Hopkins* steamed into the storm.

Author William Mueller described the captain's actions:

> … Capt. Buck, reduced speed to 3 knots. At 3 knots they would make only 72 miles in a 24-hour period. That would mean the 2400 miles they had remaining would take 33 days… The storm worsened. The waves continued to grow until they were large enough to break high up on the bridge. Captain Buck, seeing great green and white masses of water rolling

down the foredeck, looking as though they would carry away the forward masts, smashing against the bridge, knew that he and his crew were in one of the legendary storms that happen once in a hundred years. Would the ship take it?[2]

Rodger Piercy:

No one was allowed to leave the midship quarters. The wind was so great it could blow a man from the deck into the sea. The waves had begun to roll higher and higher until, I would guess, they were forty to fifty feet high. We were riding into them and one minute it seemed we were standing on our stern, and the next plunging forward down a huge wave. About every fourth wave our bow would plunge into one and the whole forepart of the ship would become submerged with tons of water which would flow right over the gunnels. The entire ship would vibrate and labor to pull her bow out into normal position, and the water would smash against the midships. I think every man in the crew felt the clutch of fear, but it was then that our officers showed their true spirit. They laughed, joked, and never once let any of their concern show to the crew. Yet we knew what problems they had.

The bow gun which was welded and bolted to the deck had been torn out and washed down to the midships. Every heavy wave that washed over the ship would smash it against the side of the hatch and gunnels. We did not dare try and secure it. Two of our lifeboats were smashed and in bad condition. The wings of the bridge tore loose from their stanchions and were curled up about two feet above where they should have been. Besides we had sprung some plates and were taking water. All the bilge pumps were kept going to try and keep the grain dry. As you know, if the grain had gotten wet and started to swell, we would have been in <u>real trouble</u>.

Because of the rough weather, the galley crew could not cook and we were eating sandwiches. We did have coffee anyway. On the third day it started calming. It seemed that the storm passed almost as quickly as it came, and we were soon cleaning up the mess. As badly as we were damaged, it did not seem so, once the seas were calm and we could get back to normal routine. It seemed everything had to be cleaned, polished or greased. There was plenty to do, but by then we were glad to be able to do it.[3]

The ferocity of the storm was unimaginable. Cadet-Midshipman Arthur Chamberlin wrote a censored letter home after arriving in Durban and included a note to his brother Robert describing the storm: "Robert, don't ever go to sea!"[4]

Due to damage to the forward deck plating, and being driven off-course approximately two hundred miles, the *Hopkins* arrived at Durban on September 3, two weeks behind schedule.

William Mueller: "... They had been presumed lost and the call letters of the ship had been cancelled [by the military], making it difficult for them to make port in Durban. After a visual inspection by port authorities, they were permitted entry."[5]

A 1943 report to Admiral Land described the voyage:

> The vessel left Port Lincoln alone and unescorted, and a after a thirty-two-day voyage, bucking heavy gales, arrived at Durban, South Africa. During the heavy weather, the lifeboats were smashed and much gear carried away. So bad was the weather that the beams running fore and aft were cracked and in many places the welding of the plates gave way. The deck-house tore loose, the welding leaving go along the bottom where it was welded. The forward ammunition hold was flooded. The bow was stove in. The forward gun mounts were wrecked and torn to hell.
>
> The vessel lay eight days at Durban discharging grain and having the welders repair the breaks and strains to the deck-house, deck plating and hull plating, also having the lifeboats replaced and repaired.
>
> The grain was all wet in No. 1 hold. All the bilges were plugged with grain; in fact the 2nd assistant engineer [Cronk], taking off a manifold to clear the lines, found the whole line plugged with grain. Sack after sack of it was taken out of the bilge and thrown overboard.[6]

In Durban, damage to the *Hopkins* was inspected and repairs made, which included the guns and their mounts.

Rodger Piercy:
It seemed only a few days before we got the cry, "Land Ho!",

and the "Dark Continent" never looked better to anyone. When we arrived off Durban Harbor, it was so crowded with allied shipping that we had to anchor outside for two days before we could go in to discharge. When we moved to the docks, they immediately started discharging and had us free in two days to move to the shipyard for repairs.

We were allowed liberty again and found Durban to be a very pretty town. It was a rest camp for allied troops, and I remember seeing part of the Free Polish Army, Free French Army, Scottish Highlanders, and many segments of various Dominion units.

The second night ashore, part of our crew got drunk in town and had found a number of big Zulu rickshaw pullers. About six of them had the Zulus riding in the rickshaws while they pulled them around town having chariot races. Needless to say, the British people were incensed at this fraternizing and eventually the police put a halt to it.

The Seaman's Institute at Durban was very cordial and many of the crew went there both for services and entertainment. I've visited the park at Durban, where they had trees from all over the world planted.

Meanwhile, the *Stephen Hopkins* moved to the shipyard, and we were completely repaired of all our storm damage and put back in top condition.

We then moved down the coast to Cape Town, South Africa. We went to berth to finish discharging our cargo [two thousand tons of sugar] and even pumped off our surplus fuel. As it turned out we were to go to Paramaribo in South America and rumor had it that we were to take a load of bauxite to New Orleans. They needed the fuel here in South Africa, and we could easily get more there. [Bauxite was an important wartime commodity and was used to manufacture aluminum airplanes.]

While we were in Cape Town, I went ashore with Karl Largergren and spent the day visiting and hunting souvenirs to bring home. It was there that Karl told me he was very despondent. He had a feeling that he would never see his home again. He told me that, "The German raiders are active in the South Atlantic, and I just feel something is going to happen. I'm not going to make it." Karl was a gunner on the bow gun under Second Officer Earl Layman.

We were in Cape Town about one week, when ordered to move on to South America. Just before we left, we had a passenger [George Townsend] come aboard through the

American consul. He told me he had been in the Middle East, and I think it was connected with oil. He had come to Cape Town on a British ship that was returning.[7]

Navy gunner Moses Barker: "At Cape Town we went ashore and do you know what kind of music we danced to? The Star Spangled Banner – it was the only music they had."[8]

Before the *Hopkins* sailed, Chief Mate Richard Moczkowski wrote a letter home to his family with the simple opening statement, "I'm on my way home!"[9]

Prior to departure, Capt. Buck was warned of possible raider action in the South Atlantic and ordered his crew to be especially vigilant. He reminded them that although they were now a seasoned crew, it was no time to let down their guard just because they were headed home. General Quarters drills were intensified to insure they remained at peak fighting condition should they come upon the enemy. This Liberty ship would fight to the end if necessary.

Piercy continues:

Back at sea we resumed our normal duties, but were instructed to be especially alert as there had been all kinds of activity in the area. All guns were to be ready for instant action; total blackout, and no horseplay of any kind.

The weather was only moderate, skies mostly overcast. Good enough for us to make fair time, and it remained about the same all week. There were no particular incidents and nothing to indicate what the future might hold. In fact, on the morning of September 27th, just after breakfast, the off-duty crew had a dice game rolling.[10]

13

TANNENFELS

TO THE

SOUTH ATLANTIC

Discharging her cargo in Yokohama, *Tannenfels* loaded rubber and other war materials for her return to Europe. Capt. Werner Haase's report (taken from Top Secret documents) describes the voyage.

On 8 August 1942, we finished taking on fuel and equipment. The ship was made ready for sailing and all official matters were taken care of according to regulations. Admiral (*Paul*) Wennecker came on board with his entourage and gave a short speech to the crew. It was a very cordial sendoff. At 2000 the last boarding party of three from HSK X (*Thor)* came on board. The anchor line was released, and under the instructions from the harbor pilot, we left Yokohama. At 2036 the harbor pilot left the ship and a marine pilot gave further instructions. At 2143 we received instruction from another marine vessel to follow it and we did anchoring at 2400 in the Tateyama-Wan anchorage.[1]

On August 9, at 0700 a Japanese Naval unit came aboard with orders for us to prepare for the delivery of a seaplane which was taken on board two hours later and correctly lashed down. At 1100 the Japanese contingent departed and we raised anchor at 1119 to continue our journey. Immediately after leaving the anchorage area a Japanese torpedo boat took up a position in front of us and we followed directly behind it. At 1640 we set a course of 224 degrees, sailing into good weather in a wind force of 4 WSW, and a lively sea and swell. Soon thereafter the Japanese ship departed and signaled us with a message, "We wish you a good voyage and return home."[2]

Our course was maintained over the next several days. Several reports were received from submarines but were meaningless to us since the subs were located too close to the Japanese islands and coastal waters. The good weather continued and there was no danger of any typhoons. On 13 August we passed Itbayat Island (west coast of the Philippines) where a course change was made to 220 degrees true. We maintained this course until 16 August whereby a storm with rain, wind, waves and swell came from the south. On 16 August we received a radio message warning that several submarines were located on our course near the Natuna Islands (midway between Malaysia and Sarawak). Later after darkness, the course was changed to the east to get well away from the danger zone.[3]

At 2100 hours on 18 August we passed the Seroetoe beacon. An hour later we saw a shadow rising on our port side. This turned out to be a warship. We received the call "NQ" and we answered with the distinct signal "D." Earlier we sighted several other Japanese vessels which were clearly distinguished as such.[4]

On 19 August at 0542, the daylight visibility prevented us from traveling the distance to Sunda Strait (between Sumatra and Java). We reduced speed and at 0600 we encountered a Japanese warship which acted in a strange way. The ship put itself in front of our bow and in such a way that we had to sail dangerously close to the island and make a large detour to avoid this vessel and the island. Passing through the Sunda Strait, we showed our distinct signal and received a response signal of "Have a good trip home."[5]

We steered a true course of 200 degrees in good weather, but the wind and sea conditions increased during the following days. The ship had to struggle to make progress and spray continued over the decks and hatches. On 23 August we changed course to 260 degrees. We followed course orders for our rendezvous with Auxiliary Cruiser X (*Thor*) which occurred exactly at the planned meeting place on 28 August. We remained at this position until midday and sighted Auxiliary Cruiser *Thor* at 1308 hours. After carefully maneuvering until 1421, everything was immediately made ready to transfer equipment. I went on board the Auxiliary Cruiser to deliver a personal report. The transfer was interrupted over the next day-and-a-half due to wind and sea conditions. Finally on the 30th, the transference of supplies was completed along with the transfer of seventy-one prisoners at 1620. Everything went well, and after I said goodbye to their commander, we set off and resumed our voyage at 1640.[6]

We traveled a course of 251 degrees and to save oil we used only one engine making a speed of 9 knots. We sailed on for the next few days into prevailing westerly winds at a force 4-7, changeable weather, and at times rough seas and swell causing the ship to struggle. On 4 September a radio signal was heard from a ship bearing 165 degrees. It was the English vessel *City of Canterbury** which was communicating with the Lorenco Marques station about arrival, passengers and cargo. A course change was not needed.[7]

On 7 September orders were received whereby we were to rendezvous with the Auxiliary Cruiser 28 (*Michel*) on 12 September. The meeting didn't seem possible because weather conditions were so bad that speed was greatly reduced in order to avoid damage to the ship. On 11 September the ship was steered directly into the sea in order to change the hatch No. 1 tarpaulin which had been torn by the waves. The ship was struggling against brutally high waves and swell into a southwesterly storm with hurricane gusts and a wind force of 10 to 12. The waves were breaking over the entire vessel. The storm weakened during the night but the next day on the 13th bad weather hit us again. A telegram was previously received on the 11th ordering us to move further north toward our waiting area and this was finally attempted on 14 September with a new direct course. Radio traffic in the South Atlantic was such that there didn't seem to be any danger. However, a new depression

---

* The merchant ship *City of Canterbury* escaped from an attack on convoy BM12 earlier in February 1942. The attack took place in the approaches to Singapore as British troops were being transferred to this area from India. The major loss in the convoy was the *Empress of Asia* which was carrying 2,200 troops of the approximately 3,800 in the convoy. She was set afire and abandoned.[8]

developed later on the 14th and due to the aforementioned order we didn't change course to avoid this storm. On 16 September the weather cleared and for the rest of the voyage the ship's forward path was not affected very much.[9]

On 20 September 1942 at 0930 we arrived at the appointed meeting place. We stopped the engines and then sailed with one engine until 1300. At 1303 the auxiliary cruiser came into view and we carefully maneuvered toward it and at 1340 we were floating on Cruiser 28's (*Michel's*) lee side. I immediately went on board to have a meeting with their commander. At their commander's recommendation, we saved fuel by shutting down our engines, but we were ready for action. On the 21st wind and sea prevented the transfer of supplies. The weather finally cleared at 0800 on 23 September and work was finally completed at 1900. We agreed to stay together and the next morning Ship 28 received a message and had to leave and meet another ship. I received a direct order to wait at my position until Auxiliary Cruiser 28 (*Michel*) returned. Orders were that I would receive important papers, nineteen men from the crew, and sixty-nine prisoners to transport back to the homeland. In addition, it was agreed that we would inform Auxiliary Cruiser 23 (*Stier*) that it should travel to the waiting

The Japanese plane delivered by Tannenfels *stowed on the deck of* Stier. National Archives.

The same plane from a different angle. National Archives.

position of Auxiliary Cruiser *Michel* and *Tannenfels*. Over the past few days we had drifted 100 sea miles to the south-southwest. At 0800 we departed to sail back to our waiting position arriving there at 1930.[10]

Auxiliary Cruiser 23 (*Stier*) came into view on 25 September at 1025. At 1200 hours we lay on Ship 23's lee side with engines stopped. I went on board at 1400, gave my report and then we started transferring supplies and the airplane. The work was completed at 1900.

The Commander and I agreed to drift in the same manner as with Auxiliary Cruiser 28, since:

1. The position was fairly secure.
2. Oil needed was to be saved at all costs.

Both commanders were in agreement that it was absolutely necessary to continue the voyage at full speed. The oil supply was however very low. We even considered the possibility of transferring oil to our ship. We drifted like this until 27 September 1942 in relatively good weather. The weather changed and at 0400 on 27 September the wind was from the east with an almost calm sea. The wind force was 1-2 with continuous fine rain. The visibility was moderate. At 1009 we saw a ship four points to starboard that suddenly came out of a rain squall. As can be seen from the sketch [p. 138], we were lying in the lee of Auxiliary Cruiser 23 (*Stier*) at about a true 110 degrees. The wind was north-northwest at 3-4 and increasing.[11]

At first we believed that the ship was Auxiliary Cruiser 28 (*Michel*). But to be safe, we ordered our engine full throttle two times. This was a safety measure, in order to be ready for any eventuality.[12]

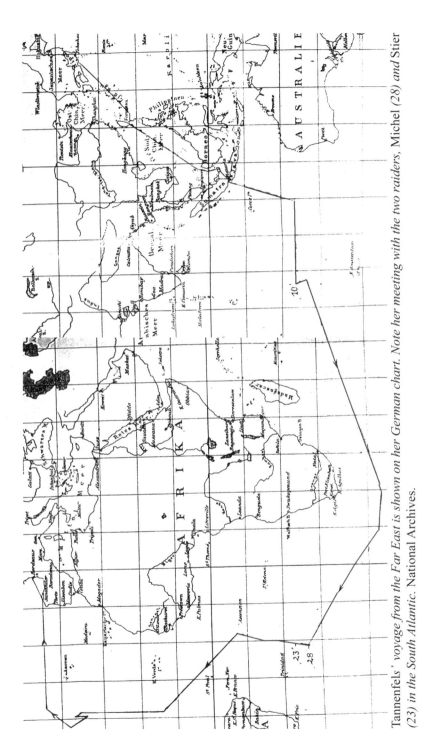

Tannenfels' voyage from the Far East is shown on her German chart. Note her meeting with the two raiders, Michel (28) and Stier (23) in the South Atlantic. National Archives.

14

ACTION

IN THE

SOUTH ATLANTIC

O n August 7, 1942, the tanker *Charlotte Schliemann* was dismissed from the area with the understanding that she would wait nearby for further instruction from SKL. At 1200, a message was received that the two raiders should separate the next day. Later that evening, both vessels carried out night exercises loading and firing their guns.[1] In his book, *The Secret Raiders*, David Woodward wrote:

> As they went they practiced exercises between the two ships and carried out drills on board. [*Stier*] Capt. Gerlach notes that his gunnery officer had brought his crews to such a pitch of efficiency that even the reserve crews of the main armament, made up of officers, petty officers, clerks and anti-aircraft gunners, could get off a minimum of fourteen rounds per minute, while the crack crew achieved a figure of eighteen and three-quarter rounds per minute."[2]

Crew of Stier *at gunnery practice.* National Archives.

The following day, SKL telegraphed both ships that the previous day's message was premature and that the wrong orders had been issued. The new order was that Ship 23 (*Stier*) would shift operation to FE. But again there was a problem with the transmission. Finally, later that evening, SKL correctly laid out the new operation plans and Capt. Gerlach sent the following transmission. "I shift my operation area after FE, FD, FK, FR." Ship 28 (*Michel*) also received a short signal from SKL ordering her to depart from Ship 23 in the early morning hours.[3] After traveling thirteen miles with *Stier*, *Michel* sailed off on a 356 degree heading at 0200 on August 9.

At 0815, the lookout announced the sighting of a mast and stack of a ship bearing 72 degrees. The vessel was identified as a commercial steamer with three masts and was keeping its course. At first *Stier* maintained a parallel course with the steamer to avoid appearing threatening. At 0840, the steamer was 9-½ to 10-½ miles off. Gerlach closed in to four miles. The steamer didn't make any course changes until 1109. She was identified as the

7,250 ton British freight steamer *Dalhousie* traveling in ballast from Cape City to Trinidad.

When the steamer was abeam she began zig-zagging in 5 to 10 degree turns. Capt. Gerlach ordered the starboard guns to prepare to fire.

At 1216 the alarm was given. The freighter immediately turned to port and *Stier* fired one salvo as a warning to stop. The *Dalhousie* sent a brief Q message at which the order was given

Stier*'s torpedo hit the* Dalhousie *at No. 5 hatch.* National Archives.

to open fire. On the fourth salvo the steamer was hit; smoke was seen in the after body. The *Dalhousie* answered with her 12.7cm gun. *Stier* fired back at a 2 for 1 ratio. It was hopeless for the steamer. The raider suspended fire several times to see what the other vessel planned to do but each time resumed her barrage as the steamer tried to run off. Finally, after twenty salvos over a thirty-two minute period, the opponent turned and signaled her surrender.

At 1248 *Stier* signaled: "Leave your ship!" The steamer's crew could be seen collecting personal items and stowing them in the lifeboats.[4] The boats were quickly launched and rowed toward the raider.

Because of the Q and R messages sent (Q = disguised merchant vessel attack and R = enemy surface warship) and the possibility of an enemy warship arriving on the scene, there was no time to search the freighter and she had to be torpedoed. A G7a torpedo was shot from the starboard pipe hitting in the area of hatch No. 5 and the ship sank tail first at 1447.

Capt. Gerlach's decision to quickly sink the *Dalhousie* was further prompted by the sighting of another vessel heading toward his ship on a course of 110 degrees. As this vessel drew closer,

The survivors were taken aboard Stier *as they came alongside.* National Archives.

The Dalhousie *immediately began sinking stern first.* National Archives.

The Dalhousie *slowly twisted counterclockwise as she went under.* National Archives.

The raider Michel *drifting with* Stier *as the vessels' captains plan future strategy.* National Archives.

however, he was relieved to see it was the raider *Michel* which was responding to the intercepted Q message. Meanwhile, the *Dalhousie*'s crew was taken on board. They included: one captain, ten officers, twenty-six crewmen, and five gunners. Among the effects in the boats were an automatic lifeboat radio beacon and receiver, ship's papers and two Atlantic sea charts on which the course and routes taken by the ship were rubbed out but still visible.[5]

At 1547, in order to be off as soon as possible, *Stier* and *Michel* left the area and traveled fourteen miles away from the sinking in a southerly direction. Both captains agreed that with the sinking of *Dalhousie* and the warnings the ship sent, transfers to new operational areas should be asked for. Capt. Gerlach requested the following Operation areas; FE; FD; FK and FR (see grid chart on p. 98). Both ships continued south awaiting new orders.[6]

According to *Stier*'s war diary, on August 10 Capt. Gerlach was very pleased with the sinking of *Dalhousie*. Reviewing the previous day's events, he realized the attack could be used as a model for future raider attacks against merchant shipping. The best aspect of the mission was that the opponent hadn't realized that his ship was a surface raider.

August 11: At 2400, *Stier* was on a 216 degree course heading for Operation area GM (Parallel with Buenos Aires and La Plata – Grid Map). At 1100, August 12, *Stier* was in an area between Cape City and La Plata, traveling crosswise during daylight to avoid enemy ships in preparation for night attacks. This was considered the safest route. The raider would then proceed to the lower right corner of GN and then go on a long zigzag to GM in preparation for searching in the west. It remained to be seen whether tanker traffic would be in the GW or GD quad. It was anticipated that the weather in that area would be moderate until the end of September.[7]

August 14: SKL sent a transmission ordering *Stier* to Operation area GM. SKL followed with another message stating that the *New York Times* had printed a story* about an American cruiser searching for raiders in the South Atlantic.[8]

With this new information an operation on the west coast of South America would be more desirable, especially after factoring in considerations of fuel and [presumably] moderate weather. Gerlach hoped SKL would consider this as an alternative. Until then, he concentrated his energies in the South Atlantic. Should the enemy cruiser be alone, *Stier*'s operation in the Cape City – La Plata track would be the best choice. Capt. Gerlach pointed his ship's bow toward Operation areas GV and GW.[9]

August 16: at 0800 there was a noticeable increase in the wind, swell and heave, as well as a rapidly falling barometer. During the night it was difficult to make headway. The engine

---

* Page 1 of the August 13, 1942 *New York Times*, the headline read, "Fight Believed On In South Atlantic: Allied Cruiser, Probably Ours, Is Pursuing German Raider After Saving Ship." The article indicated that a raider attacked a British ship and the ship probably survived after sending an SOS; that the raider was extremely fast, disappearing when the cruiser approached.[10] The ship was the 5,874 ton freighter, *Arabistan*, which was attacked on August 11, sinking on the 14th. The raider responsible was *Michel.*

Gale winds with high, heavy seas reduced Stier's *speed to almost zero.* National Archives.

was racing, potentially endangering the entire plant. The next day the weather deteriorated further and by night wind gusts were measured from the WNW at a strength of 11-12.* *Stier* was working heavily to make progress. The ship's engine registered the equivalent of 10 revolutions but the distance traveled for the day was only three miles.[11]

Although the captain expected acknowledgement of the sinking of *Dalhousie* from SKL, only a short signal was received on August 14. There was no mention of any sinking. In fact the message was confusing, describing objectives for the operational areas, with no acknowledgement of *Stier*'s success.

Capt. Gerlach was disappointed and angry. In his reply, he said that *Stier* had been 100 days at sea, fought two recognized heavy Channel engagements, was responsible for three sinkings, yet only twenty EK II (Iron Cross) honors had been awarded. He pointed out that it would be difficult to keep the crew's morale up without recognition. He emphasized that, in addition to

---

* Beaufort scale 11-12 indicates a violent storm-hurricane of 56 to over 65 knots in speed.

acknowledging the value of the *Dalhousie* sinking, honors for the crew should be immediately awarded. Such recognition would show appreciation for outstanding individual acts of courage during that event.

Gerlach also said that he considered the method and results of the *Dalhousie* sinking to be applicable in future encounters. He reminded SKL that *Stier*'s operational area had been swept clear of opponents' ships; three ships sighted and three ships sunk.[12]

August 17: A storm was quickly arising and by noon had increased to gale force with the barometer reading 29.33. The sea was extremely high and heavy. The ship worked heavily but did not take on any water.

The storm track turned counterclockwise in the evening producing further heavy and steep seas and winds played havoc with the ship's steerage. The wind was from the north-northwest slowly swinging to the west as the Beaufort force increased from 7 to 9. At midnight the storm, wind and swell began to slacken and *Stier* was able to travel ten miles by 0600 on August 18.[13]

August 18: A new transmission was received in which *Michel* was asked to evaluate local traffic conditions for SKL. *Michel* responded that there had been no traffic in the middle of the South Atlantic for over two months.

August 19: Another storm developed and *Stier*'s course was changed in order to avoid it. A message was heard from the Falkland Islands BAMS [Broadcast Allied Merchant Ships] of the sinking of *Dalhousie*.[14]

August 20: There was still a moderately severe sea and swell. In the afternoon a message from an American ship was heard telling of ten survivors from the ship sunk by the raider. The report was identified as reliable indicating that *Michel* attacked *Arabistan* and that the ship sunk afterwards. Ten men escaped. Escaped crewmen were a problem for any raider (HSK). Each raider captain was required to ensure that no prisoners escaped to avoid data about the HSK becoming known.[15]

August 21: A wireless message was received scheduling a future meeting with *Charlotte Schliemann*. The course was set at

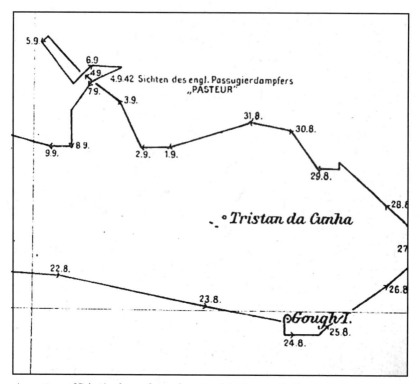

A portion of Stier's *chart shows her track before and after arriving at Gough Island, southeast of Tristan da Cunha.* National Archives.

95 degrees. *Stier* began traveling eastward toward Gough Island to explore the island for a suitable bay to urgently overhaul their machinery. A meeting with *Charlotte Schliemann* was set for August 27 to receive fuel and supplies.[16]

Capt. Gerlach compiled a list of items needed: coal was in the shortest supply, followed by water, food and spare parts. In addition, 860 tons of fuel oil were needed for normal operations over the next several months with 400 tons essential for the ship to make it back to western France. Calculation showed that *Stier* would then have enough on board to return to the Gironde by November 28th. Overall sea time could be extended to December 16 if thirty-five more tons of fuel oil were added. However, to be cautious, OKM (*Oberkommando der Kriegsmarine — Supreme Command of the Navy*) was advised that the vessel could only stay at sea until December 6th.[17]

Gough Island came into view at a distance of approximately five miles. There appeared to be no inhabitants or settlement. The only suitable anchorage was found on the north side of the island, but anchoring was almost impossible because of strong winds which increased as the vessel drew near the shore. Then an area was discovered on the southwest shore of the island where a hoist could be utilized to overhaul the machinery over a two- to three-day period. As the weather continued to deteriorate, Capt. Gerlach instructed *Charlotte Schliemann* to wait until August 27 for their scheduled oil transfer. *Stier* sailed eastward ten miles between 0300 and 0400 to move away from the island and conserve fuel by drifting at night. At 1800 a rising storm forced the ship to start her engine. The wind increased quickly and she covered only four miles, working strongly against a rising sea and swell. During the afternoon the wind climbed from force 2 to force 10. Visibility was poor as one rain squall after another combined with a rough sea and high swell out of the south.[18]

Repairs were completed and *Stier* went to her refueling appointment. At 1130 hours on August 27 the tanker *Charlotte Schliemann* came into view as prearranged. Immediate discussions were held with Capt. Rothe. The ships were maneuvered into position and after only seven minutes oil was being pumped into *Stier*. Enough oil (295 tons plus 925 tons) was taken for the ship to operate, then return to the Gironde (France). During the

Gough Island as viewed from Stier *appears dismal and inhospitable.* National Archives.

Charlotte Schliemann *transferring fuel to* Stier. *Note the fuel line running across the water from the bow of the tanker to the raider.* National Archives.

oil transfer the forty prisoners of war from *Dalhousie* (except the captain and steward) were delivered to *Charlotte Schliemann*. The *Gemstone*'s captain also was taken on board, away from his crew. *Charlotte Schliemann*'s captain informed Capt. Gerlach of his orders to sail to Japan. *Schliemann* was dismissed and a short telegram was sent stating that *Stier* had enough fuel to last until December 6. No acknowledgement of the signal was received and it was again sent on the 29th.

August 29: *Stier* set sail for the Cape City-La Plata Operations area. A short message was wired regarding this new destination and it was confirmed.[19]

September 1: At 1120 hours, *Stier* observed the third anniversary of the beginning of the war. Capt. Gerlach hoped a message would be sent commemorating the anniversary to the crew. However, nothing was received from the homeland about the anniversary, nor any congratulations to the crew for their accomplishments. Capt. Gerlach strongly felt this would be a great opportunity for his HSK to give out medals and honors, which would be greatly appreciated. This was especially important because the crew had been cut off from the homeland.[20]

Later in the day, SKL wired that an English (salvage) steamer, the *Industria,* had set out from Cape City for Montevideo. The ship was stated to be on the same course as *Stier* but had a one and-a-half day lead. Capt. Gerlach replied that, with the fuel situation as it was, they could not afford to hunt approximately three to four days at high speed to overtake the British ship. If the report had been received two days earlier a successful hunt would have been possible.[21]

September 4: At 0659 hours a ship with two masts and one funnel was sighted at 86 degrees. The steamer was traveling against the sun. Lt. z.S. Nadorff was unable to identify it since the ship was too fast. Her distance from *Stier* rapidly increased to twenty-one miles and any attempt to cut off the enemy ship became impossible.

The ship was identified as a large passenger steamer although her class was not certain. It was evident that she was from the European Union (Allies). Since action against the steamer was impossible it remained a question whether *Stier* was sighted and reported. Her superstructure could be seen clearly but no signals were heard. Capt. Gerlach said it was a case of a fast steamer showing clearly what speed is worth. An auxiliary can do only fourteen knots.

SKL reported that the 29,253 BRT large passenger liner *Pasteur* of the Cunard White Star Line of Liverpool was the ship sighted.* The steamer was on direct course to Buenos Aires.[22]

---

* The *Pasteur* was launched in 1938 in France and was considered to be the third fastest ship of her time. She could travel at a maximum speed of 25.5 knots and carry over 1,100 passengers. The *Pasteur* was so swift that she rarely sailed in a convoy. She was captured in Canada after France surrendered and carried troops and prisoners of war for the remainder of the war.[23]

September 12: During the course of the night, a very large steamer was heard. It was known that the steamer was in the vicinity because a wireless transmission had already been received from the steamer on the same wavelength earlier that evening. A second transmission gave a substantial approximation. However, nothing was seen by the lookouts because it was a very dark night.

Transmission 1712/12 was received from SKL in the afternoon ordering *Stier* southward toward Cape City [Cape Town, South Africa]. Another meeting with *Michel* was ordered for three weeks hence. Capt. Gerlach considered this meeting unnecessary, in addition to not being feasible. He replied that *Michel* should take supplies from *Uckermark* as she was already in that operations area. *Stier* would most likely take supplies from *Tannenfels*.[24]

September 16: The good weather permitted another attempt to work with the other airplane. It was lowered into the water and almost became airborne on its first attempt. However, it sagged and came to a stop. On the second attempt, the suspensions from the fuselage cracked. Both machines were now useless. It was decided they would be given to *Tannenfels* to be brought back to the Homeland.[25]

September 18: An unknown steamer was heard transmitting on wireless. Confirmation was not made. However, *Stier* tried to intercept the vessel by stopping every thirty minutes and listening to the K.D.B. (*Kristalldrehbasis – a hydrophone detection system used to pick up underwater sounds*) beginning at 2200. The vessel was pursued for a day with no sighting and pursuit was given up the next day at 1200.

The appointed meeting with *Tannenfels* for September 21 was moved to the 22nd and *Stier*'s course was changed at 1500 to meet *Tannenfels*. SKL sent a message that a longer meeting with *Uckermark* was planned in order to take on provisions and to exchange camouflage materials. However, the fuel delivery would not take place. There was a scarceness of coal and fresh water, and there was also a build-up of marine growth on the ship's hull which was slowing the ship's speed to less than thirteen knots.[26]

September 20 was a Sunday. A station was set-up aboard *Stier* for a drawing by lots and an auction to raise funds for charity. The proceeds from these activities amounted to 3,270 R.M. (*Reichmarks*) and with the cinema collected earlier amounted

The Sunday fair aboard Stier *included activities, costumes and boxing matches. It resulted in a generous donation to a German welfare fund. National Archives*

Above, a boxing match on the fore hatch. Below, crew dressed in costume for the occasion. National Archives.

to 3,809 *Reichmarks*. The total would be transferred to the K.W.H.W. (Kriegswinterhilfswerkes — War Winter Welfare Organization).

This was a German relief fund which functioned from 1933-45. Its purpose was to provide clothing and food for people in emergency situations back in the Homeland.

The captain was very pleased at the generosity of his crew, emphasizing that only five Reichmarks per person was requested and in the end, the average contributed per man was ten.

A course change was set for the meeting with *Tannen-fels*.[27]

By September 21 the *Stier* was losing speed due to the sea swell and a piston in cylinder I needing to be replaced necessitating the ship's revolutions be reduced to ten knots. Five hours later the ship began to roll due to the counter-clockwise shifting of the sea swell. Progress was difficult and the meeting with *Tannenfels* was put off to early morning of the 23rd. The weather calmed down on the 22nd and the coordinates were reached but *Tannenfels* was not at the agreed meeting place.[28]

A ship's masts came into view on the 24th which was presumed to be *Tannenfels*. A slow approach was made but it turned out to be *Michel*. *Michel*'s captain came aboard *Stier* and specific issues were discussed along with telegrams received by *Michel*. *Tannenfels* had too little fuel for transfer and instructions were given to *Stier* if possible to fuel *Tannenfels* and then to seek fuel from *Uckermark*. *Stier* however, presented the alternative to take fuel from *Tannenfels,* which could be re-fueled by *Uckermark*. *Michel* instructed *Uckermark* to stand by from 0800 on October 4 and wait for messages from *Stier.*

Further area border clarifications took place between the two ships and then *Michel* was dismissed for a breakthrough attempt back to the Homeland. *Stier* was refueled and dismissed *Uckermark,* which left for her voyage to Japan. *Stier* set a course westward to meet *Tannenfels* at the pre-arranged October 4th position. Both *Stier* and *Michel* ran apart and then diverged from each other at 1600.[29]

On the morning of September 25th a vessel came into sight on the starboard side. It was the blockade runner *Tannenfels*. Both

Tannenfels *drifting with* Stier *in the South Atlantic.* National Archives.

ships came together at 1055 and at 1125 Capt. Werner Haase of the *Tannenfels* came aboard. A discussion followed in which *Stier* was to take on additional supplies. At 2000 the engine had to be reported as inoperable and for 3½ hours a piston was pulled and repaired.[30]

September 26 saw continuing good weather and the time was used to scrape and paint the water line. After lying alongside the *Tannenfels* overnight, the next day there was delivery of additional supplies needed by *Stier* and further discussions took place. Among other items, as replacement for the two wrecked Arado 231s, the *Tannenfels* brought a seaplane that was given by the Japanese Navy to be used by a German auxiliary cruiser/raider. Since the plane's length and width dimensions turned out to be suitable, it was taken on board *Stier* and put on the extended platform in hatch No. 5 that reached down to the lower deck.

Closer inspection revealed that the plane was in a completely dilapidated state, without bombing or radio equipment, and the rest of the parts were in such poor condition that the *Stier*'s aircraft specialist reported that it would take at least three to four weeks to do a complete inspection in order to decide whether it was airworthy. The struts were rusted through, as were the anchorings

The crew of Stier *over the side scraping marine growth from the hull.* National Archives.

of the struts, and all movable parts such as pontoon supports, the hinges of the loading docks, etc., were rotted through.[31]

On September 27th Capt. Gerlach reported on the situation developing:

> On the morning of 27 September 1942 Ship 23 (*Stier*) lay at approximately Lat. 24 degrees 44' S and Long. 21 degrees 50' W, with the blockade breaker *Tannenfels* in position to await Ship 28 (*Michel*) in accordance with a previously planned rendezvous. For two days we were able to take advantage of the prevailing good weather to scrape away the growths on the ship's waterline, and then to paint. Also, on this Sunday morning since early dawn, crews were working outboard on places [on the hull] and in rubber dinghies.
> At about 0800h the first officer reported to me that because of the upcoming wind and increasingly rougher seas associated with it, as well as the rain, outside work would have to be suspended.

In addition, visibility continually became poorer, so that for this reason as well it seemed advisable to cease working, although, up to now, this area which had been under observation for a long time – appeared to be completely free of any vessel traffic. At 0850 there were only twelve men in the rubber dinghies with a few people aboard and some working outboard.

0852 – Just as I had left the bridge to go below decks, I heard the call "**Vessel**" in sight to starboard, direction 30 degrees ships bearing, which corresponds to a compass bearing of 150 degrees. Then followed an immediate alarm, calling the ship, and the realization that it was not one of our own, nor a neutral vessel, but definitely a large enemy steamer.

A flag signal "**Stop at Once**" was set.[32]

PART III

15

SEPTEMBER 27, 1942
LAT. 24° 44' S.
LONG. 21° 50' W.

0852

Stier raised the flag signal, "Stop at once."

Aboard the *Stephen Hopkins* Capt. Buck ordered the U.S. ensign run up. Immediately he commanded the helmsman to turn hard to port to both present a smaller target to the enemy and position the after gun for firing.

0853

Stier unmasked all her guns and swiveled them toward the enemy.[1] At the same time she turned hard to starboard.

0856

Stier opened fire on the *Hopkins*. The first salvos came from her 20mm and 37mm guns, raking the freighter, with their main focus on the bridge and superstructure. One minute later *Stier*'s six 5.9" guns began firing, registering immediate hits.[2]

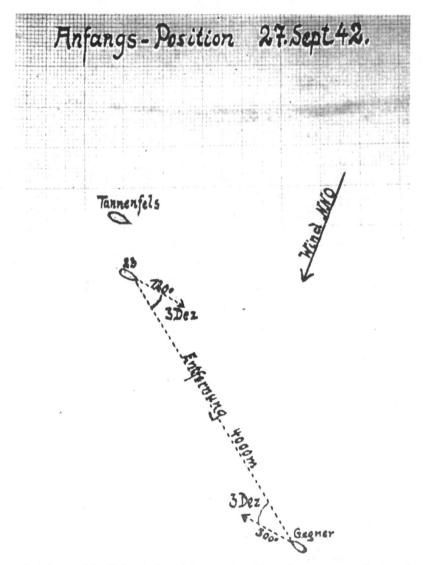

The "first position" sketch shows the vessels relationship to one another when the Hopkins *was first sighted at 0852.* Tannenfels *and* Stier *(two vessels at top) are drifting on a course of 120 degrees, the* Stephen Hopkins *is steering a course of 300 degrees. Distance between* Stier *and the* Stephen Hopkins *("gegner" or opponent) is 4,000 meters or just over two nautical miles. The wind is from the north-northeast (NNO= nord/nord ost).* National Archives.

Aboard the *Stephen Hopkins* the crew raced to their battle stations. Ordinary Seaman Rodger H. Piercy, was stationed and assisting at the stern gun along with several Navy Armed Guards and Cadet-Midshipman Edwin O'Hara.

Rodger Piercy:

> The German ships began to move out to encircle us, one to port and one to starboard. As soon as they fired, we received orders to open fire. We had our guns trained on the smaller raider and immediately let go [the time was 0900]. We knew we hit her, but did not know to what extent. From then on we had no time to do anything except load and fire. It seemed about the fifth round or so, Ensign [*Cadet-Midshipman*] O'Hara and Willett were jubilant. We caught her in the engine room and it looked like she was dead in the water, but I mean her guns were certainly active. O'Hara was in charge of our gun at the beginning as Ensign Willett had stayed on the bridge to determine if we were up against friend or foe.
>
> When he (Willett) gave orders to open fire, he left the bridge for the stern gun. On the way to the stern, he got hit in the stomach with shrapnel which sliced him open and knocked him down. He got up and came to the stern with part of his intestines hanging out.[3]

George S. Cronk, second assistant engineer:

> I stood the midnight watch shift and was sleeping when the General Quarters alarm woke me up. While trying to get dressed I recognized Chief Mate Moczkowski's voice outside my room telling someone to "Get on that gun!" "Get on that gun!" "Get on that gun!" When I opened my door the Chief Engineer Rudolph Rutz came out of his room and handed me a rack of three test tubes, so I could take boiler water samples for chemical analysis when I went on watch at noon. He said, "Here's your test tubes but I don't think you'll need them," or words to that effect. By that time we had been hit several times. I put the test rack on my desk and opened my locker for a coat. A shell hit the room next to mine; the 3rd Engineer's room (Kenneth Vaughan). He was on watch in the engine room. I walked out on the boat deck and it was in shambles. I went down to the main deck aft and saw 1st Engineer Charles Fitzgerald and two men

(I don't remember who they were) with fire hoses. The water was coming in spurts. He handed me the fire hose and said, "I will go to the engine room and see what's wrong." (I never saw him again) A few seconds later a shell hit the engine room and blew up at least one boiler. Steam and asbestos pipe covering came out of the skylights and engine room door. Making my way forward toward the officer's mess there was a lot of steam and I could not see too well. The whole area around the galley and crew's quarters was gutted. I met Wiper Henry Engel. He was holding his hip and said he was hit. I told him to go to the officer's mess as it seemed to be intact. He continued to go aft away from the mess room. (I never saw him again). As I came in the starboard door of the mess room, Chief Engineer Rutz came in the port door carrying Messman Herbert Lowe. Lowe didn't seem to be alive. Ford Stilson, the Chief Steward, was also in the messroom.[4]

Moses Barker, (Navy) seaman second class:

I was on the 4-8 watch. I got off watch at 8 in the morning and went amidships for breakfast. Just as I finished I heard the damndest explosions going off. The ship was shaking all over. I took off for the 4-inch 50 on the stern. I started out the passageway and man you wouldn't believe the machine gun bullets coming by. I mean it was something else. I was on my hands and knees running like a rabbit. Man was I moving. I got back and I can't say what was happening on the rest of the ship as I was occupied. I finally got on my 4-inch 50 and we had a pretty good time. Those Germans really knew what they were doing. Every time their guns would go off they would go off all at once and those shells would hit us every time.[5]

0900

Capt. Buck had ordered Chief Mate Richard Moczkowski to maneuver the *Hopkins* so that her stern faced *Stier,* in order to present a smaller target. While swinging, the *Hopkins* began firing on both enemy vessels. Second Mate Joseph Layman was in charge of the bow 37mm guns and his crew scored hits with the *Hopkins'* first shots.

Chief Mate Moczkowski, however, was seriously wounded by enemy fire at this time. Shot in the chest and left forearm, the mate continued at his post abaft the wheelhouse, rallying his men and directing orders to the bridge to enable the ship to keep her guns bearing on the enemy vessels. Weakened by a rapid loss of blood from a severed artery, he collapsed to the deck, but refused to stay down, and ordered a seaman to assist him to his feet and prop him in a doorway that he might discharge his duties.[6]

From a distance, *Tannenfels,* under orders to avoid risking her vital cargo, followed the action. A German war correspondent, Friedrich Weber, who was aboard *Stier,* reported:

> *Tannenfels* hardly recognizable in the fog, also fired at the enemy ship before running off. We had to lead in the battle because *Tannenfels* had traveled a long distance from Japan loaded with valuable raw materials that must reach Germany under all circumstances. At this point in time, nobody knew if the American was part of a larger group.[7]

But even at a distance the blockade runner joined the action. Capt. Haase:

> Suddenly we noticed that Auxiliary Cruiser 23 (*Stier*) was being fired at. Now we gave the alarm too. Our guns were immediately manned and at the same time received permission to fire. We turned around and saw that our ship was being fired at. The first three shots landed in our wake, about twenty to thirty meters behind our stern.[8]

Aboard the *Stephen Hopkins* Chief Steward Ford S. Stilson was in his quarters writing the menu for the following day and was not aware of the precise time:

> My first knowledge was the sound of a shot, 37mm or like type striking through the superstructure or midship section above the waterline. As there was no mistaking this sound from a shot fired from the ship I knew we were under attack and grabbed my life jacket and papers and went to my station at amidship. The general alarm rang as I was on my way. About one minute was spent assuring my men that this was not a drill and that those of them who did not have gun stations should

not go out on the boat deck until the abandon ship signal had been given. I also rallied such men as I saw amidships to their stations.

At the end of this first minute or so word was passed to me that the chief mate had been wounded. I went back to my room, secured bandages and antiseptics and proceeded to the bridge deck where I found the chief mate reclining on the deck in the thwartship passageway adjacent the wheelhouse but very active in shouting orders and advising the captain to keep her turning with the stern bearing on the enemy. The mate was shot high in the chest and in the left forearm. The chest wound did not bleed or froth much but the arm wound had touched an artery and he had lost considerable blood since he was too active and excited to keep the artery compressed. I applied a tourniquet and bandaged both wounds. I started below to get more material ready for the next casualty but returned up the ladder at the sound of severe groans. He had gotten to his feet with the aid of one of the ordinary seamen, Piercy, and had turned the opposite passage where he was again struck this time in the leg by a fragment. All this time, shells had been riddling the superstructure and our own 4-inch had started at a rapid rate about the time I was bandaging the mate.[9]

0900-0905

The *Stephen Hopkins'* second mate, Joseph E. Layman, was in charge of the 37mm bow guns and was able to score immediate hits upon *Stier.* Capt. Gerlach noted the good fire control and discipline practiced by the enemy ship:

It became immediately clear that this wasn't a normal trading vessel, especially in this untraveled area, but that of an auxiliary warship, patrol ship or perhaps even a helping cruiser or troop transporter, well-camouflaged and harmless looking. Observation of the ship concluded that the ship was similar to the British *Dalhousie* sunk on August 9, 1942 approximately 8,000 BRT and that she wasn't loaded and appeared to be sailing in ballast. The enemy ship was configured in the following assembly based on initial hits against our ship:
   (1)   – 6-inch cannon at the stern
   (2)   – four 4.7 inch cannon at the stern
   (3)   – four 4.7 inch cannon amidships.[10]

0901

The *Stephen Hopkins'* radio operator, Hudson A. Hewey, tried to transmit a "Q" message from the radio shack but the transmission frequency was immediately blocked by a transmitter aboard *Stier* for the next five minutes. *Tannenfels* confirmed no radio traffic or transmissions from the enemy ship nor repetition of "Q" messages from a land station. Hewey tried one more attempt at 0906 but this message was also blocked.[11] Radio Operator Hewey was killed shortly thereafter when the radio shack was destroyed by fire from the raider's Flak guns.*

0904-0905

The *Stephen Hopkins* turned off to port to present her stern and *Stier* turned hard to starboard so as not to let her opponent run off and escape in the mist. The entire port Flak artillery of *Stier* opened up on the freighter. The critical point was the *Hopkins'* stern cannon. Still numerous hits occurred. During one of the first salvos fired by *Stier*, one of the 5.9-inch cannon shells found its mark in the *Stephen Hopkins'* engine room, destroying the starboard boiler. Not only did this cause a huge fire but the explosion released scalding steam into the air. Caught and killed in this deadly hit while on watch were Third Asst. Engineer Kenneth Vaughan, Fireman Michael Fitzpatrick and Wiper Andrew Tsigonis. Deck Engineer Nick Makres was never seen but was believed killed also by a direct hit into his room. Oiler Gus Tsiforos was never seen by any of the survivors. Chief Engineer Rudolph Rutz and Second Engineer George Cronk "were together all the time the battle was going on carrying wounded men out of the engine room and off the decks and out of their quarters where they were shelled in their beds."[12]

---

* Actually, the messages did get through. A Secret Document issued in Berlin on December 10, 1942, stated:, "The ship delivered at 1258 (0858 local time) o'clock an SSS [under attack] message indicating location which was repeated around 1304 (0904) and 1306 (0906) as SSS and SOS. St. Helena and Falkland heard and further spread this message."

Wiper Pedro Valdez was killed and later certified by George Cronk. The resulting starboard boiler explosion caused *Hopkins* to lose engine power and her way-on was reduced to 1 knot.

When the Flak 38 stopped only briefly, *Stier*'s own firing perspective of the opponent in the limited visibility was obscured by gun smoke (*and later*) her own fires.[13]

0901-0910

During this time span, according to the German report, the *Stephen Hopkins* hit *Stier* fifteen times with larger caliber; (15cm and twelve, 7 or ten, 2 cm) whose sequence of firing couldn't be determined by *Stier.*

(*Except for machine guns, the* Stephen Hopkins *made all those hits with a single, old, World War I 4-inch gun. The marksmanship of her Navy Armed Guard and back-up merchant marine crew are a credit to both services.*)

0905

At this time *Stier* received two hits in rapid succession. Both hits in themselves could have been fatal. The first went from the starboard side into the steering engine room piercing the entire cable pit. The result was that the steering engine failed and remained in the hard-to-starboard position.

The second hit went completely through the main engine area, detonating the oil valves on the port side. The armatures, filters, and piping were torn up, the main fuel adjustment valve severely bent and several clevis mountings were torn off. These two hits made the ship un-maneuverable and the ship was stopped. After one to five minutes the port artillery was set for firing. It was also during this time (between 0905 and 0910) that *Stier* attempted to fire a torpedo, but the distance couldn't be resolved because of the loss of the entire power plant, a fact which was not yet known on the bridge.

Results of *Hopkins* hits upon *Stier*:

(1) hit in the steering engine room causing loss of steering engine.

(1) hit in the engine room port oil stores causing strong fragmentation and igniting fire in the oil gates.

(1) hit in the engine room piercing portside electrical cables causing failure of the entire electrical connection system, affecting: lighting, fire extinguisher pumps, gyroscope, stabilization, ammunitions' hoists and elevators (ammunition now had to be carried by hand from topside chambers), and emergency rudder mechanism.

(1) hit in forward engine room tank causing a leak.

(1) hit in the coal bunker causing a fire.

(1) further hit in coal bunker causing strong smoke necessitating evacuation of heating room plant.

(1) hit in the port hatch No. 2 crew compartment causing a leakage of oil out of supply tank. In a short time large fires developed in the adjacent areas with resulting overpowering smoke. Fighting them was impossible because of damage caused by hit No. 3.

(1) hit in port hatch No. 4 cargo causing strong fire.

(1) hit in the main military hospital

(1) hit in the reserve military hospital on bridge killing ship's doctor.

(1) hit on the stern.

(1) hit in the steward's quarters starting a fire.

(1) further hit into the non-commissioned officers' area in hatch No. 4.

(1) hit under the bridge by the loading officer.

(1) hit in the starboard bridge wing without detonation.

0907

The deadliest hits upon *Stier* occurred at No. 7 hatch. Fire quickly spread by leaking oil to the wood bunks, mattresses, bedding, chairs, and wood lockers causing tremendous smoke and additional fast spreading fires. The fire hoses didn't work because of the loss of pumps caused in hit No. 3. The fire extinguishers were soon empty.

Further hits came from the small caliber (4cm or 2cm) to the funnel and antennas, port 37 and 20mm Flaks.

0908

The *Stier*'s port antenna was hit by small caliber and the loss was not immediately noticed since the receivers still worked from time to time with the grounded antenna. A connection was made to the 200 watt transmitting antenna. Another hit was made to the guidance system of the starboard antenna. This was repaired in ten minutes.[14]

0900-0910

It was during this period that the heroic actions of the U.S. Navy Armed Guard gun crew and the merchant seamen assisting them took place. These actions were amongst the bravest in the history of American naval and maritime warfare. As the *Stephen Hopkins* was being continually raked by enemy fire (from two ships at times with at least four times the destructive power of the American freighter), her Armed Guard and merchant crew were being killed one by one in a hellish one-sided battle.

According to (Navy) Seaman Second Class Paul B. Porter's statement to the Navy:

> [Porter] had finished with his 4-8 am watch and had just eaten breakfast and fallen asleep in his starboard ship quarters. He was violently awakened with what sounded like a sledge-hammer banging on the deck. Porter ran to the porthole to see what the disturbance was and saw two ships; one of which was firing at the *Hopkins*. Grabbing his gear, Porter ran out of his cabin aft to his battle station which was on the .50 caliber gun. While doing so Porter passed a crewmember that had died a horrible death as he had been shot in the buttocks. (*Possibly Wiper Henry O. Engel as he was last seen wounded in the hip on the main deck*) Upon arriving to his gun mount, Porter found the gun covered by wet canvas and the gun inoperable because it was wet. He immediately left and continued on to the 4-inch gun and saw that the Armed Guard and merchant marine

backups were being killed in rapid fashion. While at this station Porter saw the forward 37mm blown up and, with it, several crew disappearing over the side.[15] One of those unfortunate members killed was Porter's friend, AB Karl Largergren who was a backup gunner. (Largergren was the seaman who said in Cape Town, "I feel something is going to happen and I'm not going to make it.")

Navy Seaman Second Class Wallace E. Breck, was the only man to survive the hit on the forward 37mm. Breck said: "They made hash out of us…" He later remembered he had been lying in his bunk studying the U.S. Navy Armed Guard *Bluejacket Manual* and running to his station at the sound of firing and seeing Lt. Willett being ripped right across the stomach with bullets but continuing to his station to take charge of the aft gun and firing about thirty-five shots before he collapsed. After being revived Willett assisted in abandoning the ship.

Breck told of a gunner who found his gun beneath a tarpaulin and immediately opened fire not bothering to take the cover off, and hitting several men aboard one of the raiders. Breck was wounded by shrapnel in the hand and in the shoulder when a shell hit his gun station:

> [It] knocked off one whole corner. One merchant seaman was killed in the blast and a Filipino mess boy was injured fatally. Most of the firing was by the smaller ship. The other was more or less of a mother ship. One of the vessels was a little smaller than our ship and the other a little larger. One raider had gun turrets. …Everything happened so fast that I didn't get a good look. The smaller ship had guns I know were over five inches. Their combined firepower must have been four times what ours was. We concentrated on the smaller raider… Shrapnel was bursting in the air above us and on us. And shells were hitting us all over. But we kept up our fire until our ship was ablaze and the deck was a shambles. The battle lasted only about fifteen or twenty minutes.[16]

During this ten minute time span and shortly thereafter, the U.S. Navy Armed Guard gun crew lost nine of its fifteen members.

Casualties reported in the Office of Naval Intelligence Navy Department Intelligence Report:

Jackson, Vernon — Last seen in wheelhouse, not wounded.

Little, Otto — Last seen in wheelhouse, not wounded.

Tingle, J.B. — Last seen headed for No.1 raft. Did not leave ship on this raft.

Beyer, William — Last seen between No. 2 and No. 3 hatches. May have been an occupant of a doughnut raft sighted later.

Yanez, Andrew — Killed at same time as William J. Adrian (*AB Seaman*).

Smith, P.E. — Killed by shell, port side aft near No. 5 hatch.

Cleveland, C.T. — Seen hit by shrapnel. Believed killed.

Demars, P.O. — Last seen on after-deck below gun platform.

Berry, Lyle — Last seen in his room under 4" gun platform, port side.

The passenger, George Townsend, was last seen entering his room starboard side main deck, near salon.[17]

0905 – 0918 (*excluding a stop in action from* **0910 – 0913**)

Stier reported that the opponent (*Hopkins*) passed through a sequence of heavy salvos despite *Stier* having ammo elevator failures. The artillery fire was heavy resulting in severe damage, creating many fires and much smoke in several places aboard the *Hopkins*. These fires would burn brightly, stop, and burn briskly again.[18]

0910

Capt. Gerlach ordered *Stier*'s crew to stop firing, to see what course of action the opponent would take. The bad weather had made the opponent's outline almost unrecognizable and the

German captain was afraid she would try to run off in the rain gusts.

Captain Gerlach:

> After the three minute halt in action, at 0913 the midship artillery was given permission to open fire again. It was reported that during the 0905-0910 and 0913-0918 time periods that approximately fifty to sixty salvos hit the opponent, mainly K2 (*nose fuse*) and a small number of Bdz (*base fuse*) – ten to fifteen per gun barrel were fired. The cannon operations control post personnel, munitions personnel, and mechanical ammunition technician personnel all worked well together for the entire battle. Finally at 0918 the following order was given, "Halt! Batterie halt!" as the opponent was considered to be overpowered.[19]

O.S. Rodger Piercy:

> We were taking an awful beating. The shrapnel was heavy, and the boys handling the aiming mechanism were being blown off their seats about every second or third round. Ensign Willett kept part of the crew under cover, and as we lost a man, another would run out and replace him. Then we would fire another round or two. Suddenly there was a terrific explosion in the engine room. They had hit a boiler because the steam blew in the air. We knew they had terrific gun power because when they would catch us with a unified salvo, our ship would almost jump out of the water and vibrate from stem to stern. The second large explosion came a while later and felt like it was right underneath us. Actually it was in the No. 5 hold near the steering engine and our ammunition locker. We could not get another shell from the locker, but still had some on deck. O'Hara ran to the gun and climbed on a seat to aim along with someone else, and the last few shells were being fired. Ensign Willett was firing. O'Hara went down and someone replaced him on the last two shots. The Captain was trying to blow "abandon ship", but without much steam it sounded pretty feeble. Ensign Willett ordered everyone to lifeboat stations. He stayed behind to check O'Hara and the rest of the crew piled around the stern gun and to see if he could help anyone.[20]

Navy Gunner Moses Barker:

We fired all the shells I had in my ready box except five of them were on top. When we had the hurricane and the water seeped into the box, they were all rusted. I tore the skin off my hands trying to get the shells out of there but I couldn't do it. So, I think the last shell I put in there because I was having to watch the machine gun bullets. I had to duck behind the gun and they would zoom by. One time they were coming so hard overhead I hollered, "fire". I had my face right against the breech. If he had pulled the trigger my head would have been a block down the street. But he was already dead. All of them were dead except me. So I ran and pulled the trigger. I didn't even look to see what I was shooting or anything. I just pulled the trigger and got behind the gun again. I couldn't get any more shells out of the ready box.

We had .50 caliber machine guns; two on each side. I went over there to try to shoot one of them. I didn't know how to. The only thing I knew how to do was the 4-inch 50. I got up there looking at it but what the hell am I going to do? I got away from it. About the same time a shell hit beneath us. I got off the gun deck and went amidship. We picked up a passenger in Cape Town. He was a soldier of fortune and he was just standing there. I was trying to get by him in the passageway so I could get my lifejacket. He said, 'Son you don't want to go there.' Steam was coming out of the engine room. He said, 'Everyone is dead.' He had a lifejacket on. He put his lifejacket on me, tied it and said get into the lifeboat. He just stayed there on the ship and went down with it.[21]

Rodger Piercy:

Several of us went forward to the boat deck to see if we could find a lifeboat. The ship was an absolute shambles. You could hear water gurgling into every hold. The entire midships were blown to pieces. Apparently they were using a magnesium shell, and even when they hit steel, it would burst into flame. The boat deck had three lifeboats smashed to pieces and a fourth was missing. The radio shack appeared smashed to shambles. Chief Officer Richard Moczkowski was lying on the boat deck dying. He was badly hit in the chest and shoulders. He had been in charge of the midship guns.

The gun on the bow had taken a direct salvo and was blown into the sea. There was only a gaping hole where it had been. Second Officer Earl Layman and his crew were gone with it. My friend Karl Largergren was one of the gunners and his hunch had been right.[22]

Chief Steward Stilson:

My impression was that these shells were all entering from the port side, at least that was where the mate was wounded the second time. I picked the mate up and carried him back to the wheelhouse door and looked to the captain for instructions as I wished to know whether to carry him to the starboard deck or not.[23]

The *Stephen Hopkins* was hit in her main boiler, after which the ship's speed was reduced to 1 knot. The second and third shell had hit the radio mast and destroyed the aerial. The steering engine room was hit by a shell and incendiary. Incendiary shells set fire to the main deck house. There was extensive fragment damage and extensive damage throughout the ship, with slow flooding. *Stier* had subjected *Stephen Hopkins* to continuous fire from machine gun and large caliber for twenty minutes. The last five minutes of salvo firing from *Stier* doomed the *Stephen Hopkins*. The death knell was a hit into the 4-inch gun's magazine which exploded. At about 0920, Captain Buck ordered Third Mate Walter Nyberg to signal "abandon ship" and to prepare the lifeboats and rafts to be dropped over the side. It was found that all the portside lifeboats and rafts had been destroyed. The only usable lifeboat was the No. 1 starboard boat. The enemy's rate of fire was two to three rounds a minute with large caliber. The fire power consisted of shrapnel, incendiary and contact fuse action shells with machine gun fire. The shells were described variously as 6-inch, 4-inch and 3-inch.[24] After the ship was abandoned, fifteen to twenty rounds were fired into her, of which seventy percent were hits.

The *Stier* reported the following artillery ammunition expended:

120 shots from the twin 3.7 cm.
180 shots from the single 3.7 cm.
Over 600 shots from the Flak 38 2 cm.[25]

One person miraculously was still alive in the wreckage surrounding the 4-inch 50 cannon on the stern gun platform of the sinking *S.S. Stephen Hopkins*: Cadet-Midshipman Edwin O'Hara. After being wounded and most likely rendered unconscious, O'Hara regained consciousness after the magazine was hit. There were five shells still left in the ready box. These shells had been stuck in the box before the magazine exploded. The explosion loosened them and O'Hara fulfilled his desire to be a gunner on the 4-inch 50 on which he had spent so many hours practicing with his friend Lt. Kenneth Willett. Cadet-Midshipman Edwin O'Hara fired the last five shells at the waterline of the *Tannenfels*.

From the *Tannenfels* report:

> The enemy fired further volleys of light and heavy weapons at us and fortunately they were too high so that they whistled over the ship at amidships and at hatch four. In the course of the conflict we managed to make two hits. The second salvo landed perfectly in the enemy's stern area. According to our head shooter, lead Bosun Schumacher of auxiliary cruiser X (*Thor*), and our observer, retired artillery Captain von Likoser, we managed two hits on the enemy ship.[26]

The final salvos tore into the stern area of the *Hopkins*. Mortally injured, Cadet-Midshipman Edwin J. O'Hara, the youngest crew member aboard, went down with his ship.

Summary Report by Survivors of the Stephen Hopkins:

> The Commanding Officer of the Armed Guard [Lt. Willett] promptly manned this gun, opened fire on this enemy raider at about 1000 yards, continued firing rapidly thirty-five 4-inch shells at close range, nearly all of which struck the raider [*Stier*] along the water line, and only broke off firing after a shell exploded his magazine. He concentrated on this ship, handling the gun himself, while badly wounded, until his magazine exploded.

The Cadet [Edwin O'Hara] then fired the remaining five shells at the other raider [*Tannenfels*], which had held her fire, except for machine guns. During this time the machine guns of the *Stephen Hopkins* kept a steady fire at close range on the decks of both raiders ... 400 – 50 caliber, 100 – 30 caliber, 35 to 40 - 37mm were fired by the *Stephen Hopkins*.[27]

Sometime between 0915 and 0920 Capt. Buck ordered "abandon ship" and Third Mate Walter Nyberg to get the lifeboats swung out and the life rafts dropped. Second Engineer George Cronk was ordered to check the condition of the lifeboats. All the port lifeboats had been destroyed and there was only one slightly damaged lifeboat left on the starboard side.

George Cronk:

At this time the abandon ship signal was given. It was barely audible because of the low steam pressure. The chief said, "Let's try and stop the main engine," as it was still turning over slowly. I never saw Chief Rutz again. I went to the emergency cut-off for the main engine which was forward of what was once the galley which had been shot away. I closed the emergency pump and went to the boat deck. Live steam was still pouring from the engine room door. The lifeboat deck was in a bad state. Three lifeboats had been shot away. The No. 1 boat was hanging in the davits. The stern of the boat was maybe three or four feet lower than the bow and the after boat fall was fouled. Several men were standing nearby. I don't know who they were. They told me that Ch. Mate Moczkowski had given orders to lower the boat and had left. The *Hopkins* was getting pretty low in the water by this time and the enemy was still firing and machine gunning. (*Note: This fire was coming from* Tannenfels, *as according to* Stier*'s log, her fire was halted at* 0918) Ordinary Seaman Rodger Piercy, and Carpenter Kuhl came from somewhere and we managed to free the after fall. Kuhl lowered the forward fall and I lowered the after fall. (I never saw Kuhl again). As the boat touched water a shell hit the ship's side killing four men and wounding four men in the boat.[28]

In a letter to the Chief Engineer Rutz's sister after the war, Cronk wrote:

When the Abandon Ship signal was given he was putting life preservers on the wounded men. He told me to go to the boat deck and that was the last anyone saw of him. I helped lower the only boat left, and then I saw the captain throw his code book overboard and walk to the other end of the bridge. I went to the other side but could not find him and by that time I was trapped by fire started by incendiary shells ...[29]

Rodger Piercy:

There was destruction everywhere. Cargo booms were splintered. The crew quarters and galley appeared to be blown to shambles. I only looked from the deck as I went back down to find something that would float. The ship was sinking fast and our life-saving gear was destroyed. One shell had hit our large life raft and it skidded into the sea. The one on the port side was smashed to pieces. On deck, I met Ensign Willett who was still on his feet. He had a couple of navy boys with him, and they were to tossing one-man rafts over the side. I did not know it, but while we were firing, Capt. Buck had seen the lifeboats being smashed and had ordered the last one lowered into the sea with a couple of men in it to drift astern and come up to rescue survivors.[30]

Chief Steward Ford Stilson picked up and carried the chief mate and brought him to the wheelhouse looking for instructions. Ford Stilson:

Instruction was not necessary however, as the captain entered the wheelhouse just at this time, carrying a box in his hand which I believe to be the code box. Upon being queried by signalman Jackson as to whether he wished to abandon ship the captain replied in the affirmative and Jackson gave the signal on the ship's whistle. I secured the aid of O.S. Piercy and carried the mate down the ladder onto the starboard side boat deck. The chief mate's boat and my own was No. 2 on the port side but I made no attempt to get him there as all the shells I had observed had entered from that side and I believed it to be a shambles and under direct machine gun fire as well. The lines were coiled on a patent drum fastened to the bulkhead which required the release of the pin to run free. An incendiary shell had landed just aft of the after drum and had started to burn and spread. I climbed up and released the pin, losing a little fuzz off my pants in the process. There were two of us on the after falls but I do not remember who the other was. After the boat was part way down quite a few men started down the knotted ropes and I again gave my attention to the chief mate. The mate had no life preserver and at this moment the chief engineer stepped out on the deck and I asked him to get a life preserver from the mate's room just behind him. This he did and aided me in putting it on the mate. We started to carry him to the rail in order to lower him into the boat but discovered that the boat had been released and was gone. I suggested lowering him into the water but he objected so strenuously to this that I did not attempt to do so. He ordered me to look to myself and as all the boats were shattered or gone and I did not believe he could survive his chest wound after exposure. I did so.

At this time, when I passed through, the captain was in the wheelhouse, at the wheel was A.B. Adrian, standing by Signalman Jackson.

As I climbed down a cable to dodge the loose gear there was a considerable number of men who seemed confused about the advisability of trusting themselves to the water. Some were on a Jacob's ladder and others at the rail. I shouted to them to let go and jump but I did not see any of them do so, nor did I see any of them in the water after I got there myself. As I was on the starboard side I did not fear the propeller which was still going.[31]

Sadly, it was the continuing motion of the propeller that killed the other Cadet-Midshipman, Arthur R. Chamberlin. Navy Armed Guard survivor, Wallace Breck, who had become good friends with Chamberlin, later wrote the Chamberlin family. Cadet-Midshipman Chamberlin's brother Robert wrote:

Wally was the one who first told us how my brother died. Breck was in a lifeboat and saw Captain Buck and Artie coming down off the bridge. Captain Buck went down from gunfire from the *Tannenfels*. He, Buck, handed something (assumed to be the ship's Log) to my brother. Artie went off the stern and was pulled into the prop which was still turning.[32]

On board the raider *Stier* seawater was brought up by hand in a futile attempt to fight the fires raging on board. So many fires were burning in the battery room machinery, coal bunker, cargo hold, storage quarters, and other places that attempts had to be made to extinguish them with water rather than chemicals or steam. The ammunition lockers and ammunition were flooded.

The greatest danger was in the torpedo storage areas beneath hatch No. 2 which was burning out of control. The valves that flooded these areas were inaccessible because of the intense heat. These two torpedo areas contained nineteen torpedoes which could no longer be reached. At 0923 the torpedo room crew was sent a message to abandon their area because of the heat and smoke.[33]

As Captain Gerlach followed the rapidly increasing fires aboard his ship, he gave instructions at 0932 to contact *Michel* to see if she was in the vicinity for possible torpedoing of the enemy. The other raider was supposed to be about 180 miles to the south monitoring the same radio wavelength as *Stier*. Earlier, the two ships had agreed to communicate 8400 Khz. But because of the uncertainty of the short wave transmission, a message was coded and sent off on 600 megawatts. *Michel* was asked to go immediately to area GD 6130. No reply was received.

At 0933 orders were given to start moving everything stowed on the starboard side forward to the bridge.[34] At the same time *Tannenfels* was ordered to stand by for an assistance tow.

Captain Haase of *Tannenfels*:

> When we left we received the order to make a wide circle around the auxiliary cruiser and to remain near it. During the conflict, I had seen that the battle went over its stern. I changed course so that we approached each other prow to prow. Visibility was at this point very poor.[35]

At 0955 Capt. Gerlach reported that the *Hopkins* had begun to sink and it disappeared stern first five minutes later. About this time the wind began increasing, intensifying the fires aboard *Stier*. The first ammunition locker had to be abandoned because of the quantity of smoke and was flooded.[36]

By 1014 the engineers got the main engine running. A jury-rigged hand rudder had been put together which was to be placed past the hard-to-starboard position to two-to-three degrees to port. The intent was to place the ship facing the wind thus preventing more draft on the fires. But the plan was abandoned when the stern hoist, tied in to the jury-rudder failed during the operation.[37]

At 1025 the main engine was stopped. Instructions were given to flood the front No. 2 and 3 ammunition lockers. The front locker could not be flooded because the valves could no longer be reached. At 1033 the emergency rudder failed causing the wind to once again fan the fires. Because of the increasing danger and expansion of fire in hatch No. 2, an order was given to leave the adjacent areas because of the heat.

Capt. Gerlach:

> I now summoned the ship's naval officers to the bridge in order to hear their opinion of the ship's preservation. All the naval officers agreed with me that it would further endanger the crew to stay aboard the ship because of the detonations and explosions. The ship was in no case to be surrendered but it was important not to have any further personnel losses. I decided to let the crew go into lifeboats and rafts and to blow up the ship.
>
> The fire which burned intensely in a bright flame and from the forepart of the torpedo deck heated the decks so much that it couldn't be entered because the deck was so hot that it was glowing.
>
> The intention now was to take *Tannenfels* alongside and to use their hoses and pumps to fight the fire but this had to be abandoned because the sea was too rough and the possibility of danger to the other ship.[38]

By 1040 instructions were given to lower the lifeboats and rafts to the water. The starboard boats were all in working condition. The port boats had been hit near hatch No. 4 and the hoist could no longer be used. Therefore they had to be thrown into the water from up above.[39]

Capt. Gerlach entry for 1042 read:

> The entire crew on the boat deck began to hear my speech of the resolution that we had to give up the ship. "Sieg-heil auf Fuehrer… Victory to our leader, native country and to Ship 23." A spontaneous singing of the national anthem was then sung.[40]

War correspondent Friedrich Weber:

> We are close together on the boat deck with fires all around us and nobody can breathe from the smoke. All the men carry fire-blackened faces and are devoted to the ship. The Commander stands and speaks to the crew his last words about the ship. The ship is sizzling with flames but Germany's song penetrates louder than these sounds. Our dead ones are committed to the sea after the old custom. The wounded ones are put in the lifeboats.[41]

Capt. Griffiths had been a prisoner-of-war since June 4 when his ship, the *Gemstone,* was sunk by *Stier*. He had been transferred twice to other German ships and was now back aboard *Stier*. At about 9:00 a.m. on September 27th, in response to an order, the sentry on duty locked the door of the room where Capt. Griffiths and the other prisoners were confined. A machine-gun on the deck directly above the room opened fire and the captives felt the raider set off at full speed. A minute later an explosion was heard and *Stier* stopped dead in the water. The raider's big gun commenced firing, but after fifteen rounds it stopped. Two more explosions were heard and then all was quiet. Half an hour later the lights went out. Smoke filled the room. Anxiety grew as Captain Griffiths and his fellow prisoners realized their dire situation — the steel door locked, no one outside, the smoke getting thicker, and the ship's ammunition magazine directly beneath them.

Some minutes later they were released by a guard wearing a gas mask. The decks of the raider were in a state of chaos. Smoke belched from ports, doors and ventilators. The supply ship was standing by a half a mile away.[42]

According to the prisoners aboard *Stier*:

> Gerlach, the *Stier*'s captain, gave an address to his crew, at the end of which they all gave three cheers for the Fuhrer and sang "Deutschland, Deutschland, uber alles." *Stier* was then abandoned... The prisoners were merely told to save themselves which they did by climbing onto to a raft. While drifting around they were joined by a German sailor who had jumped overboard."[43]

By 1053 the forward radio room had shut down. It had operated throughout the battle. The port antenna was working again so that the 800 watt transmitter could be used. Capt. Gerlach badly wanted to send a message to the homeland but couldn't because of weather conditions. [44]

At 1058 instructions were given to man the boats and rafts.

At the same time instructions were given to *Tannenfels* to lower her boats to aid in rescuing the *Stier*'s crew.

Capt. Haase of *Tannenfels*:

> When running off we received an order to make a wide circle around the auxiliary cruiser and to remain near it. Visibility at this point was very low. While moving toward each other, we received an order to tow the Cruiser, since it had become unable to maneuver. The whole crew was made ready for towing. While slowly nearing the Auxiliary Cruiser we saw that she was burning at hatch No. 2, amidships and astern. At 1136 the commander suddenly called us on the megaphone and asked us to take him and his crew on board.[45]
>
> I now saw that it was no longer possible to tow the vessel. The lines that had been thrown out were immediately drawn back, so that we would be able to maneuver again as soon as possible. Lifeboat No.1, which had been put into the water with the order to set up towing connections, was then sent to the Auxiliary Cruiser under the leadership of Second Officer H. Mueller. I then moved the *Tannenfels* away from the Auxiliary Cruiser and maneuvered to its windward side. This was the most favorable position for taking people on board. This position enabled us to observe perfectly the sinking of the raider, which was completely on fire. It was about 12 noon.[46]

Capt. Gerlach later wrote that the *Tannenfels* crew carried out this order completely and with exemplary discipline. In the *Report of the Commander* concerning personnel loses, Capt. Gerlach wrote:

> The opponent shot exclusively with its cannons and they were deadly hits. If more antiaircraft had been mixed in we might have had large personnel loses occurring. At this point only two of *Stier's* crew had died; the ship's doctor, Dr. Meyer-Hamme was hit in the belly and in the intestines leading to bleeding and death and Machine Officer Arno Gurk was shot in the right temple. Shortly thereafter Machine Officer, Hans Pallhon who had been hit in both thighs died upon being transferred to *Tannenfels*. In addition, but not known at the time, were

Stier *on fire some time before 1000 on September 27, 1942.* National Archives.

five more heavily wounded and twenty-eight men who had moderate to severe injuries.[47]

Upon leaving the ship, the transport of the heavily wounded was difficult and time consuming because there were so few transportation hammocks, partly because of the numerous hits to them. After the crew had left the ship at 1140 the demolition crew received their orders to blow up the ship at 1150.

At 1140 I left with the remainder of the officers in two boats lying alongside and the command was given at 1157. At 1157 the first detonation was set forward

At 1159 the second was set aft. The forward explosive charge set for the forward machine bulkhead was unattainable because of the heat and fire. Following the aft detonation, *Stier* (Ship 23) took on a little water aft and began to settle slowly. A large hole had been blown into the starboard side. As the stern of the ship began to dip our crew watched from *Tannenfel*'s foredeck as she began to sink faster and faster. Again I gave a short speech to my men that we should be proud of this our last opponent and 27,000 BRT [British Registered Tons] of hostile shipping tonnage had been sunk while sighting only five enemy ships from which four had been sunk. We repeated Sieg-Heil after my beautiful ship reared up and went down stern first and bow showing in dead silence. That was probably the heaviest instant emotionally for me and my men.[48]

Less than an hour later the fires are quite out of control. National Archives.

Crew of Stier *abandoning ship.* Werner Link.

The war correspondent aboard *Stier*, Friedrich Weber, reported the battle in the German newspaper *Das Reich*. The following is a translation:

The last day in the South Atlantic is an impenetrable grey. Gusts move like a piece of night pulling over the sea. You can hardly view three miles ahead. Early in the morning the siren alarms. The artillerymen do not yet have the cannons loaded. There is a ship before us out in the darkness. The distance between us is very small. This can only be the enemy. The ship rides very high out of the water and is much larger than we ourselves. Now they see us over there. From the sudden surprise the steamer stops after a few minutes. If it had maintained its course it would have run by us perhaps 50 meters off our stern. We are clearly faster getting to our stations. After the main artillery sights the enemy, the shelling starts. With all pipes we hammer the mysterious opponent's ship with full strength-salvos after she turns aft. Our fire directly covers this move. But a desperate crew on the other ship struggles for life. The enemy fires back. Heavy shells tear *Stier*'s surface up and smash the deck and superstructures. In this short distance, combat with heavy caliber is a cruel enterprise. The enemy is heavily armed; however, it doesn't arise against our 15 cm's. The enemy stops and burns. We also lie quietly. Dangerous hits have made us un-maneuverable. But the duel continues. The rate of fire becomes faster. It takes only a few minutes; but in the fires and impacts and through the haze, it seems like an eternity. Everything is over in one quarter of an hour. The ship after detonation disappears in the fog and storm. A short time, it is again visible swimming in the grey. It lasts only a moment before the opponent sinks.

The statement of the watch officer said we sank about a 10,000 ton North American auxiliary warship *Steffen Hopkins* that had been built only a few months before. We don't know exactly if it was a cruiser helping as a patrol ship or for a submarine because the ship no longer exists. In any case it was a ship well-reinforced for military tasks in the South Atlantic.

The *Stier* is unconquered. But it can travel no more as fire burns along the ship. We attack the fires with all available men. Soon it is impossible to see another man because of the biting smoke clouds coming from the ammunition chambers and torpedo loads. It would be against all human and military reason to keep *Stier* any longer afloat and stay because of the danger to the men. By self-demolition the ship will go down; and it remains in the South Atlantic. *Stier* performed its operation.[49]

The last moments of Stier *as she is seen in the distance sinking by the stern.* National Archives.

PART IV

16

THIRTY-ONE DAYS IN AN OPEN BOAT

Navy Seaman Second Class Moses Barker had gotten into the lifeboat that was already down to the water. He was given a briefcase containing the ship's papers by Captain Buck. "He said, 'Barker, take this and hold onto it,' and he threw it to me. So I did for two weeks. A metal case. I held onto it like it was a teddy bear. I wouldn't have turned that loose for nothing!"[1]

According to George Cronk, as he and Carpenter Hugh Kuhl lowered a lifeboat into the water:

> ... a shell hit the ship's side killing four men and wounding four in the boat. A shell fragment must have cut the painter, which is a line from the lifeboat's bow and secured to the ship some distance forward. The lifeboat started drifting away from the ship. I jumped overboard and swam for it. I made it but had to be helped aboard. The boat had several holes in it. Some of them were jagged and hard to plug up. The boat had also taken on a lot of water. Some of the men were in a state of shock.[2]

Rodger Piercy wrote that Captain Buck had seen the lifeboats being smashed and had ordered the last lifeboat lowered into the sea in order to drift astern and come up to rescue survivors:

Two men were killed in the lifeboat just after it was launched, but it was drifting about a half mile away. That act saved our lives. We offered to drop Ensign Willett over the side and to help him to the raft, but he declined. He was too far gone, and he knew it. He didn't want to cause anyone to lose precious time when he couldn't make it. He ordered us to throw rafts over the side, to jump into the sea, and to get away from the ship because of the suction when it went down.

When I jumped over the side, he was hanging onto the rail, and I never saw him again. When I hit the drink, I felt like I had suddenly become a Popsicle! Oh, that water was cold, and I lost sight of the raft I had thrown in, but I could see the lifeboat in the distance as it crested the waves. I started swimming toward it, and it seemed like twenty miles before I got there. From time to time, I could see other fellows in the water and on rafts. They were trying for the lifeboat, too.

As I drew near the lifeboat, I could see Ford Stilson, Chief Steward, swimming also. We pulled ourselves into the lifeboat and could see George Cronk and Archie Carlson out in the water. We got out the oars and started rowing toward them and helped them in. Then we started around to pick up anyone we could find.

The two men in the lifeboat were dead. One was A.B William J. Adrian, and the other was Navy Armed Guard S2/c Andrew P. Yanez. We had no time to check them, so we took them with us. We rowed everywhere we could see anything, and finally wound up with twenty one in the lifeboat counting Adrian and Yanez.[3]

Ford Stilson, chief steward:

I swam for about ten minutes after which I began to get close to No. 1 lifeboat. I was too tired to make it as the boat was drifting away from me at a considerable rate. I shouted for a line but by the time it was found and untangled the distance was too great. I now found another lifeboat which was drifting toward me and made for that. It had one occupant whom I took to be the third mate. This boat was somewhat damaged and had a doughnut raft lashed astern for buoyancy. I again shouted for a line but by the time it was found and uncoiled the drift had carried the boat beyond my reach. I had previously sighted a large raft in the vicinity and I now swam to intercept it, first removing my shoes and slipping partly out of my life preserver. After about fifteen minutes I made the raft. The shelling of the ship (*Tannenfels*) had continued during the first five minutes or so that I was in the water.

I was now for the first time in position to look around and sighted one slightly smaller ship on the horizon standing about a half a mile or less apart. Considerable white smoke came from the smaller and partly obscured it at times. Visibility was very poor at this time as there was slight intermittent rain from that direction. This ship smoked all day as long as I could see it. Later the larger ship closed in on the smaller. At times I could not see either as the rain obscured the vision. The only distinctive feature that I noted at the time was that the larger ship had a peculiar construction forward over one of the hatches. This was a rectangular box like the construction of different color built across the ship. It did not seem to be a turret as it seemed fixed.

After I had been on the raft what seemed to be two or three hours I saw the *Stephen Hopkins* sink. She had a dense oil fire burning as she slipped under.

At about half a mile from me I sighted a doughnut raft with five or six men on, one of these men seemed dressed in cook's clothing and was of a size to lead me to think it might be second cook Ziesel. I saw the men in the lifeboat had recovered sufficiently to row and were now steadily bearing in the direction of the doughnut raft and my own. I broke out an oar and by seating myself on one corner was able to maneuver the raft to some extent so as to converge on the boat and the doughnut raft. By signals and shouting I endeavored to get the men on the doughnut to get into the water and push their raft into the line of convergence. I was unable to make them understand and they eventually drifted out of sight in the rain. The other boat with the single occupant was on the other side of me at considerable distance and receding in the opposite direction. I could see an oar flash at regular intervals. By the time the lifeboat reached me both the single occupied boat and the doughnut raft were out of sight. Just before the lifeboat reached me I saw them jettison two bodies. The water being baled was filled with blood.

After being taken aboard I found two men with seven wounds in the arm which I dressed as well as able.[4]

George Cronk:

We put Navy gun crewman "Virgie" Bullock who had one good hand steering. Myself, and three others took to the oars. We managed to pick up several men from the water and from rafts, one of them was Chief Steward Stilson. During this time several shots came from the *Hopkins* gun. I was told by the others it was Engine Cadet Ed. O'Hara on the gun. I was rowing and had my back towards the ship. The *Hopkins* sank and we never picked up anyone after that. We might have done better had it not been for the heavy rain squalls that brought visibility to almost nil till darkness set in.[5]

Two serious problems became immediately apparent: food and water drifting away from some of the rafts and the command authority of the one lifeboat with nineteen survivors in it. In the confusion and haste to board the lifeboat no one had thought about the precious water and food aboard the liferafts. The rafts simply drifted away in the wind and rain. Now they were unreachable because the lifeboat crew was too exhausted to continue rowing after them.

A question which arose almost immediately was, "Who's in charge here?"

As the only surviving officer, Second Assistant Engineer George Cronk, Sr., assumed command and took charge of the lifeboat. He wished he didn't have to [*take command*] but he stuck with it. The decisions he made, right or wrong, were something he would have to live with.[6]

Rodger Piercy:

In the meantime, we stopped to watch our ship sink by the stern, and then resumed our hunting. The larger raider, meanwhile, had pulled up to the smaller and tied up to her. They were transferring personnel, but we had very little time to watch. The smaller raider was on fire and burning fiercely. A pall of black smoke was pouring from her. She was doomed to keep *Stephen Hopkins* company. We watched her sink ...

When the larger raider finished and cast off from the smaller, she sailed over to us and made a complete circle around our lifeboat, but no one made a sound. She seemed to look us over, but definitely made no attempt to pick us up. We sat in the lifeboat and waited to see what would happen. We had heard that Germans machine-gunned survivors to keep their position secret. We knew it was at least eight hundred miles to Africa and about twenty-five hundred to Brazil, and we couldn't swim that far! So we reasoned that if they were going to destroy the lifeboat, then we might as well be shot anyway. However, they only seemed to look us over and then took off and disappeared into the mist.

The lifeboat was equipped with a sea anchor. We put it out trying to maintain our position to see if we could find anyone else. We did find the large raft which a shell had released. The shell had ruined the food stored in it, but the water cask was intact so we took it aboard.[7]

In a later interview, George Cronk, Sr. said, "When the squalls died down, the big German raider [*Tannenfels*] circled us and we put a cover over the lifeboat. They figured everybody was dead and headed off."[8]

In his official report George Cronk gave the following statement regarding the immediate aftermath:

Then the wind started rising and the sea running high, the visibility becoming very bad. All sighted the third mate in one of the smashed lifeboats that had been blown off the *Stephen Hopkins* by shell fire. He had bolstered it up at one end by a doughnut raft, but row as hard as we could we could not get to him on account of the wind and seas. A doughnut raft went by with at least five men on it, one of which I think was the captain. We rowed for two hours until our hands were blistered and still we could not pick up the men. The wind and seas were getting higher all the time and at last poor visibility blotted out everything. In the meantime we were very near the two raiders and before the mist got so bad I observed that both were motor ships of about 4,000 and 7,000 [tons] respectively. The smaller was the heaviest armed with guns in turrets or behind shields. She looked like a converted fruit boat which ran from the West Coast of the U.S.A. to Europe such as the *Oregon* and *Washington Express* streamlined with a clipper or aireform bow and cruiser stern. The other was a motor ship, larger, lighter armed and with a high stack like she might have been converted from steam. She had three masts and one set of Samson posts aft but with no booms. She also had an extreme clipper bow and cruiser stern and the upside down cross tree such as used on all Japanese built ships. She went alongside the other one which was aflame from stem to stern listing heavily to port and way down by the stern and apparently took off the crew, although the seas were running high. She went close alongside. After about ten minutes she backed away, turned around and left. She also appeared to be down by the bow but this may have been due to a boxlike structure built on the deckhouse on the fantail which made her seem high at the stern. The funnel or stack was set in the after part of the midship house like lots of motor ships but was high like a steamship built for natural draft. The ship was probably a mother ship for a fleet of armed fast raiders. We then heard a heavy explosion out of the mist which was probably the magazine or a time bomb left behind ...[9]

Rodger Piercy:

It seemed that darkness was upon us before we knew it. We had twenty-one men on board. Two we found to be dead. Several others were wounded. Mac McDaniels had a very serious shoulder wound. The muscle of his arm and part of his shoulder was shot away. I don't know how he had gotten this far. The bone in his arm was shattered, but the artery underneath was intact, so we bandaged him up. Leonardo Romero had shrapnel wounds in his arm and side. Wallace Breck, Armed Guard, had shrapnel wounds in his shoulder and hand.

The first night was on us before we knew it, and it was bitterly cold. We huddled together to use our body warmth to the best advantage. I think it was the longest night I ever spent. Hardly anyone could sleep. We had been so busy we hardly had any time to think. Now that we could rest the horribleness of the day's events came to haunt us. Friends had been destroyed and their acts of bravery were clearly etched in our minds. Things you would like to forget, but couldn't. Things like Arthur Chamberlin, the Deck Cadet, who jumped from the boat deck when we abandoned ship and apparently forgot to tie his cork life jacket down. We think it knocked him out. He skidded along side the ship and went into the screw which was still feebly turning.[10]

George Cronk, Sr.:

    After darkness, we put out a sea anchor. We bailed water from the leaky boat all night still hoping we might find someone when morning came. Morning came bright and clear. We patched the boat up as best we could. We sighted a raft with no one on it. Messman Carlos Sanchez volunteered to board the raft and secure it to the boat. We took the provisions and water off. This may have been the deciding factor that made it possible for us to survive the 2200 [*1300 miles*] mile thirty-one day voyage to the coast of Brazil. In the afternoon we hoisted sail and set a northwest course toward South America looking for a continent not a port.[11]

When they stepped the mast and raised the sail they were disheartened to find the sail riddled with machine gun bullet holes. They had to lower the sail and patch it with the repair kit. This was done by the surviving able bodied seamen since they were experienced in using an awl and needle and twine in repairing canvas.[12]

Those in the boat were:

Merchant crew	**Armed Guard**
Bill Adrian	Moses N. Barker
Archer Carlson	Ted Barnes
George Cronk	Wallace Breck
Athonosios Demetrades	Virgil Bullock
Peter Enos	Paul Porter
George Gelogotes	Andrew Yanez
Nickolas Kokalis	
Walter Manning	
Eugene McDaniel	
Gerald McQuality	
Rodger Piercy	
August Reese	

Leonardo Romero
Carlos Sanchez
Ford Stilson

At this point Second Assistant Engineer Cronk began the Lifeboat Log.

ABANDON SHIP SIGNAL AT APPROXIMATELY 9.55 A.M.
Sunday September 27, 1942.

Log of No.1 Life Boat of SS Stephen Hopkins
Course 313

Attacked by enemy raiders in South Atlantic, approx. lat. 31, Long. 16 at 9:38 a.m. September 27th. (*This was incorrect and was probably stated like this so as not to give away the battle position. Stier's log gives the battle position as 24⁰ 44'S 21⁰ 50'W, which is correct according to her voyage map*). Shelled by two armed merchant ships for about twenty minutes. All lifeboats destroyed except No. 1. All known survivors in this boat. Ship went down in flames at about 1030. Two men killed and two wounded by shrapnel in life boat. Navy gun crewman Andrew Yanez and A.B. Seaman William Adrian killed. Buried them at sea. Eugene McDaniels, baker and 2nd cook, Athonoios Demetrades wiper, badly wounded by shell burst were given first aid by Chief Steward F. Stilson who was picked up from raft. 6 more men picked up from rafts and water. 2nd Engineer was picked up from water. 6 men were sighted on raft but could not get them due to high seas and poor visibility. Wiper Demetrades found to have broken arm. Arm was set and attended to by Chief Steward. Put out sea anchor and laid low till 12 noon next day looking for more survivors. One raider badly damaged and probably sunk by guns of *Stephen Hopkins*. Known killed by shell fire are gun crewmen Phil Smith and Andrew Yanez, A.B. Seaman William Adrian and Chas. Largergren, messman Herbert Lowe and wiper Pedro Valdez. Badly wounded and probably dead are Chief Mate Richard Moczkowski, Gunnery officer Kenneth Willett, carpenter Hugh Kuhl, Eng cadet Edwin O'Hara, deck cadet C. Chamberlain.

Signed George Cronk, 2nd Engineer

Rodger Piercy:

Then we prepared funeral services for Bill Adrian (*AB*) and Andrew Yanez (*Armed Guard*). It was very difficult as we had nothing to wrap them in, and so could only lower them into the water. We hauled in the sea anchor, raised our sails, and got under way for Brazil. Then we mentioned what we could about our departed comrades, and all repeated the Lord's Prayer aloud. We lowered them into the water and had five minutes of silent prayer with no man allowed to look behind.[13]

At daybreak we had a council to determine what course we would pursue. Captain Buck had told someone not to try to go to Africa as the wind and tide would be against you, but to take the longer route and try for Brazil... The lifeboat was equipped with sails and a compass.[14]

September 28th – Lifeboat Log

Found two abandoned rafts but no sign of men on them. Took stores and water beaker from two rafts and set sail for the coast of South America. Set course in a northwest direction steering by sun and compass and started food rationing. Making good time till sun down. Had to put out sea anchor and heave to on account of high seas.

George Cronk, Sr., later told his son that whoever decided to keep the lifeboat cover with the lifeboat when they lowered it definitely saved their lives. The lifeboat cover provided protection from the sun and wind, and was used to collect rainwater. The only navigation instrument was a boat compass. There was no sextant or charts, but one of the AB's knew something about using a watch to time the sunsets* and along with using the compass it would give you a rough latitude. This is a very, very rudimentary

---

* Because the earth is tilted on its axis in relation to the sun, the greater the latitude (north or south) one is at, the more time it takes for sunset to occur. From the amount of time it takes the sun to set one can extrapolate rough latitude. Sunset would be defined as the time interval between the lower limb or edge of the sun touching the horizon and the upper limb disappearing on the horizon.

method, which gives a person some idea of the general direction he wants to go.[15]

According to the United States Maritime Service Training Manual (1944), in addition to a specified amount of food rations and water, lifeboats were required to carry the following equipment, although some of this was lost in the attack and launching of the boat:

Two Boat Hooks — one used fore and the other aft for holding or shoving off, or for fishing a line out of the water.

One Canvas Hood and Spray Curtain — used to protect the crew from the spray of the sea and also to provide shade from the sun.

One Ditty Bag — one canvas bag containing sewing palm, needles, sail twine, marline and marlinespike.

One Fishing Kit — in good condition with hooks, fishing gear and booklet of instruction.

Two Hatchets — placed in the forward and after ends of the boat on long lanyards for emergency use.

One Life Line — with seine floats, for men in the water to hold onto.

Two Life Preservers — for anyone who cannot get to their own or who have lost theirs. They may also be thrown to persons in the water.

One Painter — 15 fathoms, 2-3/4 inch, secured to the stem for being towed and towing, coiled ready for use.

One Sea Anchor — with a storm oil container to keep the boat headed into the sea and to spread the oil so that the waves will not break on the small craft.

One gallon of storm oil — to calm the seas.

One bailer — usually made of wood or leather to bail the water out of the boat.

One bilge pump — which works by suction and sucks the water out of the boat below the floor boards.

One two-gallon bucket — for bailing the boat or for other practical purposes.

Automatic Plugs — used in draining the boat on the davits.

Twenty-five soft wood plugs — 3 inches long, 1/4 inch to 3/4 inch taper contained in a canvas bag. These are to plug up bullet holes or for similar purposes.

Six woolen blankets — to keep the wounded or sick warm or to use for men who had to get away from the ship without any clothes.

One first-aid kit — in a watertight container containing scissors, bandages, tourniquets, boric lint dressings, absorbent cotton, adhesive tape, safety pins, iodine with brush, ointment for burns, supply of splints and instructions in first aid.

Thirty fathoms of 15 thread manila line — for general use.

Mast and sails — for sailing the boat and reaching land or keeping in the sea lanes where rescue is more likely. The sails are red or yellow in color to make them visible for greater distances.

Oars — a single banked complement of oars, two spare oars, and a steering or sweep oar (painted a distinguishing color so as to be quickly recognized).

Rowlocks — must have a full set and a half.

Rodger Piercy:

Ford Stilson was to have strict charge of all supplies, both food and water. They were counted and a rationing system was devised. George Cronk, being the only officer aboard, was allowed to be the titular head of the ship. Being an engine room officer, he knew exactly nothing of navigation or sailing, and was totally dependent on the old time able seamen. We were well-trained seamen and now had to prove it. We set up sea watches exactly as we had aboard ship and maintained them to the day we landed.[16]

September 29
Took in sea anchor, rationed food and water and resumed a

northwest course. No change in condition of wounded men. Sailed all night in a general westerly direction.

September 30th

Becalmed, very slight breeze enough for steerage way. Rationed food and water, put salt water drip on wounded men's arms and changed bandages. Steering due west by sun, compass deviation by course of sun 23 degrees. Good breeze at sundown. Changed course to northwest.

Concerning the injured Wallace Breck, Rodger Piercy said:

... we cut a piece of shrapnel out of his shoulder. We made the wounded as comfortable as possible by giving them extra room and any cushioning and covering we could. They were to have double and triple food and water rations. We kept someone with them at all times.[17]

George Cronk, Sr. had to assert his authority immediately because of serious problems with some of the crew. From the very beginning several crew members were angry because he had not tried to be rescued by the Germans. They felt being alive as a prisoner was better than taking a chance crossing an ocean to be free. Cronk wasn't sure the Germans would have taken them prisoner. Rumors of Germans machine-gunning enemy survivors and leaving the scene were circulating among seamen in many ports. Nevertheless, this decision haunted him for many years because four crewmembers would die on the voyage to Brazil. They might have been saved by the German ship's medical staffs if they had actively sought to be taken prisoner.

Years later his son, George Cronk, Jr., wrote, "This he had to live with and I don't fault him for a decision made under such wartime conditions. Command decisions when lives are at stake are always hard to make and the most easily to criticize after the fact or in hindsight."[18]

An even more serious problem was dealing with the cutting of rations and water. George Cronk, Jr.:

> In the first week or so many crewmembers were very upset with my dad's decision to cut food and water rations in order to give the wounded the extra rations in the hope that it would somehow help them recover or at least provide some comfort and prolong their will to live. Some were upset enough to threaten his life and act on it if the opportunity ever presented itself. He responded by telling them, he would take them out with the flare gun if they tried to take over the lifeboat or was caught stealing rations from anyone else. He told me that he always kept the flare gun with him when he was awake and turned it over to one of the Navy gun crew when he had to sleep, with the explicit order to use it if they had to. He knew the Navy crew always followed orders and were more disciplined than the merchant crew. They were the ones he trusted most during their ordeal.[19]

October 1st

Light breeze from northwest, steering southwest. Condition of men about the same. Rationed food and water. Cut water ration to 6 ounces per day per man, so as to give more to wounded men.

October 2nd

Strong winds from Southeast. Sailing due west. Have no idea of position of ocean currents or prevailing winds as there is no South Atlantic chart in boat. Condition of wounded men the same. Rationed food and water.

Rodger Piercy:

> The days became a procession. The days were hot and the nights were cold. We had canned pemmican and Horlick's Malted Milk Tablets. One can of pemmican (*Pemmican was an emergency ration made up of pressed beef, dried fruit and fat*) had to feed five men their evening meal. Horlick's Malted Milk Tablets were four for breakfast, two for lunch, and four for dinner along with one-fifth of a can of pemmican. Water was rationed once in the morning and once in the afternoon. The

wounded were given more pemmican and water almost as they needed it.

On the hot days we went swimming, but no more than three at one time could swim while others watched closely for sharks. Believe me we saw sharks! Sometimes they would follow us for a couple of days at a time. Then we would use a helmet and take turns filling it with sea water. A friend would hold his head over the side of the lifeboat while one of us would pour water over it. "You pour fifty over me, and I'll pour fifty over you!" Anything to kill time and erase boredom.[20]

October 3rd

Making good time due west with a strong wind and following sea until about 2 a.m. Had to heave to and put out sea anchor till 6 a.m.. Set sail to the northwest wind S.S.W. Wiper Demetrades condition improved, others about the same. Rationed food and water, one water cask empty. Having trouble with whales, afraid of hitting one and capsizing. Raised water ration to 10 oz.

October 4th

Changed bandages on wounded men. Condition about the same. Strong easterly winds, making good time. Course due west by sun. Rationed food and water. Keeping sharp lookout for ships. Weather rather cool. Don't know the latitude.

October 5th

Becalmed from midnight to 6 a.m. Heavy rains, squalls, replenished water supply by catching rain in sail. Took sails; repaired them. Strong wind sprang up 1 a.m. Hoisted sail making good time but sea pretty rough. McDaniels, 2nd cook condition getting worse. Think gangrene has set in. Wiper Demetrades improving. Messman Romero about the same. Men's spirits are high so far. Steering N.N.W. by compass. Changed course to due north 4 p.m. Replenished water supply to the extent of three gallons.

Rodger Piercy:

About eight or nine days out we began to run out of water and by the eleventh day, it was getting serious. We had a meeting and decided to pray for rain, which we did. That night we had a change in the weather. The seas began to roughen up, and it began to look like rain. We were pleased not only for rain, but because we needed wind. We had to sail faster and make better time. On hot days, we would almost be becalmed and make very little time.

The winds became very strong and the seas high. We decided to keep our sails up and make all the time possible. Gus Reese, an Able Seaman, was fifty-nine years old and had sailed windjammers for seven years. He took the tiller during the storm and, at one time, would let no one touch it but himself for eighteen hours. It was like a trip on a beach roller coaster, almost without end.

Then the rain came in sheets. We let the sail down and the fresh rain washed the salt out of it. Then we caught enough to fill anything that would hold water. Being very thirsty, we drank all we could. We got soaking wet and nearly froze as this went on for days. However, as soon as we got our water supply renewed, we again hoisted sail and got under way so as not to lose precious time.[21]

October 6th

Good southeast breeze all night, making good time. Demetrades still improves, Romero and McDaniels getting worse. Ration food and water. Trying to get farther north on account of cool nights. Men have very few clothes. Course N.W. Rain water caught has bad taste due to chemical in sail cloth.

October 7th

Very little breeze, making about 2 knots N.W. McDaniels becoming delirious, Demetrades better, Romero about the same. Ration food and water. Weather getting warmer, wind from S.S.E.. McDaniels, 2nd cook died at 6:30 P.M. Stopped ship for 5 minutes and buried him at 10.30.

Rodger Piercy:

On the twelfth day, I believe it was, [actually *11th day*] Mac McDaniel died. He was about twenty-two years old [*twenty-three years old*] and had stood everything very well. We believed he developed gangrene. We held funeral services for him in the same manner as the others.[22]

Utilityman Gerald Eugene McQuality had become good friends with Eugene "Mac" McDaniel while aboard ship. After the war McQuality visited the McDaniel family in Palestine, Illinois. He was interviewed by a local newspaper reporter.

> Mac and I were very good friends, more like brothers and several times during our days together in the lifeboat he asked me if I would make this trip to Palestine. He appeared to be anxious that his folks know the true story. That is why I came.

Regarding the attack, the newspaper reported:

> I was in the ammunition room sending four-inch shells up by carriage to the gunners when the [torpedo] struck. Mac was in the galley cooking. He helped me over the side into the boat. We saw five others floating around in the rough sea on a life raft. Many others went down with the ship and ours was the only lifeboat that was not wrecked by shells.
> Before we could get away from the ship, a burst of shrapnel struck amidships, killing two of the boys in the lifeboat outright and severely wounding Mac in the upper right arm.

McQuality related how he quickly applied a tourniquet about his buddy's arm in effort to prevent the loss of additional blood. A Filipino and two Greeks were also badly wounded by the blast before the lifeboat got away headed for the Brazilian coast.

There was little McQuality could do to save his friend's life, Gangrene quickly set into the wounded arm and the salt water sprayed over the lifeboat getting into the wound and wetting the bandages. They used what bandages they had, finally tearing up their undershirts for more bandages. The lifeboat had water, some tomato juice and some concentrated foods which were rationed out to each of the survivors.

The Wisconsin sailor said he sat constantly by Mac's side, talked to him about the folks at Palestine and repeatedly promised him he would come to Palestine and tell his family of his last hours.

McQuality praised the young Palestine sailor, who though badly wounded and realizing that death was only a matter of hours and at most days, away, did not complain and seemed to appreciate the little things that were done to make him comfortable. McDaniel talked almost all the time up to the end, giving his shipmate a general idea of the town he had promised to visit.[23]

Navy seaman Moses Barker remembered early in the voyage while they were trying to row away from the battle scene and the rain and wind were increasing:

> Meanwhile, we are bailing like hell because the waves and water are getting real strong – getting ready to have a storm. We were trying to bail the water out and I threw some water on his arm and oh that really tore me up because of the salt water. He screamed like a banshee. (That hurts)![24]

Jerry McQuality:

> On the day that McDaniel died, the eighteen survivors faced the difficult task of giving him a proper burial service at sea. We did all we could in the best way we knew how... It was a sad time for me and all the others. There was no one to

Eugene Darrel McDaniel succumbed to injuries received in the attack on the Stephen Hopkins. U.S. Navy.

offer a prayer aloud but we all prayed silently. We then lowered Mac's body over the side and then stood in silent tribute. The service was not like many others, but it was our service and we all felt it deeply."[25]

Rodger Piercy:

Every night we had one man at the tiller, one man with him to make sure he stayed awake, and one man at the bow for lookout. We had hoped to sight a passing ship and get help, but we never did.

This was the lifeboat assigned to Bosun Phelps, and he had put four cartons of cigarettes in it. Although he never made the trip, (*Phelps was last seen on main deck going forward*), we thought of him every time we smoked one. They lasted over two weeks, but were strictly rationed among us. We didn't have too many matches, but did have a kerosene lamp aboard. So we would just light the lamp, let it burn, and then light cigarettes from it. We were saving matches in the event we landed on wild shores and needed to start a fire.[26]

October 8th

Good southwest wind, making good time from midnight until 8 a.m. Sailing west and northwest. Wiper Demetrades still improves. Messman Romero getting worse. Gun crewman Brock has infected shoulder from shrapnel splints. All of these shell burst wounds seem to fester and rot away. Shell must have been poisoned. Rationed food and water. Romero died at 2.30. Buried at sunset. Condition of Demetrades about the same. Arm was dressed by Chief Steward. Raised water ration to 14 oz due to extra rain water. Had good night's run, wind dies down in day time.

Rodger Piercy:

It was about this time that Leonardo Romero from the Philippine Islands died. He had been going downhill for several days, but we had run out of medical supplies and could not figure out any way to help him. The last day or two he refused to eat and would pray a good deal. He was conscious and knew what he was doing, but realized he couldn't make it. His end was very peaceful.

Once again we had funeral services, and now it was getting closer to us all. We were getting weak, and our cramped quarters did not allow for much exercise. But then exercise only developed an appetite for food we did not have. It was still raining off and on; however, we were making fine headway. We were all sure we would make land.

We kept a very close eye on the compass. We wanted to land in Brazil which we knew had a 3,500 mile coastline. We felt we would be interned there for the duration, but believed that Argentina was pro-Nazi and would be tougher on us. If we had any doubts that drift or leeway was dropping us south, we would change course a couple of degrees.[27]

October 9th

Course northwest. Hope to sight something in a few days. Wiper Demetrades about the same. Got piece of shell out of Gun Crewman Brock's shoulder. Wound looks better. Rationed food and water. Not much wind stirring N.N.W. Checked up on water and ship's stores. Romero had diamond ring, only possession, keeping it in brief case.

October 10th

Due to taking inventory, no water reduction contemplated in next ten days. Ample food for at least 25 days. Wiper Demetrades still holding on. Rationed food and water. Gun crewman's shoulder about the same. Messman Peter Enos, has infection in right knee. Not much wind. Making very slow headway to N.N.W. Good breeze at sundown till midnight. Sailing due west.

October 11th

Good breeze until 9 a.m., ran into rain squall, caught 1 gallon water. Becalmed. Something sent up a green rocket right over our mast from a very short distance. Apparently from a submarine. We answered with 2 flares from Very pistol. (*According to filed report, "There was no answer to the boat's two flares from a Very pistol"*). All this at about 3.15 A.M. Rationed food and water. Wiper Demetrades still holding on. Gun crewman Brock and Messman Enos about the same.

October 12th

George Gelogotes, fireman, died this morning without apparent reason. Buried him at noon. Had $105.00 cash money in his possession and Seaman's papers. Will turn over to Consul first port of arrival. Wind from S.E. making good time northwest. Rationed food and water. Wiper Demetrades still holding on. Gun crewman Brock and Messman Enos about the same.

Rodger Piercy:

Just before the storm ended, George Papas grew ill. (*Note: This was George Gelogotes. Papas was last seen in the wheelhouse*). He was not wounded and had been in good health, but was cracking up under the strain. I think he was about forty-five years old. He went out of his head a few times, wanted to jump overboard, and had to be restrained. Later on, he turned purple and died. We think he had a heart attack. George was a good, old, easy-going guy that everyone liked. He was the first non-wounded man to die, and it gave us all food for thought.

Once again we had to have funeral services and our fifth man was consigned to the deep from our lifeboat. Still we could not become accustomed to it, and it cast a gloomy spell over us all. The next day the storm started breaking up, and it cheered us all up. We needed some sun.

It was about this time that we had one of our odd experiences. From time to time, we would think about what we would eat if we had a chance. In fact, I even think a skunk was mentioned a time or two.[28]

Moses Barker:

After two weeks in the lifeboat – it was monotonous just sitting there. We would once in a while talk about food. We had one guy from California and he had a chicken ranch. And for about a week he would talk about the different ways he was going to fix chicken. "You all coming to stay with me and I'm going to fix you the best chicken." We weren't as hungry as we were thirsty and you know we never had any bowel movement while we were in the boat. Everything in us was used by our bodies.[29]

Rodger Piercy:

Anyway, as the skies began to clear, a rather large bird, which we decided was a sea tern, came circling out of the sky and landed right in the lifeboat with us. It had been caught in the storm and was absolutely exhausted. One of the fellows reached out, picked it up, and said, "Well, here's the meal we wanted!"

That poor bird had been fighting for its life and needed just as much help as we did. Not a man among us had nerve enough to hurt it. So we kept it with us for two days and allowed it to rest and recuperate. Then we let it fly away. Every one of us felt better for it.[30]

October 13th

Very little breeze, hot. Rationed food and water. Wiper Demetrades still holding on. Brock and Enos about the same. Steering northwest, little better breeze, at sundown.

October 14th

Fair wind, steering northwest, days getting hot. No sight of land or ships or anything else. Everyone in fair spirits. Wiper Demetrades still holding on. Gun crewman Brock and Messman Enos about the same. Rationed food and water.

October 15th

Heavy rains, squalls, caught about 12 gal rain water, wind variable from S.E. Sailing N.W. Wiper Demetrades pretty low. Gun crewman Brock and Messman Enos about the same. Rationed food and water.

October 16th

Several squalls, not much wind. Wiper Demetrades died at 7 A.M. o'clock. Buried him at 9 A.M. Only possession Seaman's papers and bank book. Caught about 1 gal of rain water. Have about 40 gal of water altogether. No sign of land or ships. Still steering a northwest course. All water beakers about full. Rationed food and water. Still steering a northwest course. Seems as if we should have sighted land. Maybe currents are against us. Heavy squalls. Before midnight put out sea anchor, hove to.

Rodger Piercy:

Andy Tsigonis had his hand shot off during the battle with the raiders. (*Note: this was Athonosios Demetrades who had broken his arm, had it reset the first day in the lifeboat. Andrew Tsigonis was listed as on watch in boiler room with 3rd Assistant Engineer Kenneth Vaughan who was "nearly certainly killed due to shell having hit starboard boiler"*). Once in the lifeboat, we had bandaged him up and stopped the bleeding. He had fared very well. He was a nice looking native of Greece and was quiet and unassuming. The week of dampness had been hard on him, and he was slipping away. He had no appetite and was giving his food ration to his friend, Nick. [*Kokalis*] I think he realized he couldn't go much further and felt the extra food might help his buddy, Nick, to make it. Anyway Andy [*Athanosio Demetrades*] died quietly and without protest. I know he realized that we did everything for him that we possibly could; little as it was.

If I remember correctly, we had funeral services for Andy on our twenty-second day [*twentieth*] out in the lifeboat. With any help or luck, we could probably have saved him. So far we had lost forty-one men from the crew of the *Stephen Hopkins*. All that remained were six from the Naval Armed Guard and nine Merchant Seamen. Still no land in sight; nor any sign.[31]

October 17th
Took in sea anchor 6 a.m. Steering northwest. Fill all water casks and empty ration tins with water. Frequent squalls during day. Rationed food and water. Steering N.N.W.

October 18th
Heavy squalls all night, good wind in morning. Sailing due west. Rationed food and water. Everybody about the same. Ordinary Seaman Piercy laid up with sore foot.

October 19th
High wind and seas, shipping lots of water, bailing all night, everybody wet from rain and spray. Most everyone has sores that won't heal. Violent squalls. Steering northwest. Hove to all night. High seas.

Rodger Piercy:

The sun came bearing down hot, and before long we were all dry again. The breeze was blowing briskly, and we had a full sail. We were making fine time. We kept a close watch on our compass heading. Since we were getting weaker, we kept two or three men watching the compass and changed men at the tiller at the slightest sign of weariness. You could tell by the sail when the man at the tiller was getting tired.

It was a couple days after we buried Andy (*Demetrades*) that we ran into a school of whales. There were nine of them, and they were tremendous in size. It seemed as if we couldn't avoid them. We dropped the sail and lashed the water casks, just in case one might flip a ponderous tail. They were the most beautiful and graceful things you could ever see in the water. It seemed they hardly moved a muscle and yet could glide through the water with an ease that was unbelievable for a mammal of such huge size. One passed so closely to the lifeboat that I think I could have reached out an oar and touched it.

However, they soon passed on and made no attempt to bother us in any manner. It had been a tense fifteen or twenty minutes for us. No one had had any experiences with whales, and we did not know what to expect. It turned out to be a happy event and gave us something new to talk about. We were all glad it happened.[32]

October 20th

Bright sun shiny day, good wind. Seas still rough. Steering a northwesterly course. Took inventory on food. Cut ration in half. All water casks full. Wind from southeast.

Rodger Piercy:

We were now about twenty-five days out in the lifeboat, and the days remained hot; the nights were cold. We kept huddled together so our body warmth would help us from freezing. The ones in the middle could sleep a little. The outside circle would wear heavy jackets. You see we only had a few jackets and had to rotate using them.

In the heat of the days, we would go swimming, but never more than three at a time while the rest of us watched for sharks. Occasionally a shark would pick us up and follow for perhaps half a day and then fall away. They were never any serious concern though.[33]

Moses Barker:

We had canned pemmican on board. We'd take a can of pemmican and cut it into four squares and each of us would get a pie shape and then throw the can over the side. The water was clear. I wish it was like that nowadays and one day a shark grabbed a can. The sucker was really moving. Before this we would soak ourselves in the water. We'd get in and get out of the boat for half a minute, but no more.

I learned never to let my feet in the water – ocean. I wouldn't even do it on a lake out here. The boat rocking like this, the sun would burn and blister us and at night we would freeze. This was daytime and my feet were over the side and the boat would be rocking in the water and come back up. I was day dreaming and all of a sudden I saw the damndest barracuda you ever seen in your life. He came out of the water at I guess ten feet from the boat and that sucker went after my feet and I just made a flip over backwards and that thing hit the boat. I thought (the boat) would turn over. Boy he hit hard. I bet it knocked its brains out. Never again did I put my feet in the water.[34]

October 21st

Seas calm, plenty of sunshine, very little wind. Just steering way. Steering west northwest. Compass variation only 11 degrees by course of sun.

October 22nd

Good breeze all night, making good time due west. Condition of men about the same. Rationed out food and water.

Rodger Piercy:

We had a fairly good breeze blowing at the time now and seemed to be making good time every day and night. We had a good spirit of optimism and grumbling was a minimum... [35]

October 23rd

Poor breeze, just steering way. Sun hot, everyone kind of weak. Cut ration in half 4 days ago. Now getting 1 oz of Pemmican, 1 oz of chocolate, ½ oz of Malted Milk tablets, 1 type C ration biscuit per man per day, water ration 20 oz per man per day due to rain water caught. No sight of land or ships. Everyone in fair spirits. Steering west, wind N.N.E.

October 24th

Been becalmed for 24 hours. Very hot, everyone very weak. Seen some kind of sediment floating in water. Saw a butterfly and two moths. All think we are near land. Very poor visibility. Repaired rudder and sail. Fair breeze at sunset. Steering west.

Rodger Piercy:

Several days passed with nothing eventful happening. Then on about the twenty-eighth day, late in the afternoon, we spotted birds. They were a land-type that lived near the seacoast. Needless to say, we were all pretty excited. We realized these birds could range fifty to one hundred miles off shore, but to us that was pretty close. Sleep did not come easily that night. The next day we spotted birds all day long, but nothing else. The following day, the water color started to change. Sometimes we would pass through yellow water that looked like boiling sulfur; a very peculiar color and seemed shallow. Then in the afternoon we spotted a beautiful butterfly. It was a large one, and we realized that an off shore breeze had probably blown it out to sea. We knew we must be really close.[36]

October 25th

Had fair breeze all night. Sea choppy, not making much time. Seen a yellow moth. Makes us think we are near land. Steering northwest, very poor visibility.

October 26th

Very good breeze, water changing color. Very near land, so we believe.

Rodger Piercy:

That night we kept a double watch to listen for the roar of the surf, in case we approached a landfall during the darkness. About six o'clock in the morning, Archie Carlson, the lookout, called out to waken everyone to see if they could hear the surf roar as he was sure he could. It was still dark and quite foggy, but we could definitely hear the surf. Man, what a happy crew! Over two thousand miles in thirty-one days!

Still it was dark and foggy. We didn't dare risk going ashore, so we turned around and put back out to sea to wait for daylight. Daylight came, but the fog didn't begin to raise until about ten o'clock in the morning. Then we could see a beautiful sandy coastline with only a moderate surf to go through... [37]

October 27th

Hurrah, sighted land 4 a.m. Landed at small Brazilian village of Barra de Itabapoana. Police notified Consul at Rio de Janeiro. Trying to arrange transportation to Rio.

G. Cronk, 2nd Engineer [38]

In later interviews, Moses Barker said that after the *Hopkins* sank,

I quit cussing and began praying and told God that if he would let us live I wouldn't ever hurt anyone again. A storm came up, and the Germans went away and we were safe. Since that day, I've never hurt another human being.[39]

I love the ocean but that was a long trip. We were just lucky we had a good crew. The merchant marine and Navy got along wonderful together. Usually you had a little conflict between the branches, but with us there were no different branches. We were all the same.[40]

17

RETURN TO THE FATHERLAND

Sept. 27, 1942. Capt. Haase, M.S. *Tannenfels***:**

> At 1209 hours our other lifeboats were lowered into the water and were immediately sent to the Auxiliary Cruiser. Neither before or at the current time did we see any shipwrecked sailors aboard lifeboats* from the enemy ship.[1]

---

* In a March 1955 issue of the German newspaper *Der Frontsoldat*, Hans Grunert, a *Tannenfels* crewmember reported, "In spite of a search of two hours we did not find any survivors of the American ship. With our flag at half-mast we made a full circle around the spot where the Liberty ship had sunk thus rendering the last honors to our brave adversary'.[2]

Herzliche Grube, a member of Kameradschaft Hilfkreuzer *Stier* (*Stier* Association), verified this in a 1984 letter written to Jean Dierkes-Carlisle, daughter of 1st Asst. Engineer, Charles L. Fitzgerald who was killed aboard the *Hopkins*. He wrote, "We looked for hours for survivors of *Hopkins* aboard *Tannenfels* but we didn't believe there would be any after we hit their ammunition chamber creating a fireball."[3]

Captain Haase:

It was raining off and on. The wind and waves continued to increase. The sea was moving in a lively manner and there was a low swell. Our lifeboat crews had a hard job to do. Meanwhile, preparations were being made on board for the reception of the comrades from the auxiliary cruiser. With the large number of jobs to be done, every one of my crewmembers did his best. In the shortest possible time, the wounded, the crew, and finally the commander with his officers were safely on *Tannenfels*. Among other things, we put up on our deck two inflatable life rafts that had been used by some crewmembers of the auxiliary cruiser who were taken into our lifeboats. We also lifted the auxiliary cruiser's motorboat up onto our deck. We lifted our own boats out of the water and maneuvered slowly forward. At 1357 hours the auxiliary cruiser, which had been blown up, sank into the deep. The position was 24° 43'S, 21° 52W. The entire crew was assembled on deck. The number saved from auxiliary cruiser 23 was immediately calculated as 326 men and eight prisoners.

Due to the threat of danger, we sailed far out toward the east and then with maximum speed toward the South in hopes of meeting up with Auxiliary Cruiser 28 or *Uckermark* at the second waiting position 28° 00'S, 22° 00'W.

In the course of the afternoon, the problem of suitable accommodation for the thirty-six wounded crewmembers (some of them badly wounded) was solved. The solution was very quick, since the officers cleared out of their cabins and the passenger cabins were also put into use. The rest

Stier*'s Capt. Horst Gerlach boards* Tannenfels *after the loss of his ship.* National Archives.

of the crewmembers were put into cabins, the forecastle and the forward bridge deck, insofar as it was possible, and provided with the most necessary items. I would like to take this opportunity to make it clear that the entire crew of the M/S *Tannenfels* acted in an outstanding manner in every way. The crew played its part in helping me find quick and satisfactory answers to the large number of questions that flooded over me. Deserving of special praise are the officers, the lifeboat crews and the ship's doctor, Assistant Naval Physician Dr. Wischeropp. There was only one very poorly-equipped hospital on board that was set up for treatment of just one seriously ill person. This means that in taking the wounded on board there were many things to be taken into consideration: such as preparing accommodations for the wounded, food preparation for sick people, obtaining medications, distribution of our supply of bandages, and the question of clothing for the sick and wounded. The wounded received strengthening drinks and a special diet: such as cognac, rum, real coffee, tea, milk, eggs, asparagus, etc.[4]

Captain Gerlach reported the following:

The taking of the crew aboard *Tannenfels* was completed in a smooth and orderly manner. Immediately afterward, Captain Werner Haase and I discussed the ship abandonment and the rescue of my crew. It took about half a day for the accommodations to be arranged. In addition there were now seventy-eight prisoners aboard *Tannenfels* including those taken from *Stier.* These POWs were moved and placed together in the large area under the bridge deck after hatch 4. The official and unofficial relationship between Captain Haase and me was the best conceivable one. Cooperation between the two of us was easy. Captain Haase had an understanding for our situation, and helped us in every possible way. The same can be said of *Tannenfels* officers and crew. Furthermore, Captain Haase has his ship and crew in perfect order. This is not a simple task and he has installed a freshness and efficiency in his sailors. He masters in a calm, safe, and considerate manner.

Captain Gerlach requests the EK II and EK I for the *Tannenfels* captain and the EK II for the remainder of the *Tannenfels* crew.

During the next day on the 28th, in order to relieve *Tannenfels'* men, *Stier*'s crew took over the lookout operations and the guard officers were replaced by *Stier*'s navy officers. Other assignments were equally divided between both the military and artillery crews. On the morning of the 28th, engineering officer Hans Pallhorn died. He was buried at sea in a solemn ceremony with a flag covering his body.[5]

Captain Haase:

> As we were getting underway, the badly wounded engine room corporal Hans Pallhorn died. He was immediately sewed up in cloth and laid out and was put to sea on 28 September 1942 at 0850 hours. The position was 25° 00'S, 18° 18'W.[6]

Captain Gerlach:

> Early in the afternoon after the rescue of the crew was completed, a course was set to try to rendezvous with *Uckermark* at maximum speed. According to my computations, Ship 28 (*Michel*) had to be in the vicinity. It was arranged that Ship 28 instruct *Uckermark* to stand by starting 4 October daily at 0800 at this prearranged position.

Both crews gathered for the solemn and formal burial-at-sea of their comrade. National Archives.

On 30 September I decided to contact Ship 28 (*Michel*) and send a radiogram with the following plain language in special code to Ship 28. "Stand on ordered meeting place 28° 00'S 22° W." The transmission to Ship 28 apparently never took place because neither of the two ships were in place. When we arrived at the point nothing was seen of either ship. I had told Captain von Ruckteschell (*Michel*'s captain) that *Tannenfels* had to fill up with at least 250 tons of fuel in order to break through on the return home going at least 14 knots and that at least one of the two ships would be needed in the return. There was still hope that at least *Uckermark* would appear on 4 October at 28° S, 22° W. We were also concerned for our own safety as we waited 1½ days and our prospects of meeting *Uckermark* shrunk [as those of being discovered by the enemy grew].[7]

Captain Haase:

On 29 September 1942 at 1000 hours we were located in the waiting area at 28° 00'S, 22° 00W. It had been agreed with the commandant that we should wait here, either until arrival of auxiliary cruiser *28*, to which a radio telegram message had been sent from auxiliary cruiser *23* just before the ship was abandoned and had been sent out one more time on 30 September 1942, or to await the arrival of the *Uckermark*, which had been ordered to sail to this position on 4 October 1942.

During this time, our position was improved every day, mornings and evenings. The weather was consistently good to changeable with moderate westerly winds and moderate sea and swell. Nothing was sighted.

From this time on we worked on providing good accommodations for the crew of auxiliary cruiser *23* for a long period of time and to make sure that the rations, which at first were very uncertain, would be as secure as possible, in case the supply ship *Uckermark* should not arrive. This succeeded better than expected. Due to a great lack of fat products, we found it necessary to break open the cargo belonging to the Reich and to take cases of lard, a case of tea and a case of egg products. All the rest of the food was rationed in such a way as to ensure a sufficient supply. I do not want to fail to express the highest praise for the kitchen personnel. They made everything possible that had seemed impossible; especially since the galley equipment and everything else that they had at their disposal was only sufficient for 150 men.

The crews of both ships shared duties (in this case peeling potatoes) as the Tannenfels *steamed toward home.* National Archives.

After it had recovered from its ordeal, the *Stier* crew was completely integrated into the vessel's operations. In terms of lookouts, only personnel from auxiliary cruiser *23* (*Stier*) were used. As the voyage progressed, a good sense of mutual understanding and teamwork was evident between the two crews.

To our great disappointment, neither *Uckermark* nor Auxiliary Cruiser *28* had appeared by 5 October 1942. Our supply of mattresses, blankets, eating utensils and tobacco products was in fact totally inadequate. Even without receiving these supplies, we found it necessary to go ahead and begin our voyage.[8]

Captain Gerlach:

On 6 October we sent the following telegram. "Schiff 23 sunk, crew saved, oil 500 tons, on *Tannenfels*, on way home, we are informing Homeland of our situation." There was the intention that *Uckermark* could deliver a more detailed message. Still no confirmation was made on 6 October. A repeated effort was abandoned for fear of betraying the ship's course.[9]

Captain Haase:

First we sailed toward our first waiting position 25 South 22° West, arriving on 6 October 1942 at 0800 hours. Not sighting anything, we continued the voyage without interruption. According to the commandant, during this day we had to traverse a dangerous area. For this reason, the engine was running at full power at 1800 hours, which produced only 84 revolutions for a short time. According to the 1st Engineer, this was the fastest speed the engine was capable of. This number of revolutions corresponds to a speed of 15.2 knots with a 5% slip.

At 1755 hours on the same day a telegram with the following text was sent to SKL: Max Ulrich sunk, crew rescued, oil 500 tons on homeward voyage with *Tannenfels*. As it turned out, this telegram was unfortunately not received.

We sailed on to midday at 7 October 1942 with 83 revolutions and from 1700 hours with 52 revolutions — one engine — and steered a northerly course at this speed until 9 October 1942.

On 9 October 1942 1128 hours, at five points to the port side, a ship was sighted. We changed course at top speed and, once the ship was out of sight, steered our old course again at 1152 hours. The weather had been very good during the last few days. Easterly winds 3-4, good visibility and moderate seas. On 10 October at 0954 hours we sighted a ship at a true 65^0 and at 1049 hours we saw another ship at 45 degrees. In both cases we were able to change course in a short time at top speed without being reported by a radio telegram.

On 12 October 1942 at 0000 hours we reached the position of 3$^°$ 00' South 22$^°$ 06' West without further incidents. From here we sailed at high speed during the day at 78 revolutions and 82 to 83 revolutions at night (due to excessive smoke production) through the Natal narrows [*narrowest point in the South Atlantic Ocean between the northeast point of Brazil and the west coast of Africa*], without sighting anything. However, on 13 October a ship came into sight at approximately 5$^°$ 00"N, 27$^°$ 30'W at 1651 hours and another ship was seen at 1840 hours. Also, here we were able to change course early enough so as not to be noticed. On 14 October we once again had to change course to avoid a ship. On 16 October 1942 at around 2000 hours we were at 15$^°$ 17'N and steered from here toward true north at 52 revolutions on one engine. From this position we sent a telegram to SKL with the message — "Rigging — 300 — with crew of *Stier.*" We immediately received confirmation that the message had been received.

During the next few days we continued our voyage at a northerly course with moderate to good weather without further incidents. The only time we had to change course to avoid being seen by another ship was on 20 October 1942 at 0825 hours at

Above, the U-boat comes into view at the scheduled rendezvous. Below, she is close alongside Tannenfels. National Archives.

26° 50'N, 38° 26'W. On the same day we received a message that we would meet up with a German U-Boat (submarine). The U-Boat was sighted on 22 October 1942 at 0908 hours. The telegram was delivered as ordered, and at 1055 hours the U-Boat boat sailed away.[10]

We continued our voyage as slowly as possible in order not to pass the reference point "rigging" before 28 October 1942. On 24 October we received telegram No. 28 with the convoy report. After linking up with the convoy, we were able to continue the voyage at a true course of 330°. At 1400 hours on same day, however, telegram No. 30 made it clear that the convoy were sailing in a westerly direction, presumably, toward North America. We then left the convoy at 1500 hours at a true course of 180°. We stayed on this course until 25 October at 0425 hours. We were now at 38° 50'N, 40° 00W, [*near the Azores*] when we received telegram No. 36. The last telegrams we received made it clear that the convoy was taking a primarily southern route - this was also confirmed by telegraph telegram No. 38 - so we took a northwesterly route, contrary to the instructions of SKL. The reason was that the route based on the position we were instructed to take

seemed to be too dangerous... We sailed at top power in a true northwest direction until 1200 hours, reached the position 40° 05'N, 41° 26'W and changed here to true north until 1500 hours. After receiving telegram No. 38, we were able to make a true 045 course from 40° 47'N, 41° 26W without any danger and continue our voyage with one engine at 52 revolutions. The weather was very good with an almost calm sea and unusually good visibility. On this day we did not see anything.

On 26 October 1942 at 0000 hours, Able Seaman August Schmidt from Ship *23* died from his wounds. [*The fourth crewmember from* Stier *to have died*]. He was ceremoniously put into the sea at 930 hours and 42° 52'N, 38° 45'W.[11]

We maintained a true course of 045 until 1900 hours and then changed to a 090 true course. On 27 October 1942, we received telegram No. 49, giving us the order not to cross 30 West longitude before 29 October 1942. We immediately changed our course to true 270. At 1600 hours we sighted a ship on our port side that we were able to bypass without any difficulty. The weather had worsened to an unusual degree. The wind was blowing from NNE at force 6-7 [*strong breeze-large waves nearing gale-mounting sea conditions*]. There was a very high north and northeast swell and the sea was quite rough. On 28 October 1942 at 0400 hours we steered again a true 090. On 29 October 1942 at 1100 hours crossed the 30° West longitude that been ordered. Unhindered and without sighting anything, we were able to continue our easterly course until the morning of 31 October 1942.

At 0732 hours several smoke clouds came into sight on the horizon. We first assumed that they came from one of the convoys that had been reported to us. We turned north and then toward the west. This change enabled us to determine that the convoy was steaming toward the south. We changed our course toward the north and resumed our old course when the convoy was out of sight. We were a little bit amazed to read in telegram No. 58 that we had changed course to evade a group of warships consisting of two aircraft carriers, a cruiser, and a destroyer, not a convoy.

With unusually good visibility, we continued the course unhindered and were flown over at 0913 and 0947 hours by a German Condor aircraft. After exchanging signals, the plane departed. At 1718 hours a Sunderland Flying Boat flew toward us at a low height. Contrary to our expectations, the Sunderland remained out of shooting range, determined our sailing speed, flew around behind us, and then disappeared in a southerly

The Focke-Wulf Fw 200 Condor was the premier long range maritime patrol aircraft used by the Luftwaffe. John MacClancy.

direction. A short time later, at 1725 and 1852 hours, a Condor aircraft once again flew toward us, exchanged signals and then immediately continued its assignment. The sighting of the Sunderland Flying Boat* was immediately reported by telegram, since we had to assume that a later attack would occur.

We continued steering our old course in order to meet up punctually at the ordered rendezvous point with torpedo boats that had been reported to us. On 1 November 1942 we passed Cap Ortega [*NNW cape in Spain*] at a distance of three miles. From here we changed our course to true 073 and then to true 049 at 0430 hours on 2 November 1942. At 0800 hours a minesweeper came into sight with several patrol boats. After a signal change, I received an order to follow the minesweeper.

At 1347 hours the ship tied up safe and well at the pier at Le Verdun.[12]

Friedrich Weber wrote the following concerning the rescue of *Stier*'s crew in a 1944 *Das Reich* issue:

---

* Seven hundred and forty-nine British Sunderlands were built. The design was so good that it remained in front line service for over twenty years. The Germans nicknamed it 'Flying Porcupine' because of its protective armament.[13] The Sunderland sank or shared credit in the sinking of twenty-seven U-Boats.[14]

A Sunderland Md.V (with French markings) underway in 1960. John Batchelor.

Now *Tannenfels* comes to pick us up out of the grey doom. It is cold and the water is rough to float in. It was hard work which called for untiring work of all the comrades, but we succeed. After heavy hours salvaging we are aboard the new ship. We are all saved after the fight is over.

The blockade runner is one of these ships that constantly sail for Germany around the world and it is an unusual ship. We notice that immediately. The enormous distance sailed by Captain Haase from the Japanese motherland into the South Atlantic undetected is reminder to all the leaders of how difficult it is to breakthrough and get back to the Homeland. The crew is made up of a handful of seasoned men from merchant shipping.

The officers and sailors aboard *Tannenfels* help us put on their remaining dry khaki pants. Life and discipline aboard the large 8,000 BRT ton freighter depends upon already established commands. The vessel has room for a 50 man crew. All other available area belongs to the 15,000 ton cargo load stored in all the holds. There are thousands of tons of lard, soybeans, food oil, spices and minerals. In addition, it carries 100 refugees from South and North America, Russia and the whole world back to the Homeland. Everyone is anxious to get back to the realm with the 200 prisoners from the English and American colonies.

It should bring fresh provisions to the *Stier*'s crew. However, *Tannenfels* now carries an additional 300 men. Our wounded are placed in the passenger chambers. We sleep in

Submarine nets, foreground, have been pulled aside to allow Tannenfels *to enter the harbor of Verdun.* National Archives.

a half-vacated loading space. Otherwise, we live on the deck. The sight aboard ship is one of multi-colored uniforms and unshaven beards for weeks. In the prisoner area aft is sighted all forms and colors. With all this freight, *Tannenfels* begins its trip back.

The homecoming becomes the most active session of our long trip. For weeks we are on the prescribed position waiting for the tanker which is to supply us with fuel for the new distance.

Tannenfels *alongside the dock at Verdun.* National Archives.

Admiral Marschall welcomes Capt. Haase and Capt. Gerlach after their ordeal. National Archives.

The tanker never arrives. We may not send messages. Thus we must sail. We still have oil but nothing comes, costing us days and weeks.

Doing half-speed at 8 knots, we run to the north. Day after day passes. The 7,000 nautical miles become less. We advance for the third time into the hot area of the equator. Hostile freighters greet us but do not interrupt us and each time it could be the end of us. We must sail and evade faster and we are constantly concerned about oil. At all hours the alarms shock us into sharp tension. Twice we run by in dark nights, so near other ships that we can completely and clearly recognize them. They regard us as one of theirs and we escape.

We have water and sufficient food supply. We live on eastern foods from the cargo. Together with the maritime service aboard we are on watch non-stop looking for the enemy. One morning northwest of the Azores a group of dark smoke clouds is seen on the horizon. The lookout announces an aircraft carrier, two heavy cruisers, and four destroyers. Our hearts beat hard. We have a cannon. It is a miracle the

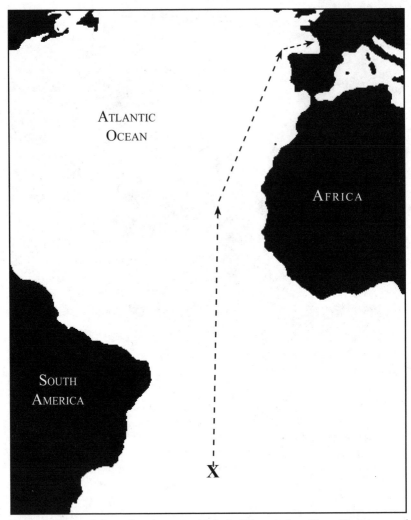

Tannenfels *track from the place at which the* Stier *sank to Cape Finistere and* Verdun.

convoy doesn't spot us. Captain Haase, supported by our commander, finds our way out of the worst situations. He has driven *Tannenfels* on the correct course in all the crucial places. The break through succeeds.

After seven weeks, Cape Finisterre (a point on the northwest coast of Spain) appears dimly through the fog. It is for us a new beginning.[15]

18

SAFE ASHORE

On October 27, 1942 the No. 1 lifeboat of the S.S. *Stephen Hopkins* came ashore at Barra de Itabapoana, Brazil with fifteen survivors. They had been at sea for thirty-one days and covered 1,300 nautical miles without navigation equipment and only the barest necessities for survival. Four men perished during a voyage filled with storms, heat and cold, illness, death and the inevitable conflicts, pressures and stresses of men thrown together in a cramped, open lifeboat, life-and-death decisions and dissensions, but they had survived.

After so much sorrow and travail, fate did deal the survivors one good card — they were fortunate to land where they did. Drifting farther south, the lifeboat would have missed the Rio de Janeiro area and would have had to sail an additional 500-odd miles to land near Sao Paulo. Had they sailed farther north and missed the northeast corner of Brazil, they would have had to

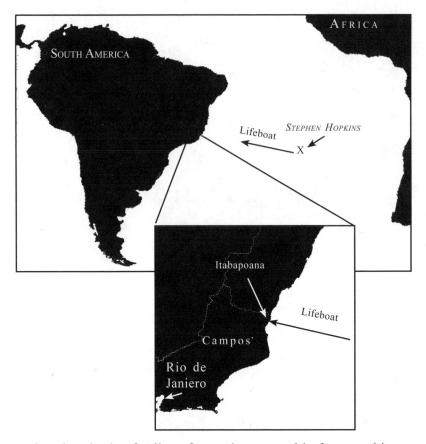

endure hundreds of miles of open boat travel before reaching a landfall in the Caribbean.

The effects of weeks of inactivity huddled in cramped quarters were apparent.

Rodger Piercy:

What a shock it was to find that I couldn't stand up, but would fall over on my face each time I tried. I finally crawled on my hands and knees, and then discovered several others doing the same. Too long cramped in the lifeboat without exercise and, of course, no food at all the last several days had taken its toll.

We pulled the lifeboat up on the beach, buried an oar, made her fast to it, and then crawled up higher in the sand to rest awhile. We had no side arms, only a Very pistol, but we didn't care. We felt we could always sail up or down the coast. We certainly needed some food. I must say for myself, and I think the entire crew, that the roller-coaster ride through the surf and skidding onto the beach was the greatest thrill of our lives! You will never know the enjoyment we had just letting the sand run through our hands unless you had made the voyage with us!

After resting a while, we called a meeting to try and decide our next move. Behind us seemed to be a small hill that became brushy and ran into timber. We decided to send some of the stronger ones on a short exploration trip. We needed wood for a night fire. Another group was to search the surf and shoreline for anything edible. Both groups were to watch for a plane or any material that would offer protection from the cold damp air. While we were planning this, one of the fellows spotted a native hiding in the brush, watching us! Upon close watch, we sighted two natives.

One of our men, Peter Enos, was Hawaiian-born Portuguese and could speak the language. Another, Carlos Sanchez, was Puerto Rican and could speak Spanish. Each of these men tried to get the natives to come and join us. It took quite a while to assure them that we were friendly North Americans in need of help and meant them no harm. They agreed to talk to one man and Peter Enos went up and met them. It only took him a little while to convince them to join us. They came down and gave us some Brazilian cigarettes. In Brazil, the native language is Portuguese, and they could easily talk with Pete.

It seemed that over the top of the hill, it dropped down to a river, and across on the other side was a small native village called Barra de Itabapoana. These men agreed to take us there. They had dugout canoes and poled them across the fairly shallow river. However, their boats would only carry two at a time and so they had to relay back and forth to get us all across. Eventually we all arrived, but by this time there was quite a gathering of natives who were very friendly and were looking us over. All of us had a month's growth of beard, ragged clothes, no shoes, and bushy hair. It would be hard to find fifteen men who looked worse than we did!

The village was small and had perhaps one hundred people with maybe another hundred farming the surrounding area. These people were poor as church mice and probably never expected to see anyone worse off than them, but here we were! I guess that is why they took us to their hearts and shared anything and everything that they had with us. I will never forget the generosity of these wonderful people.

They took us to the largest house which wasn't much as our homes go, but looked like a castle to us. They fed us boiled rice, chicken, fish, bananas, and a pudding made from mandioca (*cassava*). Wow! What a feast! Women, men, and children were all over the place and all trying to help us. It was wonderful.

A couple of young women got a hold of me and took me out in the yard. Since I couldn't understand their language, I didn't know what they were going to do. It didn't take long to find out. They had a tub of water and stripped me to the waist and gave me the works: a sponge bath, washed my face, scrubbed my hair, dried me off, and set me in a chair. Then one cut my hair and surplus beard off with scissors. A man came along and gave me a shave with a straight razor. All the time the girls were giggling, laughing, talking Portuguese, and having as much fun as watching a Barnum and Bailey circus! We were all getting the same treatment and enjoying it just as much.

After this, we were allowed to go back in the house and take naps. The beds were just wooden bunks with a blanket, but it was more than enough. By then, we were all exhausted, happy, but so nervous and keyed up we could hardly sleep.

It was about dusk when the whole community showed up. It seemed everyone wanted to see us and weren't satisfied unless they felt us, to see if we were real, I guess. We still had our Very pistol and decided to fire a star shell as a show. It was the first time these people had ever seen anything like it and were happy as children. The major-domo of the village was with us, and we let him fire a shell also. This immediately made him a village hero; so he promptly confiscated the gun. He also notified us that we were technically under arrest, could have free run of the village, but were not supposed to leave town. I never did figure out if he was the mayor or chief of police or both. He apparently had charge of the town and was respected by the people. That was good enough for us.

The party went on for several hours and everyone tried to crowd into the house. There was more food, music and a little cerveza. We all had a wonderful time even though most of us couldn't understand a word that was said. They had such friendly eyes and big smiles that we didn't really need a language. That night I slept from sheer exhaustion, and it must have been twelve or fourteen hours.

The next day was more serious. The town had no electricity and no radio or telegraph, of course. Just after our arrival they had sent a runner off to a larger town that had a telegraph to send a message to the Brazilian Minister of Marine Affairs. He in turn notified the American Consul in Rio de Janeiro, and he notified the American naval attaché in Victoria which was north of us.

That afternoon a Piper Cub plane landed on the beach. It was sent by the American consul to fly out any seriously wounded.[1]

From the "Victoria Confidential Intelligence Report" written for the *Hopkins* Navy Armed Guard report on October 31, 1942:

Trying to get to Itabapoana from Victoria to help survivors of the "STEPHEN HOPKINS" proved quite a task. The observer left Victoria at 1400 by Piper Cub plane furnished by the Aero Clube de Estado de Espirito Santo. He was grounded at Barra de Itipermerim at 1500. Left there on locomotive for Cachoeiro at 1830. Drove by taxi from Cachoeiro to Campos over a muddy and slippery road in a driving rain storm. Parts of this road overhang a valley about 200 feet deep. Arrived in Campos and arranged for another car to Barra de Itabapoana over a rougher but lower road. Arrived in Barra de Itabapoana at 0630.

Ensign Crocker of the Naval Attaché's Office had arrived at 1000 the previous evening. The survivors were in wonderful condition, considering what they'd gone through. One could not help but feel the deepest admiration for these men who had faced such odds and were never for one moment beaten. After thirty days of being battered together on a cramped lifeboat, they were still lavishing praise on one another, helping one another, and best of all, wanting to go back again. You were made to realize how small your own troubles were, and how big good humans can be.

Ensign WILLET, in charge of the Gun Crew, undoubtedly inspired these men by his heroism and courage, and memory of his deeds must have helped them when the going was toughest.

Lt. Joseph E. Rich, USNR[2]

Enclosure to Despatch No. 9187 from Rio de Janeiro dated November 24, 1942, on the subject "Survivors of the S.S. Stephen Hopkins." (Confidential)

Memorandum re: trip to Barra de Itabapoana to arrange for care and return to Rio de Janeiro of survivors of the former SS STEPHEN HOPKINS

I left Rio de Janeiro Tuesday afternoon, October 27, 1942, at 2:30 P.M. with Ensign Crocker in the Navy Douglas transport. We arrived at Campos at 3:40 P.M. and went from the airport to the Mayor's office. The Mayor was not there but his assistant told us that the survivors had landed at Barra de Itabapoana and that he thought they were coming to Campos by car, but he was not sure. As the Navy plane had to leave for Rio immediately in order to return before dark, I went back to the airport and told Commander Lanigan that the men certainly would not arrive at Campos in time to be taken back on the transport, so they left for Rio.

When I returned to town Ensign Crocker had found the Mayor, who had informed him that the men were still in Barra de Itabapoana and that he did not know as yet how or when they were coming to Campos. Knowing that the survivors had been at sea for a considerable time in the lifeboat and not knowing what condition they were in, we decided to go directly to Barra de Itabapoana and asked the Mayor to cable there and have them hold the men until we arrived.

The Mayor furnished us with a car and chauffeur and we left Campos at 6:00 P.M. arriving at Barra de Itabapoana at about 10:00 P.M. and with the help of one of the local truck drivers went directly to the pensao [*small hotel*] where the men were staying. The owner of the pensao awakened Mr. Cronk, second assistant engineer, in charge of the men, who came out and told us the following:

The total number of survivors including myself are fifteen. We arrived here this morning at about 4:30 A.M. after travelling thirty-one days in a lifeboat. The ship, S.S. STEPHEN HOPKINS, with a merchant crew of forty-one men, and armed guard of fifteen men, and a passenger named George Townsend, who came aboard in Durban, was owned by the War Shipping Administration and operated by the Luckenbach

Lines.   We were proceeding from Cape Town, South Africa to an unknown port, believed to be on the northern coast of South America.

At about 9:30 A.M. on September 27 two armed raiders suddenly came on us out of the mist and started firing immediately. One, a small raider about 4,000 tons, appeared to have four 4-inch guns which were firing simultaneously as from a fire control system; the other, a larger ship of about 7,000 tons, seemed to be a mother-ship and did not enter the battle except to keep spraying the decks with machine-gun fire. The gun crew immediately manned their guns and commenced firing at the small raider. The gunnery officer in charge, Ensign Willett, although wounded twice before reaching the gun, kept the gun trained directly on the water line of the raider and managed to fire at least thirty-five shells into the water line. The machine-guns and 37mm anti-aircraft were also manned and were firing as rapidly as possible at both ships. Most of the crew of the rear 4-inch gun were killed by explosive shells; the magazine was also blown up, but there were about five shells left in the ready box and one of the men, Cadet O'Hara, ran up and shot the five shells into the water line of the large raider. The "abandon ship" signal was given at about 9:55 but all the lifeboats except No. 1 had been hit. The No. 1 lifeboat was being lowered by the men when a shell exploded in it and killed two and wounded four of the men who were in the boat helping to lower it. However, the others succeeded in lowering the boat and getting clear of the ship. The rest of the men who were able, jumped overboard and caught doughnut rafts or else swam to the lifeboat. The men in the lifeboat then drifted near the two raiders and saw the smaller raider was down by the stern, huge clouds of smoke coming out in several different places. When they last saw the two raiders they were about bow to bow and the mother-ship seemed to be taking off the crew of the smaller ship.

They saw the S. S. STEPHEN HOPKINS go down by the stern as they were rowing away. A moment later they heard a large explosion which they took to be the magazine of the smaller raider and are confident that the ship sank. They then rowed around trying to pick up survivors until the visibility was so bad they could no longer see. They then hove to and stayed until about noon the next day hoping to find more survivors but the sea was so heavy that there was no chance of picking up anyone else, so they started out in a westerly direction. There were nineteen men in the lifeboat, five of whom were wounded by shrapnel and explosive shell — four of whom died during the trip, leaving a total of fifteen men who arrived safely. Mr. Cronk also told us that they had twenty-four gallons of water when they started the trip and arrived with fifty gallons of water which they got from catching rain water. They also had enough condensed food left to take them for another twenty days. Mr. Cronk was very anxious that a report should reach the Navy Department about the heroism of Ensign Willett, who, although wounded twice, kept the 4-inch gun trained directly on the small raider while under heavy fire from that ship. We then told Mr. Cronk to go back to bed and we would go into it further in the morning. We then went to the home of Baron von Kummer where we were to spend the night. When we arrived there we found that two of the survivors were there and had gotten out of bed to talk to us. They told substantially the same story as Mr. Cronk. There being nothing further we could do that night we went to bed and decided to take action on the following morning. The next morning we got up and found that Lieutenant Rich, the Naval Observer from Victoria had arrived about six o'clock that morning. The three of us then decided the best course would be to take the men by boat to Barra de Itapemirin where there was a good airfield and ask the Naval Attaché's office in Rio to send a Douglas transport there to take the men to Rio. If that was not feasible we could take them to Campos by truck and by plane from there to Rio. We sent a cable to the Naval Attaché's office in Rio outlining this procedure and then went down to see the survivors. They all seemed to be in good health with the exception of one, Walter Manning, who had been badly sunburned on the feet. They told us they had arrived off the coast at about 4 A.M. Tuesday morning and, hearing the breakers, had decided to stay off until daylight to see where they were. At daylight they had brought the boat over the breakers and landed on the mouth of the Paraiba River directly in front of the town. Some people from the town brought them to the nearest pensao and gave them water and food and then brought them some clothing. Shortly afterwards while we were awaiting word from Rio two small planes from the Base do Galeao in Rio arrived and landed in a nearby field. They had come to offer any possible assistance. Ensign Crocker then went to Campos in one of the planes in order to telephone Rio as we were not sure of the cable connections. On his return he found that it was impossible to send a plane to

Barra de Itapimirin because the field was too small and that we would have to take the men immediately to Campos by truck where trucks would be waiting to take them to Rio. We sent Manning, who was in the worst condition, in the small plane, and three men with wounds in the Mayor's car and then set out for Campos with the rest of the men in a truck owned by Baron von Kummer, arriving at Campos at 3 p.m. Upon arrival we found there were three small Brazilian air force planes from Base do Galeao at Rio, one of which had brought a Brazilian air force doctor who wanted to keep the wounded men in Campos overnight. They had understood that there were only six people in the group, and could take only eight men, so we sent eight men immediately to Rio in two of the planes, and took the rest to the Palace Hotel in Campos. We telephoned Rio to find out when we could get transportation. They informed us they were sending more planes on Thursday morning. On Thursday two more Brazilian air force planes arrived from Rio at 11:30 A.M. We took off from Campos with the remaining survivors at 1 P.M., arriving at Rio at 2:30 P.M. where the men were taken to the Brazilian Naval Hospital.

There are attached hereto, for further information, a list of the survivors, a copy of the log book of the lifeboat, and copies of statements made by the 2nd assistant engineer and the chief steward.

The ship's papers, consisting of articles, crew list, and register which had been placed in the lifeboat by the captain of the ship, have been turned over to the representative of the War Shipping Administration for transmission.

Timothy J. Mahoney, American Vice Consul[3]

Rodger Piercy:

They told us to hang on; help was coming. They took Wallace Breck back with them. He was a big 6-foot, 2-inch fellow that weighed about 220 lbs., but was now down to about 170 pounds. He had been hit with shrapnel pieces. We had cut one piece out of his shoulder in the lifeboat, but he still had some others that were taken out at the hospital.

That night the people gave us a party, and the main course was barbecued pig. I told the fellows not to eat the meat; anything else was OK. Some of the fellows couldn't resist, and it was nearly tragic. That greasy pork just turned them inside out. Three of them were lying on the ground in back of the house vomiting, retching, and doubled up with horrible cramps. They were trying to hide. They didn't want the people to know the food had made them ill.[4]

Moses Barker, "The villagers cooked a hog in celebration, but the hungry survivors couldn't eat it. Our stomachs had shrunk so much we couldn't eat."[5]

Rodger Piercy:

The next day we were paid a visit by a lady the natives called the "Contessa." She spoke very good English. She had a farm of several thousand acres some ten miles away. It seems her husband and she had skipped out of Romania just before Hitler took over. They had come to Brazil, bought their land in the wilderness, and started carving out a farm. She would have taken us to her home, but the American naval attaché from Victoria arrived while she was there.

The naval attaché was a young, nice fellow. He made arrangements for the people to be paid for our room, board, and for extra supplies to be sent in, including some clothing for us. We were practically nude, but it didn't seem to matter as that was the order of the day around there. Apparently clothing was for Sundays. He also arranged credit for us at the only store in town. He told us the water in the area was contaminated and to drink beer as much as possible instead.

We certainly remembered his sage advice. After he left and being fortified with newly-established credit, we promptly got half the village canned up on beer. Fortunately the store ran out of beer before things got out of hand, and everything ended happily. We were having so much fun; we didn't care whether we ever left the village. We were welcome everywhere and treated as honored guests. Sometimes when I think about it now, I wish I could have stayed there.

In a few days a flat bed pickup truck with stake sides came in with supplies and clothes for us. It was to take us out as soon as we could travel. There were no roads, just cow trails and travel would be rough. They put loose straw in the truck bed so we could lie down, and it would absorb some of the shock. Of the clothing they sent us, we took just bare necessities and gave the rest to our friends. We knew they would need them more than we would.

Our departure called for another village turnout, and we were given a grand farewell by all. They were wonderful people, and none of us will ever forget them.

We piled in back of the truck and started for Campos, Brazil. It was about sixty-five kilometers, but the roads being what they were, it was an all day trip. It was dusk when we arrived, and we were taken to the Palace Hotel. Campos was a town of about one thousand people, and the Palace Hotel had the only neon sign in town. So I guess we were traveling first class.

A vice-consul from Rio de Janeiro was waiting for us and had dinner arranged. When we arrived in Brazil, we expected to be interned for the duration of the war, but he explained that Brazil had declared war on Germany only five days before we landed. It seems German subs had sunk five Brazilian ships and really aroused the people against them. There were very proud to be allied with us.

He made arrangements for us to be flown from Campos to Rio de Janeiro. The Germans had developed and flown the Condor Air Lines, but upon declaration of war these were taken over by the Brazilian Air Force. Brazilian private pilots with very little experience replaced the German pilots. I mention this because when we came into the Rio de Janeiro airport, we landed like a Texas jackrabbit crossing hot sand. The first bounce was about five stories becoming progressively less as we slowed to a stop. The pilot was a good-natured fellow. He turned and gave us a great big grin as if to say, "I told you I could do it!" We were satisfied; we were still in one piece.

Here we were met by another consular official who loaded us up and hauled us to the waterfront. He put us on a water taxi and took us to an island in the harbor that looked like Alcatraz. It turned out to be the home base of the Brazilian Fuseleros or the equivalent of our American Marine Corps. The basement, dug out of solid rock, was the naval prison. The main floor was barracks and training grounds, while the upper floors were hospital wards. We were taken to the third floor.

We spent the next two or two-and-a-half weeks here and were very well cared for. We were given complete physical exams, vitamin shots, and treatment for any wounds or ailments. Most of us had immersion foot. Our feet had split open from constant dampness and lack of vitamins to help heal. We probably had other minor infections from lack of proper care.

The fellows were all warmly greeted by the Fuselero patients, and we soon made many friends. The nurses were

Catholic nuns and were very nice. They would try to teach us a few words of Portuguese each day, and at night just before the lights went out, they would come in and pray for us.

I think we were there about a week, when there was quite a ruckus and all the patients who could walk went to the windows that looked down into the courtyard. Two officers were led up to a wall and were executed by firing squad. This created quite a stir of excitement for all, but because we couldn't understand the language we were puzzled and a little worried.

Later when a consular official came, we asked him what was going on. He told us they were the captain and chief officer of a German ship that had been interned when Brazil declared war. I believe he said the ship was the *Windhuk*.* Brazilian officials had boarded the vessel and notified them of internment. They said the crew would be left aboard temporarily if they agreed to behave. Apparently they agreed, and a Brazilian guard was posted on the dock at the gangway to see that no one left the ship. During the next two days the German crew committed $275,000 worth of sabotage to the vessel. They completely destroyed the ship's engine and sawed the shaft in two. After the discovery, the trial was apparently of short duration, and we witnessed the penalty being meted out. Justice is meted out much more swiftly in South America than it is here.[6]

After a couple of weeks, it was felt that we were well enough to be taken to a hotel in Rio de Janeiro for the rest of our recuperation. One of my feet didn't heal too well, and I was given a pair of crutches to hobble around on. I made out-patient calls to a doctor while it healed.

Living in a hotel was quite a luxury. A maid would wake us at about six a.m. and serve us coffee and rolls in bed. This was to give us strength enough to get ready for breakfast at eight A.M. which was served in the dining room. This was my first experience with eating five times a day, instead of our usual three. I must say I enjoyed it all.

After a few days when we were strong enough to get around town, we were allowed to draw twenty-five dollars a week. The exchange rate was nineteen cruzeiros and some old milreis for

---

*   As the German *Windhuk*, the ship had seen action early in World War II as a support vessel and a raider before her internment by the Brazilians. Purchased by the U.S. Navy in 1942 and converted to a troop transport, *Lejeuene* (AP-74) began service on the transatlantic run in the aftermath of the Normandy invasion. A total of nineteen crossings were made.[7]

Shown in 1942 are some of the survivors of the Stephen Hopkins lifeboat ordeal. Top row, left to right, Virgil Bullock, Wallace Breck, Archie Carlson, Rodger Piercy; bottom row, left to right, Gerald McQuality, Ted Barnes. Courtesy of Rodger Piercy.

each American dollar. This was nearly five hundred Brazilian dollars for our twenty-five. We felt like millionaires. Our first trips were to the clothing stores. New suits, shirts, ties, shoes, and underclothing were purchased. The first day we just stood around and admired each other.

The boys from the Naval Armed Guard (*Moses N. Barker, Ted Barnes, Wallace Breck, Virgil Bullock, and Paul Porter*) were separated from us and were flown back to the United States.

They arrived home about a month or so ahead of us. We were kept behind to be sent home by ship.[8]

```
FROM:      ALUSNA RIO    302230 NCR 8695    31 OCT 42

ACTION:    OPNAV    BUPERS

INFO:      CTF 23   COMSOLANTFOR

(ACTION OPNAV BUPERS INFO COMSOLANTFOR)


ALUSNA RIO 292310. NAVY ARMED GUARD PERSONNEL IN GOOD

HEALTH WILL BE READY LEAVE AFTER WEEK'S REST.  REQUEST

DISPOSITION.  POSSIBLE SEND RECIFE VIA AIR FFT BY COM-

SOLANT FOR.  REQUEST ADVISE FAMILIES OF SAFETY THROUGH

ARMED GUARD CENTER SAN FRANCISCO.




BUPERS.....ACTION

10/11...16...23...39...

FILE
```

Telegram requesting instructions as to where to send the Hopkins' *Armed Guard survivors after they had recuperated. National Archives.*

At this point only nine merchant seamen and one officer were left from the crew of the *Stephen Hopkins*: George Cronk, Ford Stilson, Archie Carlson, Peter Enos, Nicholas Kokalis, Walter Manning, Gerald McQuality, Rodger Piercy, August Reese, and Carlos Sanchez.

Rodger Piercy:

The next month we spent at the hotel and toured all over Rio. We visited the Copacabana [*tourist beach*] and the huge statue of Christ [*Christ the Redeemer*] that overlooks the city. The statue was magnificent and when the lights are on at night,

```
                        C O P Y   DECLASSIFIED

FROM:       ALUSNA RIO DE JANEIRO    070543 NCR 3990    7 NOV 42

ACTION:     ALUSNOB BELEM BRAZIL
            ALUSNOB NATAL BRAZIL
            COM 10                                            RRRRR
            NOB TRINIDAD
            PORT DIRECTOR MIAMI

INFO:       BUPERS                                           RRRRR


GUN CREW MEN BEING TRANSFERRED DIRECT MIAMI.  VIRGIL ORVILLE BULLOCK,

WALLACE ELLSWORTH BRECK, TED EUGENE BARNES, MOSES NATHANIEL BARKER, PAUL

BOYER PORTER, E, STEPHEN HOPKINS, WILLIAM DEAN WORREL, E, AMERICA NERESSX

ALL SEAMEN 2ND.  PERSONNEL HAVE NO IDENTIFICATION EXCEPT ORDERS.  5

TRAVELLING CIVILIAN CLOTHES.  ALL LEAVING RIO NOVEMBER 7 VIA NATS.
```

Message from the Naval authorities in Rio de Janeiro informing the Bureau of Personnel where the Hopkins' *Armed Guard survivors were being sent. National Archives.*

it can be seen for fifty miles at sea. We went up Pan de Sucre (Sugarloaf Mountain) and crossed on the cable car. It was beautiful with the Valley two thousand feet below. We had lunch on the mountaintop at the restaurant there. We were taken to dinner at the Jockey Club by an American representative of the American Shoe Machinery Corp. He and his wife had been in Brazil nearly twenty years. They were wonderful people. We also had dinner at their home one night.

I must say Rio de Janeiro has more than its share of beautiful women, and we were fortunate enough to meet quite a few. In fact, the manager of the hotel had two beautiful daughters who took delight in arranging for us to meet everyone they knew. Time just flew by and, of course, by now we were all hale and healthy.

```
C O P Y


             PARAPHRASE OF TELEGRAM RECEIVED


FROM:     ALEMBASSY, Rio de Janeiro

TO:       Secretary of State, Washington

DATED:    November 19, 1942, 8 p.m.

NUMBER:   4866

        FOR WYCKOFF, WAR SHIPPING ADMINISTRATION, FROM MILLS.


        It is expected the steamer Thunderer, now in Rio,
   will be ready to sail the twenty-first of November.  Ur-
   gent authorization requested to embark ten survivors
   Stephen Hopkins, as passengers, one from Commercial Trader,
   and one member of crew of Everagra.  All twelve men are
   citizens of the United States.

        Charge War Shipping Administration


                    GAFFERY
```

Message to the Secretary of State informing him of transportation arrangements for the survivors of the Hopkins' merchant crew. National Archives.

Suddenly word came from the consular office restricting us to the hotel and to be prepared to sail at a moment's notice. The next day we were to report to his office for instructions.

While we were here, we met a Swedish seaman who had missed his ship and was to be sent to New York with us. We were to be passengers, and he was to be our messman. He had been a seaman on the Swedish liner, *Gripsholm**, which

---

* The *Gripsholm* was built in 1925 and was the first diesel-engine powered transatlantic passenger liner.[10]

```
FROM:      ALUSNA RIO


DATE:      28 NOV 42




ACTION VICE OPNAV.    INFO COMSOLANT ADVISED.

          THUNDERER, PANAMANIAN, ENROUTE SANTOS NEW YORK

VIA BAHIA AND TRINIDAD CALLED RIO TO TAKE 9 CIVILIAN

PASSENGERS, EIGHT U. S. CITIZENS, 1 GREEK, SURVIVORS

OF SS STEPHEN HOPKINS.
```

Additional message regarding transport of the merchant crew from the American Consul in Rio to the Navy. National Archives.

was an international diplomatic ship, and while she was in the harbor he had missed her. [9]

He had caught a water taxi to try and catch her as she was sailing. They couldn't and since he didn't have full fare for the round trip, when the taxi got about twenty feet off shore, the crew threw him into the water and he had to swim ashore.

Under our instructions, a ship was to sneak into the harbor at midnight and anchor out in the bay. A water taxi would take us out to board her, and we would sail immediately. That night we had all our gear stowed in the water taxi and waited around for a couple of hours for the word to go. Just before we were to leave, the Swedish seaman spotted the taxi operator who had thrown him into the bay. He said, "When you leave, hold the taxi for me. I am going to get that taxi operator just before we go!" When the word came, we all loaded aboard. The Swede went over to the taxi operator and knocked him on the seat of his pants, and then threw him off the dock into the bay. He then jumped aboard, and we shoved off and headed for the ship that was to take us home. We were all laughing and thinking of the old adage, "He who laughs last, laughs best!"

The ship was about six miles out, and we were quickly taken aboard and shown to our quarters while the crew put out to sea. We went right to bed as total blackout was in force. The next day we discovered we were on a Finnish motor vessel which had been the *Mathilda Thordin*. She ran out of Finland and escaped the Germans. She came to the United States and joined our forces. She was renamed and now was the *Thunderer*. She had been a combination freighter and passenger liner, and we were pleased to find she could do about sixteen knots. She had Krupp motors.[11]

We sailed up the Brazilian coast and entered the harbor at Recife a few days later. We stayed there a couple days and were allowed shore leave. We toured the casinos and looked the town over. The city was built up on a high bluff and from the waterfront you had to ride up on the cable car. It was undoubtedly an old town and built there as protection from pirates.

I didn't have much money and soon went broke. It was about seven o'clock in the evening, and I didn't know what to do with the rest of the time, so I sat down on the curb. A young Brazilian girl came along and spoke to me. I told her I didn't savvy Portuguese and "Hablo English." She just laughed and took me by the arm, and walked me around, showing me the sights. She wasn't really pretty, but had a wonderful sense of humor and was very friendly. She took me to her home, and I met her parents and some neighbors. We had something to eat and a lot of fun. They, trying to speak English, and me, trying my feeble Portuguese. We had a lot of laughs.

The father, daughter, and a neighbor couple all escorted me back to the ship about midnight, and we bid a pleasant goodbye. The world is full of wonderful people if you only give them a chance.

We sailed from Recife and about a week later we entered the harbor of Port-au-Spain, Trinidad. This was a hot spot at that time. As we came steaming into the harbor to our anchorage, we passed a Portuguese passenger liner loaded to the gunnels with European refugees. These people had endured hardships, made their way from all over Europe to Portugal, and were bound for South American countries for sanctuary from the horrors of war. As we steamed by with our American flag flying, these people burst into tremendous cheers, clapping, and waving victory signs. I tell you it made our hearts stand on end, and made us feel proud to be part of the American effort to end the tyranny that had uprooted these people and chased them from their homelands.

The ship was named the *Santa Maria*, I believe. It was a former American President liner that had been sold along with another ship to the Portuguese. Both ships were running refugees from Portugal to South America.

We spent about a week at anchorage in the harbor, and as things go in wartime, suddenly got word to move out alone. We kept a constant and complete watch as the German Pig boats had been very active in the Caribbean. However, we spent an uneventful week until we got off Cuba. Here we picked up a large convoy with naval protection to escort us up the American coast.

I forgot to mention that while at Port-au-Spain, we picked up a young English boy; seventeen years old as a wiper for our crew. He had left England over a year before and had been on three ships. He hadn't completed a voyage yet. We promptly nicknamed him, "The Jinx." He was good-natured, and he did complete this trip.

When we arrived off New York and started single file up the harbor, the *Queen Mary* came in and went by so fast we felt like a tugboat caught in her wash. She was a fast-stepping beauty. We moved into Pier 44 in Brooklyn and at last were back to the United States. We had left Rio a little over a month before.

We were taken by taxi to the Luckenbach Steamship Lines Office where we spent most of the day trying to straighten out affairs of the *Stephen Hopkins*. We were given fifty dollars apiece, drawn against our salaries, and left to find our own living quarters. We hired a couple of cabs and toured town looking for hotels we could get in. The cab drivers finally found us a hotel, and we spent the next seventeen days reporting to the War Shipping Administration for intensive questioning concerning lost crew members. They were trying to pay insurance claims to families of men known to be dead. We were questioned by army and navy intelligence and any other security agency you can think of.

In between time, we had opportunities to visit points of interest in New York City. We were there over Christmas and New Years. In fact, I spent New Year's Eve in Times Square and, man that was wild. You didn't need a mind of your own; you were simply forced to go the way of the crowd.

We visited the Statue of Liberty, Radio City, Madison Square Garden, and finally, Greenwich Village. To me, the

Village was the biggest nut house I ever saw without a fence around it. I guess I'm a country boy, and the big city didn't show me very much.

Finally, after seventeen days, we were paid off in Brooklyn and released to go home. We were all from the Bay area so we went to Pennsylvania Station and caught a train for San Francisco and home. Boy, what a milk run that was. We laid over one day in Chicago, and then started west. The train made every stop in every town we passed. We had no dining car, and we constantly had to jump and run for hamburgers or anything you could buy. Not only for ourselves, but anything extra for other passengers who could not move so quickly. Finally we made it to San Francisco, and it was the most beautiful sight in the world.

We had been gone a little over nine months, but believe me, I felt at least fifteen years older. As I look back now, I'm glad I made the voyage, but by choice, I would never do it again.

In thirty days time, I was back to sea and on my way back down to the South Pacific. I spent most of the next four years covering nearly all the islands, and eventually wound up at Yokohama, Japan, when the war ended.

I did come ashore long enough to go to the United States Merchant Marine Academy at Alameda, California, where I graduated a third officer and sailed the last two years in that capacity.[12]

~~~

On 31 October 1942, the U.S. Navy announced a lid of immediate secrecy on the release of information in response to the Brazilian Government Press and Propaganda Bureau's request regarding when information could be released about the *Stephen Hopkins*, how much, and to whom. OPNAV informed Brazilian authorities that any information would be released only when verified by competent U.S. naval officers, and the ship's name, tonnage, cargo, scheduled movements, the date and location of sinking must be omitted.[13]

As late as November 15 it was still not known exactly what had occurred. In a confidential *Fortnightly Summary of Current National Conditions*, OPNAV stated:

One of Germany's raiders probably was destroyed by gun fire by *Stephen Hopkins* in the South Atlantic on September 27. The *Hopkins* also damaged a large supply ship accompanying the raider. Although the *Hopkins* herself was sunk, it is noteworthy that *Hopkins* with one four-inch gun was able to damage seriously, or sink a raider, probably armed with six 5.9-inch guns.[14]

Relatives of both the Navy and merchant marine crews were also desperately seeking information. In most cases, the information was not forthcoming: for the Armed Guard, due to military security; for the merchant crew, due to the fact that three entities were involved — the operator (Luckenbach Steamship Co.), the merchant marine, which was under the auspices of the Coast Guard for the first ten months of the war, then came under the War Shipping Administration on September 1, 1942.

Cadet-Midshipman Edwin O'Hara's mother, unaware of the battle, wrote to the Luckenbach Steamship Company on 1 October 1942.

> Luckenbach Lines, San Francisco,
> 10-1-42
>
> Gentleman:
> Would you please tell me if you know if the freighter "Stephen Hopkins" is safe and unharmed?
> My son is an engineer on the ship and I haven't heard from him since Aug. 9 when he that [thought] he was to sail for home.
> My son's name is Edwin J. O'Hara, an engineer cadet of the Maritime Academy.
> I know you are not supposed to tell where the ship is now but all I want to know is "is the ship safe".
> Sincerely, Elma O'Hara[15]

Luckenbach Steamship Company sent a letter to the War Shipping Administration in San Francisco on 9 November with Mrs. O'Hara's letter enclosed:

Dear Sir:

Enclosed please find letter received ... It is our understanding that some misfortune has overtaken the ship, and it would be greatly appreciated if you could answer the enclosed letter.[16]

The War Shipping Administration answered Luckenbach on November 10:

This office is not provided with information of such nature. However in the event any cadet of the U.S. Merchant Marine Cadet Corps meets with misfortune, or apparent misfortune, at sea, the parents or nearest relatives are notified by the Navy Department in Washington, D.C. Lacking any such notification it is reasonable to assume that no such misfortune has occurred.

E.E. Thorne, Lt-Comdr, USNR
Ass't. District Merchant Marine Cadet Instructor[17]

It wasn't until just before Thanksgiving that the O'Hara family received a telegram stating that Edwin was missing. The District Merchant Marine Cadet Instructor, N.Y. Supervisor, U.S. Merchant Marine Cadet Corps filed a form on December 24, 1942 accompanied by a Supervisor's letter of December 19, 1942 that "O'Hara, Edwin J. E2 2-2398 has terminated his services for the following reason – Special termination of services."

Finally, the Commander and Supervisor of the U.S. Merchant Marine Cadet Corps, R.R. McNulty, responded to Mrs. O'Hara on December 31, 1942 with the sad news that Cadet O'Hara was lost at sea. At the end of the letter he states:

The complete story may not be told until after the war but there is sufficient evidence from eye-witness accounts to state that Cadet-Midshipman O'Hara performed an act, beyond the call of duty, which will make his name remembered by the United States Merchant Marine Corps.

We are proud of Cadet-Midshipman O'Hara.[18]

The U.S. Coast Guard did send letters to relatives of those who were lost. Vice Admiral R. Waeche of the U.S. Coast Guard notified the wife of Captain Paul Buck on November 3 that he was missing. She hadn't heard from her husband since he sent her a cablegram on September 9.

Mrs. Bertha Moczkowski, mother of the chief mate, inquired on November 4 about her son, Richard. She received a letter dated November 13 stating, "That her son was among the reported deceased." The letter gave her the names of three survivors who she could contact for first-hand information; Walter Manning, Able Seaman, George S. Cronk, 2nd Asst. Engineer and Rodger H. Piercy, Ordinary Seaman.[19]

Vice Admiral R. Waeche also signed the telegram sent to Frank McDaniel, father of 2nd cook Eugene McDaniel on November 3:

> The Navy regrets to inform you that Eugene Darrel McDaniel was killed at sea following action in the performance of his duty and in the service of his country.
> The Coast Guard extends to you its sincerest sympathy in your great loss. To prevent possible aid to our enemies please do not divulge the name of the ship.

Eugene McDaniel's death hit his Palestine, Illinois community hard. *The Palestine Register* wrote:

> The message had a noticeably sobering effect upon Eugene's Palestine friends as the word of his death was passed from one to another on the streets Tuesday night. With the shock of the telegram came a grim realization that this was the first definitely reported death of a local boy in the present war.[20]

The major newspapers did not report the battle until December 10, the day after the story was released by the Navy. The war was still going badly for the Allies — the turning point would not be reached for several months. Desirous of reporting some favorable news, the Navy skewed the information to its benefit, even changing what had already been officially reported. The *New York Times* headline subtitle, "Navy Men kept Firing

Till Magazine Blew Up, and Even Then Used Last 5 Shells ..."
The article went on to say, "The enemy shell that destroyed the
merchant ship's magazine left five shells unharmed, and Ensign
Willett personally fired these from his gun."[21] Nowhere was there
a mention of Cadet-Midshipman Edwin O'Hara's heroic actions.
To a public desperate for some news of Allied successes, the
Navy had a dramatic story and made sure that they received all
the credit.

SKL (Office of Naval Operations in Berlin) issued the following Statement after the U.S. newspapers broke the story:

> The U.S. American Fleet Department communicates that
> in September a medium-sized American trading vessel in the
> South Atlantic stood and fought with two hostile commercial
> war vessels and that one of the commercial vessels probably
> sank after being subject to moderate artillery.
>
> From the forty-one crew members of the trading vessel only
> ten survived the twenty-minute combat and after a thirty-one
> day trip in an open life raft.
>
> This is the first well-known case of combat between an
> American trading vessel and a hostile commercial raider in this
> war. The crew members saw the smaller of the two commercial
> ships in flames and this one is believed sunk. The other ship
> was damaged.

From *Stier*'s War Diary:

> The trip was a well and accomplished enterprise.
> A disadvantage was that there was insufficient airplane
> equipment which impaired considerably the amount of success.
> The assigned area of operations exhibited very little traffic and
> the only hope was by the use of air reconnaissance.
>
> A particularly large success was the sinking of *Dalhousie*
> despite the insertion of USA units being stationed along the
> eastern coast of South America in their unsuccessful attempts
> to locate raiders.
>
> The commander and crew conducted themselves
> courageously and with the best German naval and combat spirit
> to a conclusive and early end to the enemy. The destruction
> of the opponent in the fight despite heavy personal damage is

another wonderful example of the dauntless heroism employed by the auxiliary cruiser crews overseas.

Fregattenleutnant Ludolf Petersen had an important statement, "We could not but feel that we had gone down at the hands of a gallant foe ... that Liberty ship had ended a very successful raiding voyage. We could have sunk many more ships," but he added, "She may have sunk us, but she saved most of our lives. We could not have lasted much longer out there those days, and there would not have always been a *Tannenfels**, around to pick us up."[22]

Not until February 9, 1943 did Arthur R. Chamberlin, father of Cadet-Midshipman Arthur R. Chamberlin, Jr., receive more information on his son's death. He originally received a telegram in November reporting that his son was "missing and presumed to be lost in performance of his duty and service to his country." The wording seemed to indicate that his son was in the water with his lifejacket on but wasn't reachable by the lifeboat because of the heavy seas. Arthur Sr. contacted his congressman asking for more information. The official reply written to Congressman John H. Tolan, stated only that, "this vessel was torpedoed and sunk ... that Mr. Chamberlin was listed as missing."[23]

In bureaucratese, the letter said:

With reference to your statement that you have received variant versions concerning the fate of your son, you are advised that it is difficult for a survivor of a merchant vessel lost through enemy action to state definitely what happened to another member of the crew unless they happened to be together at the time of the attack.

The statement of all survivors are taken and studied in an effort to establish as near as possible the status of any missing members of the crew.

We do not usually receive survivors' reports; however, our records do show that we received a report from George S. Cronk, Second Asst. Engineer, who listed certain members

---

*   *Tannenfels* career ended on August 8, 1944. As the Allies moved westward after the Normandy landing, Germany evacuated the French ports and *Tannenfels* was scuttled in the Gironde Delta before Le Verdun.

of the crew who were badly wounded and probably dead, and your son's name was among them.[24]

On December 31, 1942, Edward Macauley, Chairman of the Maritime War Emergency Board, wrote an Order of Application requesting that the:

> ... aforesaid members of the crew of such vessel be and they hereby are declared presumptively dead and that the Secretary of the Board be authorized to issue a certificate of the presumptive death of any or all of such members of the crew. Approval came on January 6, 1943.

The tight control of information made it exceedingly difficult for families to learn what had happened and the fate of their loved ones. It was even more difficult for the merchant crews, which did not have an official department of the military responsible for them.

Many letters were exchanged and visits made between surviving crewmembers and relatives of their deceased comrades.

George Cronk, Sr. and Ordinary Seaman Walter Manning visited the O'Hara family "... and explained Edwin's heroics."[25]

Rodger Piercy was visited by Mrs. and Mr. Earl Layman when he was in Officer's Training School at Alameda, California. Their son, Joseph Earl Layman, had been second mate aboard *Hopkins*. "We had a nice visit for several hours. They told me they had just returned from dedicating their son's ship. They were very upset about the demise of their son but very proud of the way he left."[26]

Navy Armed Guard survivor Wallace Breck visited the Chamberlin family several times. According to Robert Chamberlin, brother of Cadet-Midshipman Arthur Chamberlin,

> My parents had him over for dinner two or three times. He, and my brother Artie became very close friends on board ship. Artie mentioned Wally in some of his V-mail letters home. Wally was thinking of going on to O.T.S. and asked Artie to teach him basic navigation principles, which he did. The Brecks

Armed Guard survivor Wallace Breck visited the Chamberlin family several times. U.S. Navy.

lived only 2-½ blocks from us and we never knew each other. They lived in Oakland and we lived in Piedmont. Different school districts, etc. My mother first met Mrs. Breck standing in line at a local market checkout line. Mrs. Breck was telling of her son coming home after his ship was sunk (in the South Atlantic). The two women compared notes. Hence, the discovery. Wally was the one who first told us how my brother died… Artie went off the stern and was pulled into the prop which was still turning. When my dad heard that he gave a huge sigh of relief. He finally knew that Artie had died instantly, without suffering.[27]

George Cronk Sr. wrote to Chief Engineer Rudolf Rutz's sister:

> … I am the only surviving officer. I lost over 40 pounds weight on my twenty-two hundred mile, thirty-one day trip to the coast of Brazil but I am feeling better now and will be on my way to the Pacific Coast to take out another ship soon. I want to tell you with the type of man that your brother was this country can never lose a war and you can be very proud of him for he was a square shooter and one of the merriest men I have ever known and here's hoping for you and the rest of his family the very best of luck.
> I remain your friend,
> George S. Cronk.[28]

Fulfilling the dying request of his merchant marine buddy, utility man Gerald McQuality visited the father of second cook Eugene "Mac" McDaniel. "McQuality gave the grief-stricken father a Coast Guard ring given to him just before he died… When asked if he was going back to sea, McQuality said, 'I have more reasons than ever to go back now, for the job has to be finished.'"[29]

Gerald McQuality, left, with a relative of Eugene McDaniel. Fulfilling his promise, McQuality visited the family of his close friend McDaniel. Courtesy of Maxine Spence.

PART V

19

AWARDS AND HONORS

our classes of medals were awarded to merchant seamen during World War II: the Merchant Marine Distinguished Service Medal, the Merchant Marine Meritorious Service Medal, the Mariner's Medal, and the Prisoner of War Medal.

The Merchant Marine Distinguished Service Medal was awarded to any Seaman in the U.S. Merchant Marine who distinguished himself during the war by outstanding conduct or service in the line of duty.

Six mariners from the S.S. *Stephen Hopkins* were recipients of the Merchant Marine Distinguished Service Medal:

Paul Buck, master of SS *Stephen Hopkins*
(awarded posthumously)

For distinguished service in enemy action.

Two enemy surface raiders suddenly appeared out of the mist to attack the small merchantman in which he was

Admiral E. S. Land pins the Distinguished Service Medal on 2nd Lt. Gertrude Buck, Army Nurse Corps, widow of Capt. Paul Buck. U.S. Maritime Administration.

serving as master. Heavy guns of one raider pounded his ship, and machine gun fire from the other sprayed her decks. He skillfully maneuvered his ship so that the heavier guns could be trained on the raider, and under his supervision his ship exchanged shot for shot with the enemy until the crew of one raider was forced to abandon its sinking ship, and the other enemy ship was forced to withdraw. His calmness under fire and his fearlessness in defending his ship were an inspiration to his crew. With boilers blown up and engines damaged, masts shot away, and ablaze from stem to stern, he reluctantly gave the order to abandon ship. The only serviceable lifeboat being overcrowded, he, unselfishly and heroically, remained on the bridge and went down with his battered ship.

His determination to fight his ship and his perseverance in engaging the enemy to the utmost until his ship was rendered

The USNS Paul Buck *was commissioned in 1985 and is still operating for the Military Sealift Command. U.S. Navy.*

helpless and sinking were in keeping with the finest traditions
of the United States Merchant Marine.
    For the President
    Admiral Emory Scott Land[1]

A 30,000 ton Champion Class T5 tanker (T-AOT 1122)
named USNS *Paul Buck* was commissioned in 1985 and as recently as 2006 was serving in the Military Sealift Command.

~~~

Richard Moczkowski, Chief Mate on SS *Stephen Hopkins* (awarded posthumously)

For extraordinary heroism beyond the call of duty.

The Merchant Marine Distinguished Service Medal awarded to Richard Moczkowski. Courtesy of Imogene Trembowicz.

Two enemy surface raiders suddenly appeared out of the mist to attack the small merchantman in which he was serving. Heavy guns of one raider pounded his ship, and machine gun fire from the other sprayed her decks until she was a complete wreck and afire fore and aft. The merchantman exchanged shot for shot with the enemy raiders until the crew of one raider was forced to abandon their sinking ship, and the other was forced to withdraw. The mate, shot in the chest and in the left forearm early in the action, continued at his exposed post abaft the wheelhouse rallying his men and directing orders to the bridge to enable his ship to keep her guns bearing on the enemy ships.

Weakened by rapid loss of blood from a severed artery, he collapsed to the deck, but refused to stay down, and ordered a seaman to assist him to his feet and prop him in a doorway that he might better discharge his duties. With her boilers blown up, engines destroyed, masts shot away, and ablaze from stem to stern, orders were finally given

The Liberty ship Richard Moczkowski, *launched on August 22, 1943, was named in honor of the chief mate of the* Stephen Hopkins. Courtesy of Imogene Trembowicz

to abandon the gallant merchantman. Moczkowski was carried to the boat deck, and propped against the housing while the only usable lifeboat was lowered away. His shipmates carried the mortally wounded man to the side, but seeing the crowded boat already released and clear of the ship, the mate commanded his men to leave him rather than further jeopardize their own safety.

His fearless determination to fight his ship, and his perseverance in engaging the enemy to the utmost until his ship was rendered helpless and sinking, constitute a degree of heroism which will be an enduring inspiration to seamen of the United States Merchant Marine.

For the President
Admiral Emory Scott Land[2]

The mother of the Chief Mate, Mrs. Nicholas Moczkowski received the award in April 1943 and also christened a new Liberty ship, the S.S. *George Pullman* during the ceremony. Later that year, on August 22, 1943, the Liberty ship S.S. *Richard Moczkowski* was launched at Shipyard Number two of the Permanente Metals Corporation Shipyard, Richmond, California.

~~~

Joseph E. Layman, Second Mate on SS *Stephen Hopkins* (awarded posthumously)

For distinguished service in enemy action.

Two enemy surface raiders suddenly appeared out of the morning mist to attack the small merchantman upon which he was serving. Heavy guns of one raider pounded his ship, and machine guns from the other, sprayed her decks until she was a complete wreck and afire fore and aft. His ship exchanged shot for shot with the enemy raiders until the crew of one raider was forced to abandon its sinking ship, and the other was forced to withdraw. Layman, who was in charge of the two 37mm guns forward, put shell after shell into the larger raider and courageously maintained the fire until all his shell handlers were killed and the gun platform wrecked. With her boilers blown up, engines destroyed, masts shot away, and ablaze from stem to stern, orders were finally given to abandon ship. The only serviceable lifeboat being overcrowded, Layman, unselfishly and heroically, remained on board and went down with his battered ship.

His fearless determination to fight his ship to the end, and his self-sacrifice constitute a degree of heroism which will be an enduring inspiration to seamen of the United States Merchant Marine everywhere.

For the President
Admiral Emory Scott Land[3]

The Liberty ship S.S. *Earl Layman* was built by the Southeastern Shipbuilding Corporation and launched on March 17, 1944.

Gravestone of Second mate Joseph Layman, who also had a Liberty ship named after him. Courtesy of Cecelia "Tootie" Layman.

V.J. Malone, Secretary of the Pacific Coast Marine Firemen, Oilers, Watertenders & Wipers Assn., wrote a report dated March 5, 1943 for Admiral E.S. Land of the W.S.A. concerning the loss of S.S. *Stephen Hopkins*. In the last paragraph, Malone states,

> We respectfully request, after considering the devotion to duty of George Cronk, both during the battle with the enemy raiders and in bringing the survivors to shore, that this matter be brought to the attention of the President of the United States and the aforesaid George Cronk be granted the Merchant Marine Medal of Honor [Merchant Marine Distinguished Service Medal].[4]

George Cronk, Sr. received his Distinguished Service Medal at a ceremony held at the Maritime Service Officers School at Neptune Beach, California in front of almost 1000 prospective officer candidates. The ceremony was held the day of the invasion of Sicily (July 10, 1943). Captain Macauley said,

> Thousands of our men are involved in the great struggle now in Sicily. And you may be sure they are a vital cog in the machinery of the invasion. There could be no invasion without the heroic service of the members and officers of the Maritime Service. This new school on the rim of San Francisco bay is further proof that American seamen are completely capable of

George Cronk Sr. is holding the Very pistol (Flare gun) that was aboard the lifeboat. San Francisco Call Bulletin, July 7, 1943.

George Cronk is awarded the Merchant Marine Distinguished Service Medal by Capt. Macauley (in uniform). Courtesy of George Cronk, Jr.

operating the merchant marine from the initial training period of its men to the delivery of the last cargo on armistice day.

George S. Cronk, Second Engineer on SS *Stephen Hopkins*

For meritorious service under unusual hazards.

Two enemy surface raiders attacked the merchantman upon which he was serving. Heavy guns of one raider pounded his ship, and machine gun fire from the other sprayed her decks at close quarters. Answering shot for shot, the gallant merchantman succeeded in sinking one of the raiders before she finally went under carrying many of her fighting crew with her. Engineer Cronk, sole surviving officer of the stricken ship, took command of the only lifeboat which could be launched. In heavy rain squalls and seas running high, he succeeded in rescuing six survivors who had jumped from the sinking ship.

Then, with nineteen aboard, including four badly wounded, and with no navigational instruments other than the boat compass, a westward course was set to fetch the nearest land 2,200 miles away. The small boat beat her way westward for thirty-one days. Many times heavy weather was encountered, forcing the survivors to put out a sea anchor and heave-to because of high seas. In spite of all efforts in their behalf, three of the wounded died and there were times when delirium threatened, but Cronk's firm leadership overcame all emergencies until a safe landing was made.

His courage and practical leadership, so largely contributory to the ultimate rescue of his shipmates, are in keeping with the highest traditions of the United States Merchant Marine.

For the President
Admiral Emory Scott Land[5]

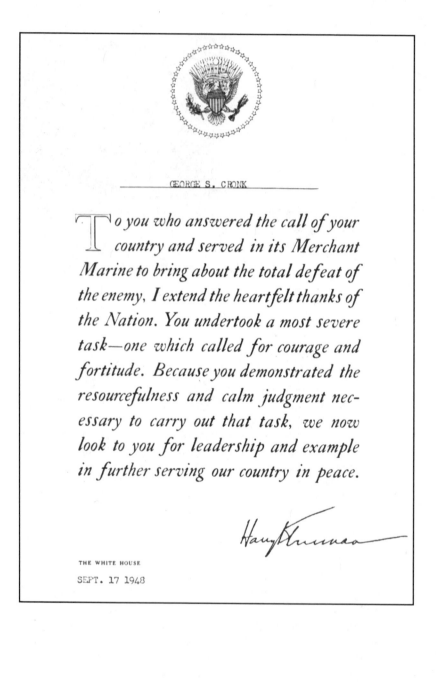

GEORGE S. CRONK

To you who answered the call of your country and served in its Merchant Marine to bring about the total defeat of the enemy, I extend the heartfelt thanks of the Nation. You undertook a most severe task—one which called for courage and fortitude. Because you demonstrated the resourcefulness and calm judgment necessary to carry out that task, we now look to you for leadership and example in further serving our country in peace.

Harry Truman

THE WHITE HOUSE

SEPT. 17 1948

Ford Stilson, on right, Capt. W.C. Tooze, USNR, Naval Reserve Director for 12th Naval District, Comdr. A.G. Ford, U.S. Maritime Service Officers' School, Alameda. Oakland California Tribune, *August 23, 1943*

Ford Stilson, Chief Steward on SS *Stephen Hopkins*

For meritorious service under unusual hazards.

Two enemy surface raiders attacked the merchantman upon which he was serving. Heavy guns of one raider pounded his ship, and machine gun fire from the other sprayed her decks at close quarters. Answering shot for shot, the gallant merchantman succeeded in sinking one of the raiders before she finally went under carrying many of her fighting crew with her. With complete disregard for his own safety, Stilson repeatedly exposed himself to heavy enemy fire in ministering to his wounded shipmates during the engagement. Later, in a lifeboat with eighteen others, he continued to attend the seriously injured and assisted materially in maintaining morale for the thirty-one days before the lifeboat succeeded in making a landing.

His courage and outstanding devotion to duty, in keeping with the highest traditions of American seamanship, will be a lasting inspiration to seamen of the United States Merchant Marine everywhere.

For the President
Admiral Emory Scott Land[6]

~~~

Edwin Joseph O'Hara. U.S. Maritime Administration.

Edwin Joseph O'Hara, Engine Cadet-Midshipman on SS *Stephen Hopkins* (awarded posthumously)

For extraordinary heroism under unusual hazards.

Two enemy surface raiders suddenly appeared out of the morning mist to attack the small merchantman upon which he was serving. Heavy guns of one raider pounded his ship, and machine guns from the other, sprayed her decks for one-half hour at close quarters. The heroic gun crew of O'Hara's ship exchanged shot for shot with the enemy, placing thirty-five shells into the waterline of one of the raiders until its crew was forced to abandon their sinking ship. The gun commander was mortally wounded early in the action, and all of the gun crew were killed or wounded when an enemy shell exploded the magazine of their gun.

At the explosion, O'Hara ran aft and single-handedly served and fired the damaged gun with five live shells remaining in the ready box, scoring direct hits near the waterline of the second raider. O'Hara was mortally wounded in this action. With boilers blown up, engines destroyed, masts shot away, and ablaze from stem to stern, the gallant merchantman finally went under carrying O'Hara and several of his fighting shipmates with her.

The magnificent courage of this young cadet constitutes a degree of heroism which will be an enduring inspiration to seamen of the United States Merchant Marine everywhere.

For the President

Admiral Emory Scott Land[7]

The Liberty ship named *Edwin Joseph O'Hara* was built by the California Shipbuilding Corporation. She was launched on July 29, 1943.

Mr. & Mrs. O'Hara survey the ship named for their son from an adjoining hull in the outfitting docks. Calship Log, *August 1943.* Courtesy of Dorothy (Mary) Norris.

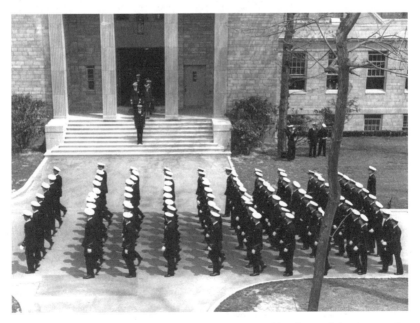

Mrs. Franklin D. Roosevelt reviews the regiment of Cadet-Midshipmen on the steps of O'Hara Hall shortly after the naming and dedication of that building. Courtesy of Dorothy O. Norris.

The O'Hara family (Mr. and Mrs., brother Donald, and sister Dorothy (Mary)) attended the christening at Calship. Edwin's mother was the sponsor and Dorothy was the Maid of Honor. The SS *Edwin Joseph O'Hara* was then turned over to the British Cunard Lines and sailed under the name *Sambo*.

On November 10, 1943 while carrying a full cargo of nitrate *Sambo*, ex-*Edwin Joseph O'Hara* was torpedoed and sunk by the Japanese submarine *I-27* while in the Gulf of Aden (Lat. 12 degrees 28' N, Long. 43 degrees 31' E). The first torpedo hit the starboard side, aft, exploding the after magazine. This was followed by a second torpedo which hit the starboard side of No. 4 hold. The ship broke in two at the after engine room bulkhead with the aft section sinking immediately. The crew abandoned in two lifeboats and rafts but one boat was smashed when what

J.C. O'Hara, father of Edwin J., and Lt. Commander D.E. Boyle of the U.S. Merchant Marine Academy viewing Edwin's Distinguished Service Medal citation in 1958, photograph, and painting by W.N. Wilson in the foyer of O'Hara Hall. The painting, entitled The Last Shot, *depicts the last actions of Cadet-Midshipman Edwin J. O'Hara during the battle.* Courtesy of Dorothy O. Norris.

remained of the ship capsized and struck it with a davit. All but two from this boat managed to reach the rafts. The master of the nearby Norwegian *Helgoy* saw the explosion and recovered the survivors, landing them at Aden. Twelve men were lost in this attack.[8]

In honor of Cadet-Midshipman Edwin O'Hara the United States Merchant Marine Academy named one of their buildings O'Hara Hall.

In July of 1958, the father of Cadet-Midshipman Edwin O'Hara, J.C. O'Hara, visited the Academy and viewed his son's citation and award, and the painting memorializing the battle.

The Navy Department Board of Decorations and Medals also sent a recommendation letter on December 31, 1943:

> 1. Awarding the Gallant Ship citation to SS *Stephen Hopkins*, "Which is somewhat similar to the Presidential Unit Citation … Citation will be accompanied by a plaque and the members of the crew will be entitled to wear a ribbon."
> 2. Since members of the Naval forces are not eligible for merchant marine decorations, the surviving members of the armed guard unit … will not participate in this citation…
> 3. In view of the above … the Board recommends that the Naval Armed Guard Unit … be awarded the Presidential Unit

The Stephen Hopkins II *laid up in New Orleans, Louisiana in October 1968. She was later sold for scrap.* San Francisco Maritime National Historical Park, Eric Steinfeldt Photographic Collection.

Citation, no merchant marine personnel to participate in the citation.

S.S. *Stephen Hopkins* was one of nine ships in World War II to earn the honor of being a Gallant Ship. This award was an executive order issued by the President of the United States and presented by the War Shipping Administrator. It was given for "outstanding action under attack or for gallant action in marine disasters or other emergencies at sea."[9]

Stephen Hopkins II was launched on May 10, 1944 and survived the war. "Following post-war service, she entered the Beaumont Reserve Fleet on December 11, 1947 and left that location on August 18, 1967. She was scrapped at New Orleans later that year."[10]

~~~

The Mariner's Medal is awarded to any seaman who while serving in a ship during the war period is wounded, suffers physical injury, or suffers through dangerous exposure as a result of an act of enemy of the United States.

Cadet-Midshipman Arthur R. Chamberlin's family received the Mariner's Medal about a year after his death.

According to the U.S. Department of Transportation, five of the ten surviving seaman were issued this medal: Archie Carlson, George S. Cronk, Walter Manning, Rodger H. Piercy, and August Reese.

The Navy Cross was the U.S. Navy's second highest medal, behind only the Congressional Medal of Honor.

Criteria
The Navy Cross may be awarded to any person who, while serving with the Navy or Marine Corps, distinguishes himself in action by extraordinary heroism.

USS Kenneth M. Willett *was named in honor of the officer in charge of the Armed Guard on the* Stephen Hopkins. U.S. Navy.

At the age of twenty-three, Lieutenant (j.g.) Kenneth M. Willett was awarded posthumously the Navy Cross for his "extraordinary heroism and conspicuous courage."

On March 12, 1943 the Navy Department issued the following Press and Radio release:

A destroyer-escort was named after Lieutenant (j.g.) Willett. "*Kenneth M. Willett* (DE-354) was launched 7 March 1944 by Consolidated Steel Corp., Orange, Tex.; sponsored by Mrs. D.C. Willett, mother of Lt. (j.g.) Willett; and commissioned 19 July 1944 at Orange, Lt. Comdr. J.M. Stuart in command."[11]

On December 10, 1942, the first paperwork was submitted to obtain suitable awards for the rest of the Navy Armed Guard crew. This was a letter sent to the Secretary of the Navy (Board of Awards).

> Subject: Consideration for Suitable Awards, U.S. Navy Armed Guard, SS *Stephen Hopkins*, 7,181 gross tons.
> References: Five documents concerning the official reports, etc. accompanied the letter. (This letter was received on December 29. It was forwarded from the Chief of Navy Personnel to Vice Chief of Naval Operations on March 13, 1943. It was acted upon on November 18, 1943 with a request to be signed by the Commander in Chief, U.S. Fleet.)

COMINCH FILE

UNITED STATES FLEET

HEADQUARTERS OF THE COMMANDER IN CHIEF
NAVY DEPARTMENT, WASHINGTON, D. C.

FF1/P15

Serial: 04223

DECLASSIFIED

CONFIDENTIAL

13 DEC 1943

FIRST ENDORSEMENT to
BuPers conf. ltr. Pers-650-Ar
QB4(928) dated March 13, 1943.

From: Commander in Chief, United States Fleet
                 and Chief of Naval Operations.
To :   The Secretary of the Navy.

Subject: Consideration for Suitable Awards, U. S.
                Navy Armed Guard SS STEPHEN HOPKINS, 7181
                gross tons.

      1.   The files of the Navy Department, Board of Decorations and Medals and the War Shipping Administration reveal that Ensign Kenneth M. Willett, U.S.N.R., has been awarded the Navy Cross, posthumously, and that thirteen members of the armed guard crew were addressed letters of commendation by the Secretary of the Navy. In addition, six officers attached to the ship were awarded Merchant Marine Distinguished Service Medals.

      2.   Although the conduct and performance of duty of the armed guard and the officers and crew of the SS STEPHEN HOPKINS was heroic and distinguished to a high degree, I am of the opinion, considering the facts enclosed herewith, that this action does not warrant the award of the Presidential Unit Citation.

E. J. KING

Armed Guard care
30 Dec 1943
7

Copy to
   Vice CNO

12 03895

RECEIVED S-C FILES
Room 2055
13 DEC 1943
ROUTE TO:-

Op File No.
Doc. No.
Copy No. of

Criteria for the Navy Presidential Citation
The Navy Presidential Unit Citation is awarded in the name of the President to units of the Armed Forces of the United States and co-belligerent nations for extraordinary heroism in action against an armed enemy. The unit must have accomplished its mission under such extremely difficult and hazardous conditions to set it apart from and above other units participating in the same campaign. The degree

of heroism required is the same as that which would be required for award of a Navy Cross to an individual.

However, consideration for this citation was cancelled by the Commander in Chief, U.S. Fleet and Chief of Naval Operations, Admiral E.J. King in a letter dated December 13, 1943.

Admiral King forwarded another letter on January 7, 1944 to the Secretary of the Navy Frank Knox stating,

> I am constrained to reiterate my previous recommendation that the award of the Presidential Unit Citation to the Naval Armed Guard Unit of the *Stephen Hopkins* is not appropriate. If, however, after further study and investigation, the Board of Decorations and Medals is able to determine that the action of certain individuals of the Armed Guard Unit was distinguished to a degree higher than the heroic standard of the others, it is recommended that such individuals be awarded the Silver Star medal in lieu of the letter of commendation.

The Navy Department Board of Decorations and Medals concurred with Admiral King's letter and subsequently on January 19, 1944 Secretary of the Navy Frank Knox approved the recommendation that the Armed Guard Unit "not be awarded ..."

One additional attempt was made but was turned down in January 1945.

Nevertheless, a tribute to the *Stephen Hopkins* merchant marine and Armed Guard crew came out of the Office of the Chief of Naval Operations:

> The extraordinary heroism and outstanding devotion to duty of the officers and crew of the Armed Guard and the ship's company were in keeping with the highest tradition of American seamanship. Their fearless determination to fight their ship, and perseverance to engage the enemy to the utmost until their ship was rendered useless, aflame and in a sinking condition, demonstrated conduct beyond the call of duty.[12]

AFTERWORD

Jean Dierkes-Carlisle is the daughter of the S.S. *Stephen Hopkins* 1ˢᵗ Assistant Engineer, Charles L. Fitzgerald. She was ten years old when her father was killed. There was a blackout on information during the war and there wasn't much information forthcoming after the war. Later in life, she began to research the battle and discovered how important the entire story was, especially for the people living in San Francisco and California. A good part of the crew was from California, the ship was built in California and *Hopkins'* home port was San Francisco.

In 1996 she was instrumental in getting the mayor of San Francisco to issue a proclamation designating September 27, 1996 as S.S. *Stephen Hopkins* Day – Honoring the ship and its crew.

~~~

Congresswoman Nancy Pelosi of California introduced the following statement in the U.S. House of Representatives on September 29, 1997:

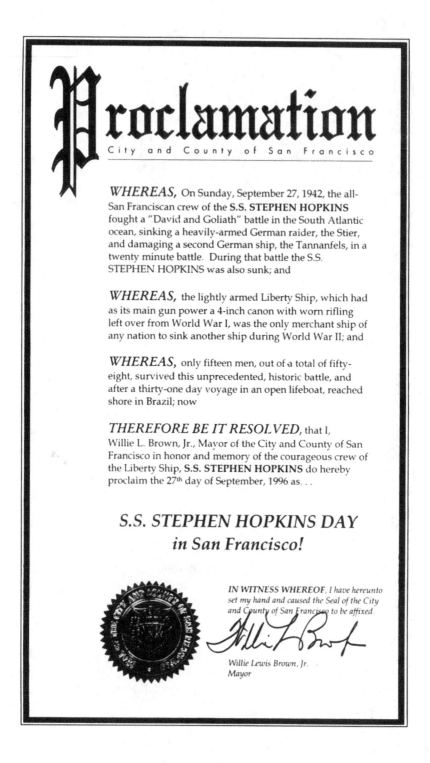

Proclamation
City and County of San Francisco

WHEREAS, On Sunday, September 27, 1942, the all-San Franciscan crew of the **S.S. STEPHEN HOPKINS** fought a "David and Goliath" battle in the South Atlantic ocean, sinking a heavily-armed German raider, the Stier, and damaging a second German ship, the Tannanfels, in a twenty minute battle. During that battle the S.S. STEPHEN HOPKINS was also sunk; and

WHEREAS, the lightly armed Liberty Ship, which had as its main gun power a 4-inch canon with worn rifling left over from World War I, was the only merchant ship of any nation to sink another ship during World War II; and

WHEREAS, only fifteen men, out of a total of fifty-eight, survived this unprecedented, historic battle, and after a thirty-one day voyage in an open lifeboat, reached shore in Brazil; now

THEREFORE BE IT RESOLVED, that I, Willie L. Brown, Jr., Mayor of the City and County of San Francisco in honor and memory of the courageous crew of the Liberty Ship, **S.S. STEPHEN HOPKINS** do hereby proclaim the 27th day of September, 1996 as . . .

S.S. STEPHEN HOPKINS DAY
in San Francisco!

IN WITNESS WHEREOF, I have hereunto set my hand and caused the Seal of the City and County of San Francisco to be affixed.

Willie Lewis Brown, Jr.
Mayor

In Honor of the SS *Stephen Hopkins*
September 27, 1997

Mr. Speaker, I rise today to honor the memory of the distinguished service of the S.S. *Stephen Hopkins,* an American merchant vessel, who sailed during World War II....

Mr. Speaker on behalf of the Congress, let us join the veteran merchant mariners and San Francisco community in commemorating the service of the SS *Stephen Hopkins* and the brave crew who sailed her into history.

~~~

On September 27, 2000, Mayor Rudolph W. Guiliani, Mayor, City of New York, signed this Proclamation:

... Now therefore I, Rudolph W. Guiliani, Mayor of the City of New York, in recognition of this great American, do hereby proclaim Wednesday, September 27, 2000 in the City of New York
"Cadet Edwin J. O'Hara Day"

~~~

On February 26, 2003, the New York State Conspicuous Service Medal and Certificate for bravery and heroic service performed during World War II was awarded to Midshipman Edwin O'Hara, signed by George Pataki, Governor of New York. The medal and certificate was presented to Vice Admiral Joseph Stewart of the United States Merchant Marine Academy to be on permanent display in O'Hara Hall.

~~~

On October 4, 2003, the Mariner Monument dedication took place at the U.S. Merchant Marine Academy. The monument honors "the 142" who lost their lives in World War II and the past, present and future midshipman of the Academy. Life-size figures

Top, the monument honoring the 142 Kings Point cadets who lost their lives during World War II. Above, left, detail of plaque honoring O'Hara. Above, right, the names of the 142. Author.

adorn the monument with Cadet-Midshipman Edwin O'Hara at the top loading a four inch shell.

~~~

On November 8, 2004, Peter Tirschwell, Vice President and Editorial Director of Commonwealth Business Media's Magazine Division, wrote an editorial for the *Journal of Commerce.* Excerpts:

> Yet there is one piece of unfinished business. The highest military honor is the Congressional Medal of Honor, and to date no merchant mariner has received the award. But the efforts are under way to get that recognition for someone whom is particularly deserving – Edwin O'Hara, an engine cadet-midshipman on the Liberty ship *Stephen Hopkins,* operated by the Luckenbach Steamship Co. of San Francisco.
>
> Shortly after the war, O'Hara was posthumously awarded the Merchant Marine Distinguished Service Medal, the highest honor to which he would have been entitled. Now, with the

---

CRITERIA FOR AWARD

The Medal of Honor, established by Joint Resolution of Congress 12 July 1862 (amended by Act of 9 July 1918 and Act of 25 July 1963) is awarded in the name of Congress to a person who, while a member of the Armed Forces, distinguishes himself conspicuously by gallantry and intrepidity at the risk of his life above and beyond the call of duty while engaged in an action against any enemy of the United States, while engaged in military operations involving conflict with an opposing foreign force; or while serving with friendly foreign forces engaged in an armed conflict against an opposing armed force in which the United States is not a belligerent party. The deed performed must have been one of personal bravery or self-sacrifice so conspicuous as to clearly distinguish the individual above his comrades and must have involved risk of life. Incontestable proof of the performance of service is exacted and each recommendation for award of this decoration is considered on the standard of extraordinary merit. Eligibility is limited to members of the Armed Forces of the United States in active Federal military service.

Oath as Midshipman in the Naval Reserve is administered to Cadet-Midshipmen at the cadet basic school, Pass Christian, Miss.

merchant marines acknowledged as veterans and as full contributors to the military victory in World War II, it is fitting that he be awarded the Medal of Honor.[1]

Cadet-Midshipman Edwin O'Hara should posthumously be awarded the Congressional Medal of Honor.

O'Hara, according to definition, was enrolled in the U.S. Naval Reserve. The inscription in the above photograph states, "Oath as Midshipman in the Naval Reserve is administered to Cadet-Midshipmen at the cadet basic school, Pass Christian, Miss."

Furthermore, according to the *Cadet-Midshipmen Information Booklet for Ship's Officers and Shore Officials* ...it states on p. 56, "A successful candidate, who has passed the Naval Reserve physical examination, shall be appointed a Cadet-Midshipman by the Supervisor and assigned by the District supervisor to preliminary training and basic Naval Science classes at a designated Basic School or the Academy."

Cadet-Midshipman Edwin O'Hara wore the insignia of Cadets and Merchant Marine officers who were Merchant Marine Reserve, United States Naval Reserve. This insignia can be seen on O'Hara's breast pocket in the photograph beneath his Distinguished Service Medal.

No person in the U.S. Merchant Marine has ever been awarded the Congressional Medal of Honor. O'Hara being in the U.S. Naval Reserve was subject to Military Rules and Regulations. An integral piece of the Merchant Marine Act of 1936 stated, "The United States shall have a merchant marine ... [to] serve as a naval or military auxiliary in time of war or national emergency ..." Maritime author and historian Charles Dana Gibson wrote:

"Throughout the entire war, military discipline ... encompassed those merchant seamen who were on ships engaged in the carriage of military cargo or personnel ... A merchant seaman assigned by a ship's master to a battle station under the control of a Naval gunnery officer subsequently came under the direct command and discipline of that officer...American merchant seamen who served in oceangoing service during World War II performed their duties under a legal framework which, in light of all recognized international law, placed them into the role of combatants integrated within the armed forces of the United States."[2]

O'Hara was taught ordinance and he used this training to man the gun while engaged in an action against an enemy of the United States. This action took place during the battle and at the very end by his firing the last five shots. He was observed at the beginning of the battle and by several eyewitnesses in the lifeboat. The lifeboat account of Cadet-Midshipman O'Hara firing the last rounds was officially documented from eyewitnesses by 2nd Engineer George S. Cronk and is on file. The deed performed was one of personal bravery, self-sacrifice, and so conspicuous that it clearly distinguished Cadet-Midshipman above his comrades. He was killed in the process. It is time for Congress to award its first Congressional Medal of Honor to a merchant mariner, Cadet-Midshipman Edwin J. O'Hara.

~~~

The Liberty ship *Stephen Hopkins* and the German raider *Stier* lie close to each other on the floor of the South Atlantic some 2,000 fathoms below the surface. Both ships fulfilled their missions; both crews did their duty for their country. If one could see the two vessels, their ensigns might still be waving in the sea currents, the spirits of their crews at their battle stations. For extraordinary acts of valor and heroism transcend their time and pass into legend that inspires generations.

Stier's War Diary paid tribute to the courage, skill, and perseverance of the Liberty ship's crew, "We could not but feel that we had gone down at the hands of a gallant foe…"

It was not until after the war that the details of the battle became known, but, as with all battles from time immemorial, no one can ever know everything about what happened.

END NOTES

BIBLIOGRAPHY

INDEX

END NOTES

Chapter 1 – The Liberty Ship

1. L.A. Sawyer and W.H. Mitchell, *The Liberty Ships* 2nd ed. (London: Lloyds of London Press, Ltd, 1985), 2.

2. U.S. Department of Commerce Maritime Administration, *The United States Merchant Marine: A Brief History* (Washington, D.C., 1972), 3.

3. William H. Langenberg, "An Ugly Duckling Turns Warrior," *Sea History* Winter 1999-2000, 21.

4. U.S. Maritime Commission and War Shipping Administration, "Fast Fact Sheet Issued on National Maritime Day, May 22, 1945," 14 December 2001 http://marad.dot.gov/Education/history/facts.html

5. Sawyer, 140.

6. U.S. Maritime Commission and War Shipping Adm., "Fast Fact Sheet," Ibid.

7. Sawyer, 141.

Chapter 2 – The German Raider

1. Paul Schmalenbach, *German Raiders: A history of auxiliary cruisers of the German Navy 1895-1945* (Cambridge: Great Britain: Patrick Stephens, 1979), 141.

2. David Woodward, *The Secret Raiders: The Story of the German Armed Raiders* ... (New York: W.W. Norton & Company, 1955), 13.

3. August Karl Muggenthaler, *German Raiders of World War II* (Englewood Cliffs, NJ: Prentice-Hall, Inc., 1977), vii.

4. John Asmussen, "Hilfskreuzer." *Absolute all about Hilfskreuzer (Auxiliary Cruiser/Raider)* 9 September 2003 http://www.scharnhorst-class.dk/miscellaneous/hilfkreuzer/hilfskreuzer_introduction.html

5. Clay Blair, *Hitler's U-Boat War: The Hunters, 1939-1942* (New York: Modern Library, 1996), 733-734.

6. William H. Langenberg, "An Ugly Duckling Turns Warrior," *Sea History* 91 Winter 1999-2000, 22.

7. Felix Riesenberg, *Sea War; the Story of the U.S. Merchant Marine in World War II* (Westport, CT: Greenwood Press, 1974), 166.

8. Muggenthaler, 211.

9. Ricky Law, "Arado AR-231," *Arsenal of Dictatorship: Online Encyclopedia of German WW II Weapons* 22 February 2004 http://www.geocities.com/pentagon/2833/luftwaffe/seaplane/ar231/ar231.html

Chapter 3 – The S.S. *Stephen Hopkins*

1. Dan & Toni Horodysky eds. "Chronological List of Ships Sunk or Damaged During January-December 1942," *American Merchant Marine At War*, 21 February 2005 http://www.usmm.org/shipsunkdamaged.html.

2. Ibid, "U.S. Merchant Marine in World War II," Ibid, http://www.usmm.org/ww2.html

3. Ibid, "Allied Merchant Ship Loses 1939 to 1943," Ibid, (Advance Release OWI 3789) http://www.usmm.net/shiplost.html

4. "Port Director's Report Arming Merchant Vessels," S.S. *Stephen Hopkins* File," (Serial PD 1747), (Armed Guard Report, Box 626, National Archives, College Park, MD.).

Chapter 4 - The German Raider *Stier*
1. Gudmundur Helgason, ed. "The U-boat War in Maps: Bay of Biscay," *uboat.net* 29 July 2004 <http:uboat.net/maps/biscay. htm>

Chapter 5 – The Blockade Runner *Tannenfels*
1. Peter Mueller, "Fischdampfer as Vorpostenboote," *Warship Building with Ssw* (*Seebeckwerft warship building*) *1. and 2. World War* 13 October 2004 http://www.werften.fichtown. de/ssw4.html

Chapter 6 – SS *Stephen Hopkins*: The Merchant Crew
1. "Merrimac Man Missing," (Newspaper article) 4 November 1942.
2. Carl Nolte, "Gallant Heroes of Liberty Ship *Hopkins* Are Aboard in Spirit," *San Francisco Chronicle* 29 April 1994.
3. George S. Cronk, Sr., Letter to James Patrick Conroy, 28 November 1974.
4. Dan and Toni Horodysky, "U.S. Merchant Marine Casualties during WW II." *American Merchant Marine at War* 28 December 2003 http://www.usmm.org/casualty.html
5. James Patrick Conroy, *So Gallantly Streaming* (Unpublished manuscript) 2003: 100.
6. Ian A. Millar, "A Footnote to History: The *Stephen Hopkins* Epilogue," *Sea Classics* November 1984, 29. http://www.armed-guard.com/hoppy.thml
7. V.J. Malone, "Report for Admiral E.S. Land," 5 March 1943.
8. Jean Dierkes-Carlisle, Telephone interview with author, 1 December 2003.
9. Malone.
10. Conroy, 139.

11. Jean Dierkes-Carlisle, Letter to author, 23 October 2004.

12. Rodger H. Piercy, Letter to author, 26 March 2001.

13. "The Battle Standard," U.S. Merchant Marine Academy.

14. Dorothy O. Norris, Letter to author, 26 October 2002.

15. Ibid.

16. Robert T. Chamberlin, Letter to author, 4 October 2003.

Chapter 7 – SS *Stephen Hopkins*: The Armed Guard

1. Justin F. Gleichauf, *Unsung Heroes: The Naval Armed Guard in World War II* (Annapolis, MD: Naval Institute Press, 1990), 10.

2. "Guns for American Ships," *Scholastic* 1 December 1941, 6.

3. Agnes Bridger and Tom Bowerman, *United States Navy Armed Guard World War I and II*. *U.S. Navy Armed Guard Veterans – Vol. I* 31 October 2002 http://armed-guard.com/agv1a.html

4. Samuel Eliot Morison, *History Of The United States Naval Operations In World War II*. *Vol. I* (Boston: Little, Brown And Company, 1966), 392.

5. Frank Knox, "Instructions for Scuttling Merchant Ships - To Master of S.S. *Stephen Hopkins*," 30 March 1942. [S.S. *Stephen Hopkins* File, U.S. Coast Guard National Maritime Center, Arlington, VA.]

6. Bridger, Ibid.

7. Ibid.

8. Ibid.

9. Ibid., 9.

10. James L. Mooney, ed. "Kenneth M. Willett," *Dictionary of American Naval Fighting Ships. Vol. 3* (Washington, D.C.: U.S.G.P.O., 1968), 622.

11. Moses N. Barker, Telephone interview with author, 21 December 2003.

12. Paul Porter, Telephone interview with author, 21 December 2003.

13. Opal Bullock, Telephone interview with author, 21 December 2003.

14. William Mueller, "S.S. Stephen Hopkins Duel to the Death," 23 September 2003 http://www.armed-guard.com/hoppy.html, 26.

15. Robert C. Ruark, "They called 'Em Fish Food,'" *Saturday Evening Post*, 6 May 1944, 24.

16. James Patrick Conroy, *So Gallantly Streaming: A True Story Of The Merchant Marine In World War II.* (Unpublished manuscript), 158-59.

17. Department Of The Navy – Naval Historical Center, "Articles for the Government of the United States Navy, 1930," Department of the Navy, Washington, DC: USGPO, 1932 http://history.navy.mil/faqs/faq59-7.htm

18. Dan and Toni Horodysky, "U.S. Merchant Marine Casualties during WW II." *American Merchant Marine at War* 24 July 2006 http://www.usmm.org/armedguard.html

Chapter 8 – *Stier* Breaks Out

1. Mackenzie J. Gregory, "Marauders of the Sea, German Armed Merchant Ships During W.W. 2 – Michel," *Ahoy-Mac's Web Log* 5 April 2004 < http://www.ahoy.tk-jk.net/MaraudersWW2/15Michel.html>

2. Jon Guttman, "The Ship That Avenged Herself," *Defiance at Sea: Stories Dramatic Naval Warfare* (London: Arms & Armour Press, 1995), 124.

3. German Naval High Command, "*Ship 23 – Auxiliary Cruiser Stier War Diary* 1 May 1942, 44 (Microfilm –U.S. National Archives, p. 70898, T-1022, Rolls 3048-49) Modern Military Records – Textual Archives Services Division.

4. Ibid, 4 May 1942, 46.

5. Michael Emmerich, "Sperrbrecher History," *German Naval History* 18 April 2004 http://www.german-navy.de/kriegsmarine/ships/minehunter/sperrbrecher/

6. German Naval High Command, Ibid, 6-7 May 1942, 48.

7. John Campbell, "Naval Weapons of World War Two," *German Torpedoes of World War II* 4 May 2004 http://www.warships.com/Weapons /WTGER_WWII.htm

8. German Naval High Command, Ibid, 8 May 1942, 48.

9. Ibid, 9-10 May, 49.

10. Ibid, 50.

11. Ibid, 12 May, 52.

12. Ibid, 52-53.

13. Ibid, 13 May, 54.

14. Ibid.

15. Ibid, 55.

16. Ibid.

17. Ibid, 56.

18. R.J. Witt and P.M. Heaton, *The Gallant Ship "Stephen Hopkins."* (R.J. Witt and P.M. Heaton, 1990), 8.

19. German Naval High Command, May 1942, 56-57.

20. Ibid, 60-61.

Chapter 9 – *Stephen Hopkins* to the South Pacific

1. Rodger H. Piercy, *The Journey of the Stephen Hopkins* (Unpublished manuscript 1966), 1.

2. Ibid.

3. Ibid.

4. James Patrick Conroy, *So Gallantly Streaming: A True Story of the Merchant Marine During World War II* (Unpublished manuscript), 164-65.

5. Piercy, 2-3.

6. Dorothy O. Norris, Letter to author, 26 October 2002.

7. Robert T. Chamberlin, Letter to author, 24 March 2004.

8. "Armed Guard Center Report of Materials Furnished to Armed Guard Units." (Serial No. PP 1747.) 25 May 1942.

9. Piercy, 3.

10. Ibid, 4.

11. Ibid, 4-5.

12. Ibid, 5-6.

13. Ibid, 6.

14. Dorothy O. Norris, Letter to author, 26 October 2002.

15. "Former Tech Grid Star Gives Vivid Picture of Fight With Sea Raiders," *Oakland Tribune* 10 December 1942, 1.

16. Piercy, 7.

Chapter 10 – Atlantic Hunting Grounds

1. Dan and Toni Horodysky, "U.S. Ships Sunk or Damaged in South Atlantic …" *American Merchant Marine at War* 28 December 2003 http://www.usmm.org/satlantic.html

2. German Naval High Command, 4 June 1942, 83-84.

3. Ibid, 84.

4. Ibid, 85-86.

5. Ibid, 86-87.

6. Ibid, 88-89.

7. Ibid, 89.

8. Ibid, 90-91.

9. Arthur R. Moore, *A Careless Word……A Needless Sinking* 7th ed. (New Jersey: Dennis Roland Chapter of the N.J. American Merchant Marine Veterans, 1998), 262.

10. German Naval High Command, Ibid, 7-8 June 1942, 92-93.

11. Ibid, 10-11 June, 95-97.

12. 3 July, 114-115.

13. 115-116.

14. 116.

15. 7-8 July, 120-122.

16. 9-10 July, 122-123.

17. 10-18 July, 123-130.

18. 21 July, 133-135.

Chapter 11 – *Stier* To the Atlantic Narrows

1. German Naval High Command, 21-28 July, 135-139.

2. 29 July, 140.

3. 30-31 July and 1 August, 142-144.

4. 2-3 August, 144-145.

5. 6 August 1942, 148-149.

Chapter 12 – *Stephen Hopkins* to the South Atlantic

1. Rodger H. Piercy, *The Journey of the Stephen Hopkins* (Unpublished manuscript 1966), 8.

2. William Mueller, "S.S. *Stephen Hopkins* Duel to the Death," 23 September 2003 http://www.armed-guard.com/hoppy.html

3. Piercy, 8-9.

4. Robert T. Chamberlin, Letter to author, 4 October 2003.

5. Mueller.

6. V.J. Malone, Report for Admiral E.S. Land, Administrator, War Shipping Administration, 5 March 1943.

7. Piercy, 9-10.

8. Moses Barker, "Moses Barker Tells of Harrowing Experience in Battle and in Lifeboat for 31 Days," *Liberty Log Newsletter*: *Stephen Hopkin's* Chapter (AMMV), April 1997, 5.

9. "5 Bay Area Men Safe in Sea Duel," *Oakland Tribune* 10 December 1942, 1.

10. Piercy, 11.

Chapter 13 – *Tannenfels* To the South Atlantic

1. Werner Haase, *Report on the Voyage of the M/S **Tannenfels** from Yokohama to Bordeaux, 1942,* 2 (Microfilm- U.S. National Archives T-1022, Roll 2830) Modern Military Records – Textual Archive Services Division.

2. Ibid.

3. Ibid.

4. Ibid, 2-3.

5. Ibid, 3.

6. Ibid.

7. Ibid, 3-4.

8. "Canadian Pacific's Empress of Asia," *Empress of Asia Voyages* 24 December 2004 http://www.greentrails.ca/empressofasia/voyages/

9. Haase, 4.

10. Ibid, 4-5.

11. Ibid, 5.

12. Ibid.

Chapter 14 – Action in the South Atlantic

1. German Naval High Command, 7 August 1942, 150.

2. David Woodward, *The Secret Raiders:* (New York: W.W. Norton & Company, Inc., 1955), 266.

3. German Naval High Command, 8 August 1942, 151.

4. Ibid, 9 August, 152-154.

5. Ibid, 153-154.

6. Ibid, 155.

7. 10 August,155-157.

8. 14 August, 159.

9. Ibid, 159.

10. "Fight Believed On In The South Atlantic," *New York Times* 13 August 1942:1.

11. German Naval High Command, 16-17 August, 161-162.

12. 17 August, 162-163.

13. 17-18 August, 163-164.

14. 18-19 August, 164-165.

15. 20 August, 166.

16. 21 August, 167.

17. 23 August, 168-169.

18. 24-25 August, 170-171.

19. 27-29 August, 172-173.

20. 1 September, 178.

21. Ibid, 178-179.

22. 4 September, 180-181

23. Hal Stoen, "The Long Voyage of the Ship *Pasteur*," 26 August 2004 http://stoenworks.com/Louis%20Pasteur.html

24. German Naval High Command, 12 September 1942, 189.

25. Ibid, 16 September, 1942.

26. 18-19 September, 196-198.

27. 20 September, 198.

28. 21-22 September, 199-200.

29. 23 September, 201-202.

30. 25 September, 202-203.

31. 26 September, 203-294.

32. "Report of the Commander of Ship 23 About the Last Successful Fight of the Ship and Its Sinking," *German Naval High Command: Ship 23 – Auxiliary Cruiser War Diary,* Microfilm Roll 3049..., 1-2.

Chapter 15 - September 27, 1942

1. "Report of the Commander of Ship 23 About the Last Successful Fight of the Ship and Its Sinking," *German Naval High Command: Ship 23 – Auxiliary Cruiser War Diary,* Microfilm Roll 3049, 1-2,14.

2. Ibid, 15.

3. Rodger H. Piercy, *The Journey of the Stephen Hopkins* (Unpublished manuscript) 1966, 11-12.

4. George S. Cronk, Letter to James P. Conroy, 14 November 1975.

5. Moses N. Barker, "Moses Barker's Talk to the S.S. *Stephen Hopkins* Chapter of the American Merchant Marine Veterans," (Audio-tape) March 2001.

6. Emory Scott Land, "Citation: For Extraordinary Heroism Beyond the Call of Duty – Richard Moczkowski, Chief Mate."

7. Friedrich Weber, "DIE ARGONAUTENFAHRT DES STIER" Vom Hilfskreuzerkreig im Suedatlantik," *Das Reich* 6 August 1944: 5.

8. Werner Haase, *Report on the Voyage of the M/S* Tannenfels *from Yokohama to Bordeaux, 1942,* 4.

9. Ford Stilson, "Personal Account of Ford Stilson," in S.S. *Stephen Hopkins* File, Timothy J. Mahoney, "Memorandum – Survivors of S.S. *Stephen Hopkins*, 24 November 1942."

10. "Report of the Commander...," 2-3.

11. Ibid, 3, 17.

12. George S. Cronk, Letter to Rudolph Rutz's sister.

13. "Report of the Commander ...," 3, 16.

14. Ibid, 4-6, 17-18.

15. Paul B. Porter, Telephone interview, 21 December 2003.

16. "Former Tech Grid Star Gives Vivid Picture of Fight With Sea Raiders," *Oakland Tribune* 10 December 1942, 1.

17. Office of Naval Intelligence, *Navy Department Intelligence Report – Enemy Attacks On Merchant Ships- S.S.* Stephen Hopkins – *U.S. Gun Crew Casualties*, 5 November 1942.

18. "Report of the Commander...," 3-4.

19. Ibid, 15.

20. Piercy, 12.

21. Barker (audiotape).

22. Piercy, 13.

23. Stilson.

24. H.V. Stebbins, Navy Department Office of the Chief of Naval Operations, "Memorandum For File: Summary Statements by Survivors of S.S. Stephen Hopkins, *U.S. Freighter*..., 1-2.

25. "Report of the Commander ...," 16.

26. Haase, 4.

27. Stebbins, 1.

28. George S. Cronk, Sr., Letter to author James P. Conroy, 14 November 1975.

29. George S. Cronk, Sr., Letter to Rudolph Rutz's sister.

30. Rodger H. Piercy, *The Journey of the Stephen Hopkins* (Unpublished manuscript), 1966, 13.

31. Ford Stilson, "Personal Account of Ford Stilson," Timothy J. Mahoney, S.S. *Stephen Hopkins* File, "Memorandum ... 24, November 1942.

32. Robert T. Chamberlin, Letter to author, 24 March 2004.

33. "Report of the Commander of Ship 23 About the Last Successful Fight of the Ship and Its Sinking," Microfilm Roll 3049, 5-6.

34. "Report of the Commander," 6, 18.

35. Werner Haase, *Report on the Voyage of the M/S Tannenfels from Yokohama - Bordeaux*, 1942, 4.

36. "Report of the Commander," 4, 15.

37. "Report of the Commander," 6-7.

38. Ibid, 7-8

39. Ibid, 8.

40. Ibid.

41. Friedrich Weber, "DIE ARGONAUTENFAHRT DES STIER" Vom Hilfskreuzerkreig im Suedatlantik," *Das Reich* 6 August 1944: 5.

42. Gabe Thomas, *MILAG: Captives of the Kriegsmarine: Merchant Navy Personnel 1939-1945* (Milay Prisoner of War Association, 1995), 58.

43. Thomas, 58.

44. "Report of the Commander," 19.

45. Werner Haase, 4.

46. Ibid, 5.

47. "Report of the Commander," 8-11.

48. Ibid, 12.

49. Weber

Chapter 16- Thirty-One Days in an Open Boat

1. Moses N. Barker, "Moses Barker's Talk to the S.S. *Stephen Hopkins* Chapter of the American Merchant Marine Veterans," (Audio-tape), March 2001.

2. George Cronk, Sr., Letter to James Conroy, 14 November 1975.

3. Rodger H. Piercy, *The Journey of the Stephen Hopkins*, (Unpublished Manuscript), 1966, 13-14.

4. Ford Stilson,"Personal Account of Ford Stilson," Timothy J. Mahoney, S.S. *Stephen Hopkins* File, "Memorandum ..." 24 November 1942.

5. Cronk, Sr., Ibid.

6. George Cronk, Jr., Letter to author, 4 February 2005.

7. Piercy, 15.

8. James Warren, "Survivor remembers sea battle," *Chicago Sun Times* 31 July 1978, 9.

9. "George Cronk Account," Timothy J. Mahoney, Ibid.

10. Piercy, 15-16.

11. Cronk, Sr., Letter to James Conroy ...

12. Cronk, Jr., Letter to author ...

13. Piercy, 17.

14. Ibid, 16-17.

15. Cronk, Jr., Ibid.

16. Piercy, 17.

17. Ibid, 16.

18. Cronk, Jr., Ibid.

19. Ibid.

20. Piercy, 17-18.

21. Ibid, 18-19.

22. Ibid, 18.

23. George H. McCarty, "Fulfills Dying Request Of Palestine Sailor," *Robinson Daily News* 12 February 1943, 1.

24. Barker.

25. McCarty.

26. Piercy, 19.

27. Ibid, 19-20.

28. Ibid, 20.

29. Barker.

30. Piercy, 20-21.

31. Ibid, 21.

32. Ibid, 22.

33. Ibid, 23.

34. Barker.

35. Piercy, 23.

36. Ibid.

37. Ibid, 24.

38. George S. Cronk, *Log of No. 1 Lifeboat of S.S.* Stephen Hopkins, Timothy J. Mahoney, S.S. *Stephen Hopkins* File ... Ibid.

39. "Courage on the High Seas: Veteran marks 55th year since ship honored for battle," *The 15th Annual Convention of the American Merchant Marine Veterans*, 11-15 May 2001, 42.

40. Barker.

Chapter 17 - Return to the Fatherland

1. Werner Haase, *Report on the Voyage of M/S* Tannenfels *from Yokohama – Bordeaux*, 1942, 5 (Microfilm – U.S. National

Archives T-1022, Roll 2830) Modern Military Records – Textual Archive Services Division.

2. Felix Riesenberg, *Sea War: The Story of the U.S. Merchant Marine in World War II* (Westport, Conn.: Greenwood Press, 1974), 169.

3. Herzliche Grube, Letter to Jean Dierkes-Carlisle, 10 August 1984.

4. Haase, 5.

5. "Report of the Commander of Ship 23 About the Last Successful Fight of the ship and Its Sinking,"*German Naval High Command – Ship 23 – Auxiliary Cruiser War Diary* (Microfilm U.S. National Archives Roll 3029, 22-33) Modern Military Records – Textual Archive Services Division.

6. Haase, Ibid.

7. "Report of the Commander," 23-24.

8. Haase.

9. "Report of the Commander," 24.

10. Haase, 6-7.

11. Ibid, 7.

12. Haase, 18.

13. "Short Sunderland MR-5," *Royal Air Force Museum* 10 April 2005 http://www.rafmuseum.org.uk/short-sunderland-mr5.htm

14. Emmanuel Gustin, "Short Sunderland," *uboat.net* 10 April 2005 http://uboat.net/allies/sunderland.htm

15. Friedrich Weber, "DIE ARGONAUTENFAHRT DES STIER" Vom Hilfskreuzerkreig im Suedatlantik," *Das Reich* 6 August 1944: 5.

Chapter 18 - Safe Ashore

1. Rodger H. Piercy, *The Journey of the Stephen Hopkins* (Unpublished manuscript) 1966, 24-28.

2. Joseph R. Rich, "Victoria Confidential Intelligence Report," *U.S. Naval Observer*, Serial 219-42, 31 October 1942. (Armed Guard Report, SS *Stephen Hopkins*, Box 626, National Archives, College Park, MD.).

3. Timothy J. Mahoney, S.S. *Stephen Hopkins* File "Survivors of the S.S. *Stephen Hopkins,* Memorandum re: Trip to Barra de Itabapoana to arrange for care and return ..."

4. Piercy, 28.

5. "Courage on the High Seas: Veteran marks 55th year since ship honored for battle," *The 15th Annual Convention of the American Merchant Marine Veterans*, 11-15 May 2001, 42.

6. Piercy, 28-32.

7. James L. Mooney, ed., "Lejeuene," *Dictionary of American Naval Fighting Ships Vol. IV* (Washington, D.C., 1969), 84.

8. Piercy, 32-33.

9. Piercy, 33-34.

10."Gripsholm-Berlin," *Gripsholm Berlin Ocean Liner Postcard – Norddeutsche Lloyd* 26 April 2005 http://www.simplonpc. co.uk/Gripsholm_Berlin.html

11. Piercy, 34-35.

12. Ibid, 35-38.

13. OPNAV, ALUSA Rio de Janeiro, Brazil, # 312131 NCR 842, 31 October 1942.

14. Excerpt From Fortnightly Summary Of Current National Situations, Serial No. 48, 15 November 1942.

15. Elma O'Hara, Letter to Luckenbach Steamship Lines, 1 October 1942.

16 W.G. Perow, Letter to Lt. McDonald – W.S.A., 9 November 1942.

17. E.E. Thorne, Letter to Mrs. Elma O'Hara, 10 November 1942.

18. R.R. McNulty, Letter to Mrs. O'Hara, 31 December 1942. In *Lindsay Gazette* 22 January 1943, 1.

19. C.W. Sanders, Letter to Mrs. Bertha Moczkowski, 13 November 1942.

20. "Eugene McDaniel Is Killed At Sea In Country's Service," *The Palestine Register* 5 November 1942, 1.

21. "Merchant Ship's Gun Crew Battles 2 Raiders, Sinking 1: Navy Men Kept Firing Till Magazine Blew Up, and Even Then

Used Last 5 Shells – 15 Survivors Land in South America," *New York Times* 10 December 1942, 1.

22. "Marauders of the Sea: *Stier* (Ship 23)," *Compunews* 14 October 2004 http://www.compunews.com/qships/p.52

23. C.W. Sanders, Letter to the Honorable John H. Tolen, 20 November 1942.

24. Ibid, Letter to Arthur R. Chamberlin, 9 February 1943.

25. Dorothy O. Norris, interview with author, 5 September 2000.

26. Rodger H. Piercy, Letter to author, [2001]

27. Robert T. Chamberlin, Letter to author, 24 March 2004.

28. George S. Cronk, Sr., Letter to Rudolph Rutz's sister.

29. McCarty, George H. "Fulfills Dying Request Of Palestine Sailor," *Robinson Daily News* 12 February 1943, 1.

Chapter 19 - Awards and Honors

1. "Merchant Marine Heroes: Citation for Distinguished Service Medal Awarded for "Heroism Beyond the Call of Duty" During World War: Paul Buck," *American Merchant Marine at War* 9 June 2005 http://www.usmm.org/heroes.html

2. "Merchant Marine Heroes: Citation for Distinguished Service Medal: Richard Moczkowski," *American Merchant Marine at War*, Ibid.

3. "Merchant Marine Heroes: Citation for Distinguished Service Medal: Joseph E. Layman," Ibid.

4. V.J. Malone, Report for Admiral E.J. Land, Administrator, War Shipping Administration, 5 March 1943, 6.

5. "Merchant Marine Heroes: Citation for George S. Cronk," Ibid.

6. "Merchant Marine Heroes: Citation for Ford Stilson," Ibid.

7. "Merchant Marine Heroes: Citation for Edwin Joseph O'Hara," Ibid.

8. Walter W. Jaffee, *The Liberty Ships: From A to Z* (Palo Alto, CA: The Glencannon Press, 2004), 81.

9. Arthur R. Moore, *A Careless Word......A Needless Sinking* 7th ed. (New Jersey: Dennis Roland Chapter of the N.J. American Merchant Marine Veterans, 1998), 551.

10. Jaffee, 291.

11. James L. Mooney, ed., "Kenneth M. Willett," *Dictionary of American Naval Fighting Ships Vol. 3*. Washington, D.C.: USGPO, 1968, 622.

12. Robert L. Vargas, *"The* Gallantry *of an* "Ugly Duckling," *American Heritage* December 1969.

Afterword

1. Peter Tirschwell, "Recognition long overdue," *Journal of Commerce* 8 November 2004.

2. Charles Dana Gibson, *Merchantman? Or Ship Of War* (Camden, ME: Ensign Press, 1986), 127-128.

BIBLIOGRAPHY

"Armed Guard Center Report / Materials Furnished to Armed Guard Units," (Serial No. PP1747) (Armed Guard Report, S.S. *Stephen Hopkins*, Box 626, National Archives, College Park, MD.).

Asmussen, John. "Hilfskreuzer." *Absolute all about Hilfskreuzer (Auxiliary Cruiser/Raider)* 9 September 2003 <http://www.scharnhorst-class.dk/miscellaneous/hilfskreuzer/hilfskreuzer_introduction.html

Barker, Moses N.. "Moses Barker's Talk to the S.S. *Stephen Hopkins* Chapter of the American Merchant Marine Veterans (Audiotape) March 2001. (Courtesy of William Bentley and the S.S. *Stephen Hopkins* Chapter).

___, "Moses Barker Tells of His Harrowing Experience in Battle and in a Lifeboat For 31 Days." *Liberty Log Newsletter: S.S. Stephen Hopkins Chapter*, April 1997, 5. (Courtesy of Linda Pizzuto).

___, Telephone interview with author, 21 December 2003.

"The Battle Standard," U.S. Merchant Marine Academy.

Blair, Clay. *Hitler's U-Boat War: The Hunters, 1939-1942*. New York: Modern Library, 1998.

___, *Hitler's U-Boat War: The Hunted, 1942-1945*. New York: Modern Library, 1998.

Bridger, Agnes & Tom Bowerman, eds. "United States Navy Armed Guard World War I and II," *U.S. Navy Armed Guard Veterans – Vol. I.* 31 October 2002 http://www.armed-guard.com/agv1a.html

Bullock, Opal. Telephone interview with author, 21 December 2003.

Bunker, John Gorley. *Liberty Ships, The Ugly Ducklings of World War II.* Annapolis, MD: Naval Institute Press, 1972.

Campbell, John. "Naval Weapons of World War Two," *German Torpedoes of World War II.* 5 April 2004 http://www.navweaps.com/Weapons/WTGER_WWII.htm

"Canadian Pacific's *Empress of Asia*," *Empress of Asia Voyages.* 24 December 2004 http://www.greentrails.ca/empres-sofasia/voyages/

Cantwell, Alice. "50 Years Later, Navy Salutes Wartime Cadets," *The Journal of Commerce* 10 November 1992.

Chamberlin, Robert T. Letter to author, 4 October 2003.

___, Letter to author, 24 March 2004.

Conroy, James Patrick. *So Gallantly Streaming: A True Story Of The Merchant Marine During World War II.* (Unpublished manuscript). 2003.

"Courage on the High Seas: Veteran marks 55th year since ship honored for battle," *The 15th Annual Convention of the American Merchant Marine Veterans*, 11-15 May 2001, 42.

Cronk, George S. Sr. Letter to James Patrick Conroy, 28 November 1974. (Courtesy of George Cronk, Jr.).

___, Letter to James Patrick Conroy, 14 November 1975. (Courtesy of George Cronk, Jr.).

___, Letter to Rudolph Rutz's sister. (In "A Footnote to History: The *Stephen Hopkins* Epilogue," by Ian A. Millar) *Sea Classics* Vol. 17 #6 November 1984, 29. (Courtesy of Ian A. Millar)

___, "Log of No. 1 Lifeboat of S.S. *Stephen Hopkins* , Timothy J. Mahoney, S.S. *Stephen Hopkins* File, U.S. Coast Guard. National Maritime Center, Arlington, Va.

Crump, Irving. *Our Merchant Marine Academy.* New York: Dodd, Mead, 1958.

Department of the Navy – National Historical Center, "Articles for the Government of the United States Navy, 1930,"

Washington, DC: USGPO, 1932, 7 March 2004 http://www.history.navy.mil/faqs/faq59-7.htm

___, "Naval Armed Guard Service in World War II," 18 January 2002 http://www.history.navy.mil/faqs/faq104-1htm

Dierkes-Carlisle, Jean. Letter to author, 23 October 2004.

___, Telephone interview with author, 1 December 2003.

___, Letter to author, 2 November 2003.

Edwards, Bernard. *Salvo! Classic Naval Gun Actions.* Annapolis, MD: Naval Institute Press, 1995.

Emmerich, Michael. "Sperrbrecker History," *German Naval History* 18 April 2004 <http://www.german-navy.de/kriegsmarine/ships/minehunter/sperrbrecher/>

"Eugene McDaniel Is Killed At Sea In Country's Service," *The Palestine Register* 5 November 1942, 1.

"Excerpt From Fortnightly Summary of Current National Situations," Serial No. 48, 15 November 1942. Rep.0006c-Rg-38, Armed Guard Report, S.S. *Stephen Hopkins*, Box 626, National Archives, College Park, MD.

"Fight Believed On In The South Atlantic." *New York Times* 13 August 1942, 1.

"5 Bay Area Men Safe in Sea Duel," *Oakland Tribune* 10 December 1942, 1. (Courtesy of Imogene Trembowicz).

"Former Tech Grid Star Gives Vivid Picture of Fight With Sea Raiders," *Oakland Tribune* 10 December 1942, 1.

German Naval High Command. "Ship 23 – *Auxiliary Cruiser Stier War Diary.* 1 May 1942 (Microfilm – U.S. National Archives, T-1022, Rolls 3048-49, Modern Military Records –Textual Archives Services Division).

Gibson, Charles Dana. *Merchantman? Or Ship Of War.* Camden, ME: Ensign Press, 1986.

Gleichauf, Justin F. *Unsung Sailors: The Naval Armed Guard in World War II.* Annapolis, MD: Naval Institute Press, 1990.

Gregory, Mackensie J. "Marauders of the Sea, German Armed Merchant Ships During W.W. 2 – Michel." *Ahoy Mac's*

Web Log. 5 April 2004 http://www.ahoy.tk-jk.net/ MaraudersWW2/15Michel.html

"Gripsholm-Berlin," *Gripsholm Berlin Ocean Liner Postcard – Norddeutsche Lloyd.* 26 April 2005 http://www.simplonpc.co.uk/Gripsholm_Berlin.html

Grube, Herzliche. Letter to Jean Dierkes-Carlisle, 10 August 1984. (Courtesy of Jean Dierkes-Carlisle).

"Guns for American Ships," *Scholastic* 1 December 1941, 6.

Gustin, Emmanuel. "Short Sunderland," *uboat.net* 10 April 2005 http://www.uboat.net/allies/sunderland.htm

Guttman, Jon. "The Ship That Avenged Herself," *Defiance at Sea: Stories of Dramatic Naval Warfare.* London: Arms and Armour Press, 1995.

Haase, Werner. *Report on the Voyage of the M/S Tannenfels from Yokohama to Bordeaux, 1942.* (Microfilm – U.S. National Archives, T-1022, Roll 2830, Modern Military Records – Textual Archives Services Division).

Helgason, Gudmundur. "The War in Maps: The Bay of Biscay," *uboat.net* 28 February 2004 http://uboat.net/maps/biscay.htm

Horodysky, Dan and Toni, eds. "Allied Merchant Ship Loses 1939 to 1943, (Advance Release OWI 3789) *American Merchant Marine at War* 21 February 2005 http://www.usmm.net/shiplost.html

___, "Chronological List of Ships Sunk or Damaged During January-December 1942," Ibid http://www.usmm.org/shipsunkdamaged.html

___, "Merchant Marine Heroes: Citations for Distinguished Service Medal Awarded for "Heroism Beyond the Call of Duty" During World War: Ibid, 9 June 2005 <http:www.usmm.org/heroes.html>

___, "U.S. Merchant Marine Casualties During WW II," Ibid 28 December 2003 http://www.usmm.org/casualty.html

___, "U.S. Merchant Marine in World War II," Ibid 21 February 2005 http://www.usmm.org/ww2.html

___, "U.S. Ships Sunk or Damaged in South Atlantic …," Ibid http://www.usmm.org/satlantic.html>

Jaffee, Walter W. *The Liberty Ships: From A* (*A.B. Hammomd*) *to Z* (*Zona Gale*) Palo Alto, CA: The Glencannon Press, 2004.

Klein, Sandor S. "Ocean-War Glory Saga: U.S. Merchant Ship Batters 2 Raiders in Epic Sea Battle," *Times-Herald* 10 December 1942. (S.S. *Stephen Hopkins* File – U.S. Coast Guard Maritime Center, Arlington, VA.).

Knox, Frank. "Instructions for Scuttling Merchant Ships - To Master Paul Buck of S.S. *Stephen Hopkins*," 30 March 1942. (S.S. *Stephen Hopkins* File - U.S. Coast Guard Maritime Center, Arlington, Va.).

Land, Emory Scott. "Citation: For Extraordinary Heroism Beyond the Call of Duty Richard Moczkowski, Chief Mate." *American Merchant Marine at War* http://www.usmm. org/heroes.html

Langenberg, William H. "An Ugly Duckling Turns Warrior," *Sea History* 91,Winter 1999-2000.

Law, Ricky, ed. "Arado AR 231," *Arsenal of Dictatorship: Online Encyclopedia of German WW II Weapons.* 22 February 2004 http://www.geocities.com/pentagon/2833/luftwaffe/ seaplane/ar231/ar231.html

Lowe, Stan, ed. "1942, The Only Time." *The Fighting Merchant Marine And Navy Armed Guard* 14 December 2001 http:// www.merchant-marine.com/only_once.htm

Mahoney, Timothy J. S.S. "Survivors of the S.S. *Stephen Hopkins*, Memorandum re: Trip to Barra de Itabapoana to arrange for care and return to Rio de Janeiro of survivors of the former S.S. *Stephen Hopkins*." (*Stephen Hopkins* File – U.S. Coast Guard Maritime Center, Arlington, Va.)

Malone, V.J. "Report for Admiral E.S. Land, Administrator, War Shipping Administration," 5 March 1943. (Courtesy of Dan and Toni Horodysky, eds. *American Merchant Marine at War* website).

"Marauders of the Sea: *Stier* (Ship 23)," *Compunews* 14 October 2004 http://www.compunews.com/qships/p.52

Martin, Rodney J. "Marinequadratkarte map," *Silent Runner – Wolfgang Heyda, U-boat Commander* 15 July 2005 http://www.u-434.com

McCarty, George H. "Fulfills Dying Request of Palestine Sailor," *Robinson Daily News* 12 February 1943, 1.

McNulty, R.R. Letter to Mrs. O'Hara, 31 December 1942 (In *Lindsey Gazette* 22 January 1943, 1).

"Merchant Ship's Gun Crew Battles 2 Raiders Sinking 1: Navy Men Kept Firing Till Magazine Blew Up, and Even Then Used Last 5 Shells – 15 Survivors Land in South America," *New York Times* 10 December 1942, 1.

"Merrimac Man Missing," (Newspaper article), 4 November 1942.

Millar, Ian A. "At His Post To The End," *Nautical Brass Magazine* July/August 1990, 18.

___, "California's Gallant Ship." *Military Collector's Club of Canada* Summer, 1989, 63.

___, "A Footnote to History: The *Stephen Hopkins* Epilogue," *Sea Classics* Vol. 17 #6 November 1984, 29.

___, "One Hundred Forty Two Reasons to Observe Veterans Day," *Western Viking* 6 November 1998.

___, Telephone interview with author, 3 January 2004.

___, "The Type of Man Your Brother Was…" *Sea History* Vol. 35, Spring 1985. (Courtesy of Ian A. Millar).

Mooney, James L. ed. "Kenneth M. Willett," *Dictionary of American Naval Fighting Ships* Vol 3. Washington D.C.: USGPO, 1968, 622.

___, "Lejeune," Ibid, Vol. 4. 1969, 84.

Moore, Arthur R. *A Careless Word ...A Needless Sinking* 7th ed. New Jersey: Dennis Roland Chapter of the N.J. American Merchant Marine Veterans, 1998.

Morison, Samuel Eliot. *History Of The United States Naval Operations In World War II.* Vol.1. Boston: Little, Brown And Company, 1966.

Mueller, Peter. "Fischdampfer as Vorpostenboote," *Warship Building with Ssw (Seebeckwerft Warship Building)* 1. *and 2. World War* 13 October 2004 http://www.werften.fichtown.de/ssw4.html

Mueller, William. "S.S. *Stephen Hopkins – Duel to the Death*," United States Navy Armed Guard World War I and II 23 September 2003 http://www.armed-guard.com/hoppy.html

Muggenthaler, August Karl. *German Raiders of World War II* Englewood Clifts, NJ: Prentice Hall Inc., 1977.

Navy Department. "Commander Of Armed Guard Aboard Merchant Vessel That Fought It Out With Two Raiders Awarded Navy Cross," (Press and Radio Release) 12 March 1943. (Armed Guard Report, S.S. *Stephen Hopkins*, Box 626, National Archives, College Park, MD).

Navy Department. *Ordinance And Gunnery Instructions for Naval Armed Guards on Merchant Ships 1942* Washington, D.C.: USGPO, 1942.

"Neutrality Act," of August 31, 1935. Joint Resolution," 49 Stat. 1081; 22 U.S.C. 441 note, 25 November 2002. http://www.mtholyoke.edu/acad/intel/interwar/neutralityact.htm

Nolte, Carl. "Gallant Heroes of Liberty Ship *Hopkins* Are Aboard in Spirit," *San Francisco Chronicle* 29 April 1994.

Norris, Dorothy O. Letter to author, 6 June 2005.

___, Telephone interview with author, 8 December 2003.

___, Letter to author, 26 October 2002.

___, Telephone interview with author, 5 September 2000.

Office of Naval Intelligence. "Navy Department Intelligence Report – Enemy Attacks On Merchant Ships – S.S. *Stephen Hopkins* - U.S. Gun Crew Casualties," 5 November 1942. (Armed Guard Report, S.S. *Stephen Hopkins*, Box 626, National Archives, College Park, MD.).

O'Hara, Elma. Letter to Luckenbach Steamship Lines, 1 October 1942. (Edwin O'Hara File, Schuyler Otis Bland Library, U.S. Merchant Marine Academy).

Oliver, Edward F. "The Last Five Shells," *True* November 1957.

OPNAV, ALUSNA Rio de Janeiro, Brazil # 312131, NCR842, 31 October 1942. Rep. 0006c-RG-38 (Armed Guard Report, S.S. *Stephen Hopkins*, Box 626, National Archives, College Park, MD.).

Perow, W.G. Letter to Lt. McDonald – W.S.A., 9 November 1942. (Edwin O'Hara File, Schuyler Otis Bland Library, U.S. Merchant Marine Academy).

Piercy, Rodger H. *The Journey of the **Stephen Hopkins*** (Unpublished manuscript) 1966. (Courtesy of Rodger H. Piercy).

___, Letter to author, 16 November 2001.

___, Letter to author, March 2001.

___, Letter to author, [n.d.], 2001.

"Port Directors Report Arming Merchant Vessels," (Armed Guard Report, S.S. *Stephen Hopkins*, Box 626, National Archives, College Park, MD.).

Porter, Paul B. Telephone interview with author, 21 December 2003.

Reed, Jim. "Starving Sailors Spare Ailing Bird," *The 15th Annual Convention of the American Merchant Marine Veterans* 11-15 May, 2001, 43.

Reminick, Gerald. *Death's Railway: A Merchant Mariner POW on the River Kwai.* Palo Alto, California: The Glencannon Press, 2002.

"Report of the Commander of Ship 23 about Last Successful Fight of the Ship," *German Naval High Command: Ship 23 – Auxiliary Cruiser War Diary.* (Microfilm - U.S. National Archives, T-1022, Roll 3049, Modern Military Records –Textual Archives Services Division.).

Rich, Joseph R. "Victoria Confidential Intelligence Report," *U.S. Naval Observer* Serial 219-42, 31 October 1942. (Armed Guard Report, S.S. *Stephen Hopkins*, Box 626, National Archives, College Park, MD.).

Riesenberg, Felix. *Sea War: the Story of the U.S. Merchant Marine in World War II* Westport, Ct.: Greenwood Press, 1974.

"Roosevelt and Hull on Neutrality Repeal," *Current History* January 1942, 399.

Ruark, Robert C. "They Called 'Em Fish Food,'" *Saturday Evening Post* 6 may 1944.

S.S. *Stephen Hopkins* File, (Naval Armed Guard Casualty File, Box 40/470/55/09/02, National Archives, College Park, MD.).

___, (Naval Armed Guard, Box 626/370/12/35/3, National Archives, College Park, MD.).

Sanders, C.W. Letter to Arthur R. Chamberlin, 9 February 1943. (S.S. *Stephen Hopkins* File, U.S. Coast Guard, National Maritime Center, Arlington, VA.).

___, Letter to The Honorable John H. Tolan, 20 November 1942. (S.S. *Stephen Hopkins* File, U.S. Coast Guard, National Maritime Center, Arlington, Va.).

___, Letter to Mrs. Bertha Moczkowski, 13 November 1942, (S.S. *Stephen Hopkins* File, U.S. Coast Guard, National Maritime Center, Arlington, VA.).

Sawyer, L.A. and W.H. Mitchell. *The Liberty Ships* 2nd ed., London: Lloyds of London Press Ltd., 1985.

Schmalenbach, Paul. *German Raiders: A history of auxiliary cruisers of the German Navy 1895-1945*. Cambridge, Great Britain: Patrick Stephens, 1979.

"Short Sunderland MR-5," *Royal Air Force Museum* 10 April 2005 http://www.rafmuseum.org/uk/short-sunderland-mr5.htm

Stanford, Peter. "How an Ugly Duckling Fought Back and Sank Her Assailant." *Sea History* Spring 1985.

Stebbins, H.V. Navy Department Office of the Chief of Naval Operations, Memorandum for File: "Summary of Statements by Survivors of S.S. *Stephen Hopkins*, U.S. Freighter 7181 G.T., War Shipping Administration, Charterer Luckenbach Steamship Co.," 27 November 1942. (S.S. Stephen Hopkins File, U.S. Coast Guard, National Maritime Center, Arlington, VA.).

Stilson, Ford. "Personal Account of Ford Stilson, Chief Steward, S.S. *Stephen Hopkins*: September 27, about 9:30-10AM," "Memorandum for File:… (S.S. *Stephen Hopkins* File, U.S. Coast Guard, National Maritime Center, Arlington, VA.).

Stoen, Hal. "The Long Voyage of the Ship *Pasteur*," 26 August 2004 http://stoenworks.com/Louis%20Pasteur.html

Thomas, Gabe. *MILAG: Captives of the Kriegsmarine Merchant Navy Prisoners, of War Germany 1939-1945*, Pontardawe: The Milag Prisoner of War Association, 1995.

Thorne, E.E. Letter to Mrs. Elma O'Hara, 10 November 1942. (Edwin O'Hara File, Schuyler Otis Bland Library, U.S. Merchant Marine Academy.

Tirschwell, Peter. "Recognition Long Overdue," *Journal of Commerce* 8 November 2004.

U.S. Department of Commerce Maritime Administration. *The United States Merchant Marine: A Brief History*. Washington, DC., 1972.

U.S. Maritime Commission and War Shipping Administration. "Fast Fact Sheet – Issued on National Maritime Day, 22 May 1945," 14 December 2001 http://www.marad.dot.gov/Education/history/facts.html

USNS *Paul Buck.* (Photograph) Military Sealift Command 5 June 2005 http://www.msc.navy.mil/inventory/smallpics/small.paulbuck.jpg

Vargas, Robert L. "The Gallantry of an 'Ugly Duckling,'" *American Heritage* December 1969.

War Shipping Administration. "General Equipment of a Lifeboat," *United States Maritime Service Training Manual*. Cornell Maritime Press, 1943-44.http://www.usmm.net/lifeboat2.html

Warren, James. "Survivor remembers sea battle", *Chicago Sun Times* 31 July 1978, 9.

Weber, Friedrich. "DIE ARGONAUTTENFAHRT DES *STIER*," *Vom Hilfskreuzerkreig im Suedatlantic*," *Das Reich* 6 August 1944, 5.

Witt, R.J. and P.M. Heaton. *The Gallant Ship "Stephen Hopkins*," R.J. Witt and P.M. Heaton, 1990.

Wittenberg, Edward. "Raiders," *Auxiliary Cruisers – German Raiders* 9 September 2003 http://www.geocities.com/kriegsmarine1939/raiders.htm

Wolfe, Bernard. "Getting the Convoys Through," *Popular Science* May 1943, 112.

Woodward, David. *The Secret Raiders: The Story Of The German Armed Merchant Raiders In The Second World War*. New York: W.W. Norton and Company, Inc., 1955.

INDEX